D1095145

CITATION ANALYSIS IN RESEARCH EVALUATION

Information Science and Knowledge Management

Volume 9

Editor-in-Chief:

J. Mackenzie Owen, *University of Amsterdam, Amsterdam*

Editorial Board:

M. Bates, *University of California, Los Angeles*
P. Bruza, *The University of Queensland, Brisbane*
R. Capurro, *Hochschule der Medien, Stuttgart University of Applied Sciences, Stuttgart*
E. Davenport, *Napier University, Edinburgh*
R. Day, *Wayne State University, Detroit*
M. Hedstrom, *University of Michigan, Ann Arbor*
A.M. Paci, *Istituto di Studi Sulla Ricerca e Documentazione Scientifica, Roma*
C. Tenopir, *University of Tennessee, Knoxville*
M. Thelwall, *University of Wolverhampton, Wolverhampton*

CITATION ANALYSIS IN RESEARCH EVALUATION

HENK F. MOED

 Springer

A C.I.P. Catalogue record for this book is available from the Library of Congress.

ISBN-10   1-4020-3713-9 (HB)
ISBN-13   978-1-4020-3713-9 (HB)
ISBN-10   1-4020-3714-7 (e-book)
ISBN-13   978-1-4020-37146 (e-book)

Published by Springer,
P.O. Box 17, 3300 AA Dordrecht, The Netherlands.

www.springeronline.com

Printed on acid-free paper

All Rights Reserved
© 2005 Springer
No part of this work may be reproduced, stored in a retrieval system, or transmitted
in any form or by any means, electronic, mechanical, photocopying, microfilming, recording
or otherwise, without written permission from the Publisher, with the exception
of any material supplied specifically for the purpose of being entered
and executed on a computer system, for exclusive use by the purchaser of the work.

Printed in the Netherlands.

Contents

Preface

This book is written for members of the scholarly research community, and for persons involved in research evaluation and research policy. More specifically, it is directed towards the following four main groups of readers:

– All scientists and scholars who have been or will be subjected to a quantitative assessment of research performance using citation analysis.
– Research policy makers and managers who wish to become conversant with the basic features of citation analysis, and about its potentialities and limitations.
– Members of peer review committees and other evaluators, who consider the use of citation analysis as a tool in their assessments.
– Practitioners and students in the field of quantitative science and technology studies, informetrics, and library and information science.

Citation analysis involves the construction and application of a series of indicators of the 'impact', 'influence' or 'quality' of scholarly work, derived from citation data, i.e. data on references cited in footnotes or bibliographies of scholarly research publications. Such indicators are applied both in the study of scholarly communication and in the assessment of research performance. The term 'scholarly' comprises all domains of science and scholarship, including not only those fields that are normally denoted as science – the natural and life sciences, mathematical and technical sciences – but also social sciences and humanities.

The term 'research policy' in this book is used in a broad sense, and comprises policies at various levels: science policy of a national government by ministers responsible for scholarly research; research policy at the level of research organisations or institutions dealing with quality control and the allocation of research funds; and research management, carried out by directors of research groups or departments, including hiring, promoting and retaining individual scholars.

This book deals with a crucial aspect of research performance: the contribution of scholarly work to the advancement of scholarly knowledge. Its principal question is: how can citation analysis be used properly as a tool in the assessment of such a contribution? Although the major part of the analysis relates to the basic science – a domain in which citation analysis is used most frequently – this book also addresses its uses and limits in the applied and technical sciences, social sciences and humanities.

It provides a wide range of important 'facts', and corrects a number of common misunderstandings about citation analysis. It introduces basic notions and distinctions, and deals both with theoretical and technical aspects, and with its applicability in various contexts, at the level of individual scholars, research groups, departments, institutions, national scholarly systems, disciplines or subfields, and scholarly journals. It reveals the enormous potential of quantitative, bibliometric analyses of the scholarly literature for a deeper understanding of scholarly activity and performance, and highlights their policy relevance. But this book is also critical, underlines the limits of citation analysis in research evaluation, and issues warnings for potential misuse. It proposes criteria for proper use of citation analysis as a research evaluation tool.

It describes primarily the use of data extracted from *the Science Citation Index* and related Citation Indexes published by the *Institute for Scientific Information* (ISI). Although this institute's name was recently changed to *Thomson Scientific*, its original name is still used throughout this book. It focuses on the use of the ISI Citation Indexes in the study of the scholarly communication system, and particularly in research evaluation, rather than on their outstanding usefulness in scholarly literature retrieval. But many aspects to which this book dedicates attention relate to citation analysis in general, regardless from which databases the analysed bibliographical data is extracted.

Quantitative studies of science and technology is a rapidly developing field, and its development is closely linked to a number of general tendencies in the global scholarly system. National governments and research organisations and institutions need systematic evaluations for optimising their research allocations, re-orienting their research support, rationalising research organisations, restructuring research in particular fields, or augmenting research productivity. *Evaluative bibliometrics* is a subfield of quantitative science and technology studies, aimed to construct indicators of research performance from a quantitative analysis of scholarly documents. Citation analysis is one of its key methodologies.

Whereas in the USA companies such as *ISI/Thomson Scientific* and *CHI Research* were the primary contributors to evaluative bibliometric methodologies, in other countries, particularly in Europe and in Australia, these were mainly further developed in academic research departments. The aim of this book is to further contribute to an *academic basis* for evaluative bibliometrics, by presenting it as a multi-disciplinary scientific–scholarly activity, with its own methodologies and theoretical debates.

Applying citation analysis in research evaluation in a proper way requires a high level of competence. It is not something that anyone with access to the ISI Citation Indexes can do easily. On the contrary, this book illustrates that one needs detailed technical knowledge and theoretical understanding to carry out citation analysis properly. The book does not, however, provide a detailed technical manual of how to carry out citation analysis. Instead, it focuses on its main lines, basic principles and assumptions, and its uses and limits in the various domains of scholarship.

It is up to the members of the scholarly community and the policy arena, and *not* to the author, to decide whether or not citation analysis is to be used for evaluative purposes. In order to make such a decision properly, it is essential that all participants have insight into the nature of citation analysis, how its indicators are constructed and calculated, what the various theoretical positions state about what they measure, and what are their potentialities and limitations in scholarly research evaluation. This book aims at providing such insight.

Structure of the book

This book presents a number of studies undertaken by the author, some in collaboration with his colleagues at the Centre for Science and Technology Studies (CWTS) at Leiden University (the Netherlands), and building upon the earlier works of many other scholars in the field. The following table provides an overview of the general structure, and indicates the primary target audience for each part.

Part	Primary target audience
Executive Summary	Research policy makers, managers and evaluators
Part 1: General Introduction and Main Conclusions	Interested scholars from all domains of scholarship
Part 2: Empirical and Theoretical Chapters	Practitioners and students in quantitative science studies

Part 1 provides an introduction, and presents the basic notions and main conclusions as regards the use of citation analysis in research evaluation. Moreover, it includes a synopsis providing summaries of all later chapters, each briefly introducing the main topics and conclusions in each chapter, but excluding most of the technical details. Part 1 aims at presenting the reader, particularly those who are not active in the field of quantitative science studies, what this book is all about and its conclusions.

Part 2 presents more detailed conclusions of 24 empirical and theoretical chapters, arranged into 8 sub-parts (Parts 2.1–2.8):

Part Number	Part Title
2.1	Assessing basic science research departments and scientific journals
2.2	The ISI Citation Indexes
2.3	Assessing social sciences and humanities
2.4	Accuracy aspects
2.5	Theoretical aspects
2.6	Citation analysis and peer review
2.7	Macro studies
2.8	New developments

Part 2.1 provides a further introduction to later parts, discussing a large number of issues as regards the types of citation analysis that are applied most frequently: the assessment of the past performance of research departments in basic science, and the measurement of journal impact using journal impact factors and related citation measures.

Acknowledgements

I wish to thank the following colleagues for their most valuable comments on draft versions of particular chapters: Maarten Coolen, University of Amsterdam, the Netherlands (Chapter 2); Henry Small, Thomson Scientific, USA (Chapters 6, 7, 12, 13, 14); Paul Wouters, Royal Netherlands Academy of Arts and Sciences (Chapters 15 and 16); Liv Langfeldt, Norwegian Institute for Studies in Research and Higher Education (Chapter 18); Marc Luwel, Ministry of the Flemish Community, Belgium (Chapters 19 and 20); Jan Reedijk, Leiden University, the Netherlands (Chapters 19 and 21); Rolf Lehming, National Science Foundation, USA (Chapter 22); and Abraham Bookstein, University of Chicago, USA (Chapter 24).

In addition I am grateful to the following co-authors of journal articles that played an important role in this book: Anthony van Raan, CWTS (Chapter 4); Thed van Leeuwen, CWTS (Chapters 4 and 5); Renger de Bruin, former CWTS, Centraal Museum, Utrecht, the Netherlands (Chapter

4); Jan Reedijk, Leiden University, the Netherlands (Chapter 5); Wolfgang Glänzel, Steunpunt O&O Statistieken, Leuven, Belgium (Chapter 5); Martijn Visser, CWTS (Chapters 8 and 10); Marc Luwel, Ministry of the Flemish Community, Belgium (Chapters 4 and 11); and Anton Nederhof, CWTS (Chapter 11).

I am also grateful to my employing institution (Leiden University) and to Anthony van Raan (Director of CWTS) for giving me the opportunity to write this book and to use CWTS resources, to Suze van der Luijt (CWTS) for clerical assistance in its preparation, and to Peter Negenborn and Erik van Wijk (CWTS) for their efforts in creating and maintaining at CWTS the bibliometric database version of the ISI Citation Indexes applied in numerous chapters.

A substantial part of this book is based upon a series of lectures I delivered in 2003 and 2004 at the CWTS Graduate Course on Measuring Science. I acknowledge the Ministry of the Flemish Community, The Netherlands Organisation for Scientific Research (NWO) and the scientific publishing company Elsevier for funding parts of the work described in this book.

Finally I wish to express my gratitude to Eugene Garfield (Chairman-Emeritus, Institute for Scientific Information, USA), for his strong support during the preparation of this book, for writing a note on accuracy issues included in Chapter 12, and for his most valuable comments on the book's structure and on all chapters.

EXECUTIVE SUMMARY

This book is about scientific, or more generally, scholarly research. It focuses on a type of research that is characterised as 'basic', 'fundamental' or 'strategic'. It recognises its crucial importance for global economic progress and social welfare, but at the same time it acknowledges that a firm political or societal basis for this type of research can be maintained only by further developing a system of internal quality control and performance enhancement. This book aims at showing that citation analysis is a useful tool in such a system.

It primarily concerns the assessment of the contributions scholars make in their research publications to the advancement of valid scholarly knowledge. It deals with the assessment of research performance of individual scholars, research groups, departments and institutions, scholarly journals and national scholarly systems, and with the analysis of general characteristics of global science and scholarship.

It explores the uses and limits of citation analysis, involving the construction and application of a wide range of 'bibliometric' indicators of the 'impact', 'influence' or 'quality' of scholarly work, and derived from citation data, i.e. data on references cited in footnotes or bibliographies of scholarly research papers. It focuses on the Citation Indexes produced by the Institute for Scientific Information (ISI, currently Thomson Scientific), but many findings are also relevant in the use of other citation indexes.

This book aims to provide useful information for members of the scholarly community and research policy officials about basic technical aspects of citation analysis, what it measures, and how it can be properly applied in research evaluation and policy processes, by systematically discussing numerous statements about its value made by scholars and policy makers, correcting misunderstandings and illustrating its strengths and limits, particularly in relation to peer review.

It is argued that the use of citation analysis in the evaluation of individuals, groups and institutions is more appropriate the more it is:

– Formal – i.e., previously known to evaluators or decision makers and to scholars or institutions subjected to evaluation that indicators are used as one of the sources of information.
– Open – those subjected to the bibliometric analysis have the opportunity to examine the accuracy of underlying data, and to provide background information that in their view is relevant for a proper interpretation of the quantitative outcomes.
– Scholarly founded – that bibliometric investigators present their outcomes within a scholarly framework, discuss issues of validity, explicitly state theoretical assumptions, and underline their potentialities and limits.
– Supplemented with expert and background knowledge about the substantive contents of the work under evaluation, the conditions under which evaluated scholars operated, and their research objectives.
– Carried out in a clear policy context – i.e., applied in the framework of an evaluation procedure of which both the evaluative perspective and the objectives are clear to all participants.
– Stimulating users to explicitly state basic notions of scholarly quality, its dimensions and how they were operationalised and weighted.
– Enlightening rather than formulaic – the indicators are used to obtain insight in a particular aspect addressed in the process, rather than as inputs in formulas designed to algorithmically generate the process' outcomes.

Application of citation analysis in the assessment of past research performance in basic science and of scientific journals has reached a *high level of sophistication*. This book discusses numerous issues raised by scientists subjected to citation analysis, by journal editors and policy makers, and shows how such issues can in principle be accounted for or solved technically.

The extent to which citation analysis based on the ISI Citation Indexes can be validly applied in all domains of scholarship, including the applied and technical sciences, social sciences and humanities, is often debated. This book thoroughly examines differences in the *structure of the written communication systems* among the various domains of scholarship, and the extent to which these systems are *covered by the ISI Citation Indexes*.

The ISI Indexes do not claim to have complete journal coverage, but rather to include the most important. Their founder, Eugene Garfield, developed a powerful and unique criterion for expanding the database beyond the core of journals whose importance to a given field is obvious: the frequency at which journals are cited in those sources that are already included in the index.

Applying a 'database internal' criterion, this book shows that ISI coverage tends to be *excellent* in physics, chemistry, molecular biology and biochemistry, biological sciences related to humans and clinical medicine; *good*, yet not excellent, in applied and engineering sciences, biological sciences related to animals and plants, geosciences, mathematics, psychology and other social sciences related to medicine and health; and *moderate* in other social sciences including sociology, political science, anthropology and educational sciences, and particularly in humanities.

A principal cause of non-excellent coverage is the importance of sources other than international journals, such as books and conference proceedings. In fields with a moderate ISI coverage, language or national barriers play a much greater role than they do in other domains of science and scholarship. In addition, research activities may be fragmented into distinct schools of thought, each with their own 'paradigms'.

This book distinguishes and illustrates *four types of bibliometric studies* in which the ISI database plays different roles. The decision as to which type of study is appropriate in a discipline depends upon the extent to which it is covered by the ISI Indexes. Compared to a 'standard' analysis in fields with excellent coverage, this database may be expanded in several ways in fields with good but not excellent coverage, or it may play a limited role or no role at all when field coverage is moderate.

If the extent to which research findings reach beyond a purely national or local viewpoint and are exposed to criticisms from a wide international scholarly audience is considered as a relevant criterion of research quality in social sciences and humanities, a major task would be to develop for the various subfields valid indicators of this aspect of research performance. This book argues that it cannot be taken for granted that the ISI Citation Indexes provide such indicators in all subfields of these domains of scholarship. A challenge would be to systematically explore alternative data sources and methodologies. The expertise and perceptions of scholars active in the various subfields should play an important role in such an exploration.

As regards *journal impact factors*, this book provides a technical and historical explanation of how ISI impact factors are calculated, and highlights a number of problems affecting their accuracy and applicability. It illustrates how alternative journal impact measures solve many of these problems, but at the same time underlines that there is no single 'perfect' indicator of journal performance. Although the status of the journals in which a research group publishes is an aspect of research performance in its own right, journal impact factors should not be used as surrogates of citation impact of a group's publications.

Data accuracy is a next crucial issue. It is illustrated how uninformed data collection and analysis may substantially distort the outcomes of citation analysis. Use of inaccurate data may not only distort results for particular groups, but also affect the credibility and hence the usefulness of a bibliometric study as a whole. But accuracy problems can be overcome in advanced data handling and in data verification procedures involving evaluated scholars and their institutions.

The next key issue concerns *what citations measure*. Outcomes of citation analysis of basic science research groups tend to statistically correlate in a positive way with peer ratings of the groups' past performance. This book presents more empirical case studies revealing such a positive correlation. Findings provide a further theoretical justification for applying citation analysis in research evaluation, but correlations are not perfect.

It is argued that citation counts can be conceived as manifestations of intellectual influence, but the concepts of citation impact and intellectual influence do not coincide. Distinct notions of the concept of intellectual influence may exist, and evaluators assessing scholarly work may have different views upon which are the most crucial aspects to be taken into account. Outcomes of citation analysis must be *valued* in terms of a qualitative, evaluative framework that takes into account the substantive contents of the works under evaluation.

The interpretation of citation impact involves a quest for possible biases. It is therefore crucial at which level of aggregation citation analysis is carried out. Evaluating aggregates of entities can be carried out in such a way that the effects of special characteristics and circumstances of individual entities to some extent cancel out. It must be underlined that systematic biases as regards the aggregate as a whole may still occur and should be taken into account.

The conditions for proper use of bibliometric indicators at the level of individual scholars, research groups or departments tend to be more readily satisfied in a *peer review* context than in a policy context. It can therefore be argued that bibliometric analyses at such lower aggregation levels normally best find their way to the policy arena through peer assessments. But it does *not* follow that citation analysis is *merely* a tool to be used by peers.

This book illustrates the use of citation analysis as a tool to *assess peer review procedures* and to keep the peer review process honest. From the latter perspective, it is a tool for policy decision makers as well. It shows that citation analysis has its strengths and limits, and that the same is true for peer review. The challenge is to combine the two methodologies in a proper, productive way.

A study of *research assessment exercises*, in which a small peer committee evaluated research departments in an entire national discipline, raised the question whether such exercises are capable of identifying truly excellent or 'top' research departments. This finding underlines the need for research policy makers to thoroughly reflect upon the objectives of such exercises, taking into account their cost effectiveness.

This study also provided evidence that a peer rating system (e.g., in terms of 'excellent', 'good', 'less good', 'poor') tends to generate a distribution of ratings among departments that depends upon the rating system itself, and that is to some extent independent of the overall performance level of the departments under evaluation.

A study of funding procedures of a *national research council* provided evidence that proximity relationships between applicants and expert committees responsible for the evaluation of grant proposals made their outcomes inequitable. It illustrates how quantitative, bibliometric methods can fruitfully contribute to an *internal* debate within a funding agency about funding procedures and evaluation criteria, and to a *public* debate between a funding agency and the national science policy sphere.

Citation analysis is a most valuable tool in policy studies addressing general issues regarding the academic system, with a complexity that reaches beyond the capabilities of expert panels. Studies of the global academic system and 'macro' studies of national academic systems are excellent examples. This book presents four studies that deal with 'classical' issues in the field of quantitative science studies and that have a high policy relevance:

– Did scientists' global publication productivity increase during the 1980s and 1990s?
– How to measure trends in national publication output?
– Does international scientific collaboration pay?
– Do US scientists overcite papers from their own country?

A first macro study presented in this book examined trends during the 1980s and 1990s in *global publication productivity*, defined as the total number of articles published in a year per scientist active in that year. It was found that, although an 'average' individual scientist can justly claim to have published in recent years more research articles than in the past, from a global perspective scientific publication productivity did not increase during the past two decades. One interpretation is that raising both the internal productivity of the science system, its economic relevance and collaboration, are to some extent conflicting policy objectives for basic science.

Nowadays many countries publish National Science Indicators Reports and analyse what bibliometric macro indicators express about the state of *a nation's research system*, and about the level of its research performance. Not infrequently, the various indicators and methodologies seem to lead to different conclusions. This makes bibliometric indicators vulnerable to selective use and manipulation. A second macro study presented in this book provides technical information as regards the construction and interpretation of publication based macro indicators.

Assessing the trend in a single country's publication output, it explores a categorisation of publishing authors into *domestic* (i.e., working in institutions located in the country itself) and *foreign* (active in other countries). Indicators are considered that give an answer to the following questions: did the country's scientific workforce expand or shrink, and did the number of papers in which it participated per domestic author increase or decline? It concludes that it is essential to calculate a *series* of indicators and to provide them with a consistent interpretation. Isolating a single measure from the others may distort the results and lead to biased conclusions.

A third macro study addressed the 'classical' issue '*Does international scientific collaboration pay*?' It concludes that when scientifically advanced countries collaborate with one another, they profit in around 7 out of 10 cases from such bi-lateral collaboration, in the sense that both raise their citation impact compared to that of their 'purely domestic' papers. But when advanced countries contribute in bi-lateral international collaboration to the development of scientifically less advanced countries – and thus to the advancement of science in the longer term than the perspective normally adopted in research evaluation – this activity tends to negatively affect their short-term citation impact, particularly when their role is secondary.

It has been claimed that US authors excessively cite other US colleagues. This would lead to a *US bias* in the selection of journals for the ISI Citation Indexes and would distort the outcomes of citation analysis. This book argues that the crucial issue at stake is the adequacy of the norm against which referencing practices of US scientists is evaluated. A fourth macro study found *no* conclusive evidence that US scientists in science fields excessively cite papers originating from their own country.

Finally, this book discusses *recent trends* in the development of indicators and in scholarly publication. The need is emphasised to carry out systematic studies of the *conditions* under which citation analysis is actually applied in research evaluation, and of the *effects* of its use upon the scholarly community, its evaluators and the policy arena. Such insights may contribute to the further development of the 'critical' potential of citation analysis as a research evaluation tool.

Analyses of changes in publication and citation practices are illuminating, but the principal question is not whether or not scholars' practices change under the influence of the use of bibliometric indicators, but rather whether or not the application of such measures as a research evaluation tool enhances research performance and scholarly progress in general.

As more and more scholarly documents become available in electronic form through the World Wide Web, their use as sources in citation analysis is expected to increase in the near future. From the perspective of research evaluation, including more sources does not necessarily lead to more valid assessments of the contributions scholars make to the advancement of scholarly knowledge. The extent to which the sources' documents contain new knowledge and meet professional quality standards is a critical issue.

Outcomes of citation analysis are often presented to the 'outside world' in the form of *rankings* of entities such as individual scholars, research departments or institutions. This also occurs with outcomes of peer reviews. It is argued that the need for policy makers and the wider public to obtain insight into the scholarly quality of the various groups is legitimate, but that scholarly quality is not as straightforwardly measured and ranked as performance is in many other societal domains. Moreover, rankings disregard how the performance of one entity depends upon that of others. Bibliometric investigators should look for means to express these notions in the outcomes they produce.

PART 1

GENERAL INTRODUCTION AND MAIN CONCLUSIONS

Chapter 1

GENERAL INTRODUCTION

1.1 The ISI Citation Indexes as search and research tools

Eugene Garfield's book *Citation Indexing* starts with the following paragraph that describes the basic concept underlying a journal citation index:

> The concept of citation indexing is simple. Almost all the papers, notes, reviews, corrections and correspondence published in scientific journals contain citations. They cite – generally by title, author and where and when published – documents that support, provide evidence for, illustrate, or elaborate on what the author has to say. Citations are the formal, explicit linkages between papers that have particular points in common. A citation index is built around these linkages. It lists publications that have been cited and identifies the sources of the citations. Anyone conducting a literature search can find from one to dozens of additional papers on a subject just by knowing one that has been cited. And every paper that is found provides a list of new citations with which to continue the search (Garfield, 1979, p. 1.).

Eugene Garfield Associates was founded in 1954 and launched numerous editions of *Current Contents* by 1960. In that year, the company name was changed to the Institute for Scientific Information (ISI). In 1964, ISI launched the *Science Citation Index* (*SCI*), as a quarterly multidisciplinary index covering at that time some 600 scientific journals (Garfield, 1964). From 1964 onwards, the *SCI* expanded rapidly. Subsequently, ISI began publishing indexes covering the social sciences (the *Social Sciences Citation Index*, *SSCI*) and the Arts and Humanities (*Arts and Humanities Citation Index*, *A&HCI*). In 1988, the printed indexes were supplemented by CD-ROM editions, then in 1997, ISI began the *Web of Science*, a comprehensive citation index made available to subscribers through the Internet, and covering some 7,500 scholarly journals from all areas of scholarship.

Throughout this book the term 'ISI Citation Indexes' is used to denote the various information products based on citation indexing of scholarly literature, produced during the past 50 years by the Institute for Scientific Information. ISI recently changed its name to Thomson Scientific, Inc. The ISI Citation Indexes were designed primarily for the purpose of retrieval and dissemination of scholarly literature. Citation indexing is used to augment traditional natural language (titles) by utilising cited references (citations) as indexing terms. Such use of the author, journal, title, and citation indexing elements can be characterised as *bibliographic*.

Garfield viewed the cited work as symbolic of specific content, such as a method, a concept, a fruitful hypothesis, or specific data. The citing papers one retrieves from a citation index search are assumed to have a subject relevance to the idea symbolised by the cited item targeted for the search. Citations can be viewed as indicators of document content, as document descriptors, or indexing terms.

Once citation indexing became available for bibliographic research, it was apparent that it could be used to answer inquiries into the nature of scholarly activity: how it is structured, how it develops and how its actors perform. Garfield expressed this as follows:

> If the literature of science reflects the activities of science, a comprehensive, multidisciplinary citation index can provide an interesting view of these activities. This view can shed some useful light on both the structure of science and the process of scientific development (Garfield, 1979, p. 62).

It was Derek de Solla Price (1970) who underlined that science on the one hand and humanities on the other are two distinct domains of scholarship with essentially different substantive contents. According to Price, the different substantive contents in science and humanities have "erected different social apparatuses of information pooling and exchange".

> Scholarship is a conspiracy to pool the capabilities of many men, and science is an even more radical conspiracy that structures this pooling so that the totality of this sort of knowledge can grow more rapidly than any individual can move by himself. The humanities, by resting with the capability of the individual, eschew this growth rate and certainty (Price, 1970, p. 6).

He conceived a scholarly publication as not merely a piece of information but also as an expression of "the state of a scholar or group of scholars at a particular time" and hypothesised:

If the paper is an expression of a person or several persons working at the research front, we can tell something about the relations among the people from the papers themselves (Price, 1970, pp. 6–7).

For a historical account of the creation and application of the ISI Citation Indexes, the reader is referred to Wouters (1999). During the past four decades, hundreds if not thousands of studies have used data from the citation indexes to provide some type of quantitative, statistical analysis. These applications can be denoted as *bibliometric*, as they extract, aggregate and analyse quantitative aspects of bibliographic information. As statistics related to scholarship are applied mainly in the sciences, the term scientometric is also often used.

The use of the *SCI* as a search tool is well documented in numerous publications, for which the book *Citation Indexing* (1979) provides an excellent introduction. While it did discuss various non-bibliometric uses, when the book was published the bibliometric use of *SCI* for evaluation and study of scholarly activities had not yet fully matured. The current book takes into account what has been learned about the bibliometric uses of *SCI*, and in particular, the study of scholarly communication and research performance.

A good example of the use of the ISI citation indexes for studying *the structure of the scholarly communication system* is the following statement by Garfield in which counts of cited references from the *SCI* are related to a concept of 'quality' of a scientific journal.

> Since authors refer to previous material to support, illustrate, or elaborate on a particular point, the act of citing is an expression of the importance of the material. The total number of such expressions is about the most objective measure there is of the material's importance to current research. The number of times all the material in a given journal has been cited is an equally objective and enlightening measure of the quality of a journal as a medium for communicating research results (Garfield, 1979, pp. 23–24).

This statement should be viewed in the context of his original and illuminative studies of the scientific communication system, in which relationships among journals were analysed in terms of citations from one journal to another, and core journals and more peripheral ones were identified. Equally important, his analysis provided the basis for a unique and highly useful 'internal' monitor of the adequacy of coverage of the *SCI* itself.

The journal statistics he derived were soon isolated from the study context and published by ISI in rankings of journals by impact factor, probably the bibliometric construct most widely used in the scholarly and publishing community. Journal impact factors found their way into the arena of research policy, research management and library collection management. Nowadays they are used to evaluate scholars, to develop publication strategies and to monitor library collections.

Citation counts are used to study not only communication artefacts such as scholarly journals, but also individual scholars, research groups, departments and institutions, scholarly disciplines and entire nations. In the 1960s, sociologists recognised the usefulness of bibliometric statistics in sociological research. In their important paper 'Measuring the quality of sociological research: Problems in the use of the Science Citation Index', Jonathan and Stephen Cole stated:

> The problem of assessing the "quality" of scientific publications has long been a major impediment to progress in the sociology of science ... The invention of the Science Citation Index (*SCI*) a few years ago provides a new and reliable tool to measure the significance of individual scientists' contributions ... The number of citations an individual receives may be tabulated and used as an indicator of the relative scientific significance or "quality" of that individual's publication ... This should lead to major advances in the sociology of sociology (Cole and Cole, 1971, p. 23).

The use of bibliometric data in research performance assessments went far beyond the boundaries of sociological research, but soon entered the policy arena in many countries. The application of performance indicators, however, was – and still is – controversial.

A distinction can be made between two contexts of use of bibliometric data or indicators in the study of scholarly activity: a *scholarly research context*, and a *policy context*. This distinction clearly emerges from the following statements by Stephen Cole:

> A crucial distinction must be made between using citations as a rough indicator of quality among a relatively large sample of scientists and in using citations to measure the quality of a particular individual's work (Cole, 1989, pp. 9, 11). In sociological studies our goal is not to examine individuals but to examine the relationships among variables (ibid., p. 11). Citations are a very good measure of the quality of scientific work for use in sociological studies of science; but because the measure is far from perfect it would be an error to reify it and use it to make individual decisions (ibid., p. 12).

Citation indicators in *a scholarly research context* are used as tools in testing hypotheses or examining universal relationships among variables within a theoretical framework. It is the validity of a particular hypothesis that is at stake. In a *policy context*, citation indicators may be used in reaching some type of policy decision. This decision may relate to an individual, but also to aggregates of individuals such as research groups, institutes or disciplines. Outcomes of citation analysis may have *practical consequences* for the position of individual scholars and the institutions in which they carry out their research.

1.2   Quantitative science and technology studies

Quantitative studies of science and technology is a rapidly developing field. Its development is closely linked to a number of general tendencies in the global scholarly system. During the past few decades, research institutions have been subjected to new influences and pressures emerging from the increasing need for accountability in scholarly research and training of students.

In most OECD countries, there is an increasing emphasis on the effectiveness and efficiency of government-supported research. Governments need systematic evaluations for optimising their research allocations, re-orienting their research support, rationalising research organisations, restructuring research in particular fields, or augmenting research productivity. In view of this, they have stimulated or imposed evaluation activities.

Universities have become more diverse in structure and are more oriented towards economic and industrial needs. In most member states of the Organisation for Economic Cooperation and Development (OECD) the following trends in the university system were identified (OECD Group on the Science System, 1998).

- Declining government R&D finance: Government research and development (R&D) budgets have been reduced in a number of OECD countries.
- Changing nature of government finance: Government funding for academic research is more and more mission-oriented and contract-based, and more dependent upon performance criteria.
- Increasing industry R&D finance: Private industries are funding an increasing proportion of university research.
- Growing demand for economic relevance: Universities are expected to contribute more and more to their national innovation systems.
- Increasing systemic linkages: Universities are encouraged to enter into joint ventures and co-operative research with industry and other research institutions, in order to improve the effectiveness of networks in national innovation systems.
- Growing research personnel concerns: Both ageing of the workforce and the declining interest in some fields of science by young people in a number of countries raise concerns about the availability of sufficient numbers of well-trained researchers in the future.

– Internationalisation of university research: Globalisation, stemming partly from advances in information and communication technologies (e.g., the Internet), influences research activities and networks.

On the one hand, *quantitative studies of science and technology* explore and apply methodologies enabling policy makers to carry out their research and innovation policies; on the other, they provide tools to critically assess the effectiveness of such policies. As a result, science and technology indicators are becoming increasingly important in research policy. This trend is clearly illustrated in the recently published *Handbook of Quantitative Science and Technology Research* (Moed et al., 2004).

All chapters in the *Handbook* deal with the study of conditions that positively or negatively influence scientific and technological performance, defined in terms of the needs and criteria expressed by the societies in which these systems are embedded. The basic assumption underlying these studies is that one must have a proper insight into how an S&T system works in order to design effective policies aimed at improving its performance. Five broad, partly overlapping themes can be identified that apply bibliometric methodologies and focus on *scholarly research*.

1. *The assessment of the contribution made by various bodies in the scholarly system to the advancement of scholarly knowledge.* Typical examples of such bodies are individual scholars, research groups or departments, research institutions such as universities, and national systems. The contribution to scholarly knowledge does not merely relate to the progress achieved in a particular research specialty, but also to the extent to which it contributes to surrounding research areas. This theme comprises comparative assessments of research performance, and particularly the citation impact of their publications on the international research front (van Raan, 2004a). Studies of research groups and departments play a role in national research assessment exercises of scholarly disciplines (van Leeuwen, 2004b).

2. *Analyses of the global scholarly system.* These analyses comprise studies of various characteristics of the scholarly system and their relationships to research performance, including its internationalisation and globalisation, (Zitt and Bassecoulard, 2004), scholarly collaboration networks (e.g., Glänzel and Schubert, 2004), multi- and inter-disciplinarity (Bordons et al., 2004), the dissemination of scholarly information (Arunachalam, 2004), and the participation of women (Naldi et al., 2004). Several authors applied approaches from statistical physics describing the behaviour of complex physical systems to the science and technology system and use bibliometric data to characterise it (e.g., van Raan, 1990; Katz, 1999; van Raan, 2000; Amaral et al., 2001).

3. *Analyses of scholarly fields*. This theme involves mapping of the structure of scholarly or technological fields or disciplines and their development over time on the basis of quantitative, bibliometric analysis of their literatures. Typical examples are co-citation (e.g., Small, 1973; Small, 1977), co-word (Callon et al., 1983; Noyons, 2004) and author co-citation analysis (White and McCain, 1998). Analysing co-occurrence matrices, such studies aim at identifying and analysing emerging research specialties or 'hot' topics of great strategic or technological importance, their principal actors, and their relationships to other areas of research.

4. *Analyses of the science–technology interface and the economic contributions of science*. This theme focuses on the role of science in innovation processes and on assessments of the economic outputs of basic research. There are many ways to analyse bibliometrically the science–technology interface (Bassecoulard and Zitt, 2004). Combined analysis of scientific publications and patents reveals knowledge networks among academic scientists and industrial researchers. The study of references in patents to the scientific literature sheds light upon the science base of modern technology (e.g., Carpenter and Narin, 1983). Studies of inventors of patents reveal the extent to which basic scientists employed in academic institutions contributed to technological developments (Noyons et al., 2003; Schmoch, 2004; Tijssen, 2004).

5. *Assessment of educational, social and cultural contributions of basic research*. This theme comprises a variety of topics that may be closely related to the economic function of scientific research. To the extent that analyses of documents play a role, these topics include assessments of the citation impact of basic medical research upon medical practice and the wider public, by analysing citations to basic science papers that are given in clinical guidelines, textbooks, government policy documents, international or national regulations and newspaper articles (Lewison, 2004). Other approaches examine the extent to which globalisation of research leads to more general welfare, particularly in developing countries (Arunachalam, 2004; da Motta e Albuquerque, 2004). As regards the contribution of social sciences and humanities, their enlightenment function towards the general public constitutes an important topic (e.g., Nederhof and Zwaan, 1991).

Table 1.1 presents an overview of how *citation analysis* can be used to study the science and technology system and the relationships between science and technology. In the former, citations from the scientific literature are analysed, particularly from journals processed for the ISI Citation Indexes, and in the latter those from the patent literature obtained from major patent offices such as the *US Patent and Trademark Office* and the *European Patent Office.*

Pioneering work on the analysis of patent citations was carried out by Francis Narin and co-workers (Carpenter and Narin, 1983; Albert et al., 1991; Narin, 1994; Narin et al., 1997). One basic hypothesis underlying their work is that the number of times a patent is cited from other patents provides an indication of its technological importance. Citations from one patent to another are even used to assess the economic value of patents (Sampat and Ziedonis, 2004), knowledge networks in innovation (Breschi and Lissoni, 2004), and a patent holder's stock market performance (Narin et al., 2004).

Table 1.1. The role of citation analysis in the study of the relationships between science and technology

Influencing / cited	Influenced / citing	
	Science	*Technology*
Science	Contribution of science groups to scientific progress *Citations in science papers to other science papers (this book)*	The science base of technology *Citations in patents to scientific literature*
Technology	The influence of technology upon scientific development *Citation gap*	Contribution of technologies to technological progress *Citations in patents to other patents*

A second hypothesis holds that citations in patents in a field to the scientific literature reflect that field's science base. This hypothesis was further developed in many subsequent publications (e.g., van Vianen et al., 1990; Schmoch, 1993; Meyer, 2000; Tijssen et al., 2000).

It was Cees Le Pair (1988) who underlined that the influence of technology and instrumentation upon scientific development is not properly reflected in cited references in the scientific literature. Valuable technical products such as the electron microscope are heavily used in the research described in numerous scientific publications (Bakker, 1977). The term *citation gap* indicates that, although publishing authors may mention the product in the full texts of their papers, they do not *cite* it in the papers' reference lists. Citations to patents in the scientific literature are relatively rare (Glänzel and Meyer, 2003) and their significance and usefulness are not yet fully explored.

1.3 Scope and structure of the book

This book concerns primarily the assessment of the contributions made by scholars in their research publications to the advancement of valid scholarly knowledge. In terms of the distinction in main themes presented in the previous section, it focuses on the first and second; in terms of citation relationships among documents, it explores references made in scholarly documents to other scholarly documents. The core of this book deals with the assessment of research performance of individual scholars, research groups, departments, institutions and countries, and with the analysis of general characteristics of the global scholarly system.

Basic research can be defined as the type of research that is primarily carried out to increase scholarly knowledge. Following Salter and Martin (2001), it includes both 'curiosity-driven' – sometimes also denoted as 'pure' – as well as 'strategic' or 'application oriented' research. The latter is undertaken in a quest for a particular application, even though its precise details are not yet known. A large part of this book is dedicated to the use of citation analysis in the assessment of basic research. However, it also addresses its usefulness and limits in the applied and technical sciences. In addition, it focuses on 'science', but also dedicates attention to the social sciences and humanities.

Table 1.2. Classification of scientific–scholarly activities into three broad domains

Aggregate term	Disciplines (non-exhaustive list)
Science	Natural sciences, including chemistry, physics, astronomy, geosciences
	Life sciences, including biological sciences, clinical medicine
	Mathematics
	Applied and technical sciences, including engineering
Social sciences	Psychology, psychiatry
	Economics
	Sociology, political sciences, education, pedagogical sciences, anthropology
Humanities	Law, literature, language and linguistics, historical sciences, philosophy
Scholarship	All domains of science, social sciences and humanities

The concepts *'science'*, *'social science'*, *'humanities'* and *'scholarship'* may cover different aggregates of substantive contents in different countries or cultures. In this book the term science is used to indicate research activities in the natural sciences, biological and life sciences, mathematics, and the applied and technical sciences. Social sciences include amongst others psychology, economics and sociology, and humanities comprise amongst others law, literature, language, history and philosophy. Table 1.2 presents an overview. This classification does *not* fully coincide with the arrangement of disciplines into the three Citation Indexes: *Science Citation Index*, *Social Science Citation Index* and *Arts and Humanities Citation Index*. One of the main differences is that in this book the field of law is categorised as a part of the humanities.

In any assessment of research quality, two fundamental dimensions must be clarified: its time horizon, and its scope. The first relates to the time period taken into account in an assessment of the quality of a piece of work under evaluation. Although historical studies of scholarly development may cover a time period of several decades, in many current research assessment exercises it is often much shorter than that. This book focuses on research assessments adopting a time horizon of 5 to 10 years, but also underlines the relevance of analyses covering longer time periods.

The scope of an assessment can be further specified on the basis of distinctions made by Alvin Weinberg in his classic paper 'Criteria for scientific choice' (Weinberg, 1962). He distinguished between internal and external evaluation criteria. The first relate to the quality of research (and the researchers undertaking it) compared to that of other research activities in the same research (sub)field or specialty. External criteria are generated outside the (sub)field and relate to the question "why pursue this particular science?". Weinberg distinguished technological, social and scientific merit. He sharpened the latter criterion as follows: "that field has the most scientific merit which contributes most heavily to and illuminates most brightly its neighboring scientific disciplines." The core of this book deals with the application of citation analysis in research evaluations based on internal criteria, but it also dedicates attention to its use as a tool to assess the external, scientific merit, as proposed by Weinberg.

It is assumed that in science the *research group* is the 'natural' *unit of scientific activity*. Its scientific staff normally includes a group leader, one or more senior researchers, postdoctoral researchers and several PhD students. Members of research groups tend to interact intensively one with another, and jointly carry out the group's research programme. In many areas of social sciences and humanities the organisational structure of research activities tends to be different from that in science. Scholarly research tends to be more an individual activity. The term *research department* is used to indicate an institutionalised aggregate of research groups or individual scholars covering the same subfield, normally reflected in the departments' name. In science, it may include a single or several research groups.

Citation analysis comprises a variety of ways to analyse references cited in scholarly publications. This book focuses on simple and sophisticated 'counting' of citations to particular sets of scholarly publications, but also on aspects of citing articles other than their sheer number, such as their country or discipline of origin, their subject breadth or trans-disciplinary nature. In addition, it dedicates attention to the use of citation data in analysing cognitive or social structures through a technique denoted as *co-citation analysis*, and to the study of the context of references in the text in which they are given, denoted as *citation context analysis*.

This book recognises the crucial importance of scholarly research, and particularly of basic research, for global economic and cultural progress. But it acknowledges at the same time that a firm political or social basis for this type of research can be maintained only by further developing a system of internal scholarly quality control and performance enhancement. This book aims to show that citation analysis is a useful tool in such a system, and underlines both its *potentialities* and its *limits*.

The term research policy is used here in a broad sense, and comprises policies at various levels: science policy of a national government by ministers responsible for scholarly research; research policy at the level of research organisations or institutions dealing with quality control and the allocation of research funds; and research management, carried out by directors of research groups or departments, including hiring, promoting and retaining individual scholars.

As outlined in the Preface, this book presents a number of studies undertaken by the author, some in collaboration with his colleagues at the Centre for Science and Technology Studies (CWTS) at Leiden University (the Netherlands). In these studies a 'bibliometric' version was used of the ISI Citation Indexes on CD-ROM created at CWTS. Part 2 presents the details of these empirical and theoretical studies in 24 chapters, arranged into 8 subparts (Parts 2.1–2.8).

- Part 2.1: Assessing basic science research departments and journals.
- Part 2.2: The ISI Citation Indexes.
- Part 2.3: Assessing social sciences and humanities.
- Part 2.4. Accuracy aspects.
- Part 2.5: Theoretical aspects.
- Part 2.6: Citation analysis and peer review.
- Part 2.7: Macro studies.
- Part 2.8: New developments.

Chapter 2 in *Part 1* presents basic notions and assumptions underlying the book and its main conclusions as regards the use of citation analysis in research evaluation. Chapter 3 presents short *summaries* of each of the empirical and theoretical chapters included in Part 2.

Part 2.1 discusses a number of statements, questions and misunderstandings regarding the use of citation analysis to assess the 'citation impact' that research groups generate, ranging from 'does citation analysis count citations to first authors only?' via 'does it make peer judgements superfluous?' to 'what are criteria for its proper use?' This part provides an introduction to numerous issues discussed in later chapters. Moreover, it presents advanced citation impact indicators, but refers for technical details to other publications. It focuses on research performance in basic science. Part 2.1 also critically discusses a bibliometric construct widely dispersed among the scholarly community and its librarians: the *journal impact factor*. It explains why this measure is constructed in the way it is, discusses the validity of several assumptions underlying it, and proposes alternative measures. It underlines the questionability of whether a concept as complex as journal performance can be properly expressed in a single indicator.

In order to evaluate whether or not it is appropriate to apply citation analysis in a particular discipline, insight into the basic assumptions and principles of a citation index is essential. *Part 2.2* provides such knowledge, and introduces important technical concepts. One of the most important issues regarding the ISI Citation Indexes is their adequacy of coverage in the various scholarly disciplines. Part 2.2 therefore presents a detailed analysis of the structure of the written communication system in the various disciplines, and the extent to which it is covered by the ISI Indexes. It characterises a discipline's coverage in terms of 'excellent', 'good yet not excellent' and 'moderate'. It distinguishes four types of bibliometric studies in which the ISI Citation Indexes play different roles. The decision as to which type of study should be carried out in a discipline depends upon the extent to which the latter is covered by the ISI Indexes.

Coverage of the ISI Citation Indexes was found to be moderate in certain sectors of social sciences and humanities. *Part 2.3* presents two studies assessing research performance in these domains of scholarship, applying methodologies that are rather different from those normally applied in an assessment of research departments in basic physics or chemistry. Both studies relate to academic research in a Western-European country. A study of research departments in the field of *economics* shows how the set of publications subjected to a citation analysis can be expanded to include books and other written communication media *not* covered by the ISI Indexes. The methodology applied in this study is expected to be valuable in the applied sciences and engineering as well. A second study dealing with the field of *law* illustrates how one can contribute to the development of appropriate performance indicators *without* using citation analysis.

Part 2.4 deals with accuracy issues in citation analysis. It addresses technical problems involved in counting citations to individual papers, and publications of individual scholars and their institutions, without presenting too many technical details. It illustrates how these problems can seriously distort the counts, but at the same time shows how they can be solved in a sophisticated citation analysis.

Part 2.5 concerns the validity of citation based indicators, and addresses the issue: what do citations measure? It summarises and discusses the notions of a number of important scholars in the field who related citation counts to 'utility' or 'intellectual influence' of a cited work, but also to the latter's 'authoritativeness' or 'rhetorical power' It proposes building blocks of a 'theory of citation', and discusses their implications for the use of citation counts in research evaluation. Citation analysis often focuses on the evaluation of entities such as individual scholars, research groups or departments, and scholarly institutions. Often *rankings* of such entities are compiled that not only have an impact on the scholarly community or on the policy sphere, but also upon the wider public. In daily newspapers rankings are quite popular. From publications in the press a picture tends to emerge suggesting that citation analysis is merely a ranking instrument, but this book shows that it is much more powerful than that.

Part 2.6 shows how citation analysis can be used to monitor and evaluate peer review processes, particularly peer review of grant proposals submitted to funding agencies, and of the past performance of research departments in national research assessment exercises. The presented studies raise questions about the validity of peer review. A general point made in this part is that not only citation analysis but also peer review of research performance has its particular strengths and limitations.

Part 2.7 illustrates how citation analysis can be applied in examining general aspects of the global scholarly system. Four empirical studies address 'classical' issues with a high policy relevance that are fiercely debated among members of the scholarly community and the policy arena. These issues are: Did global scholarly publication productivity increase during the 1980s and 1990s? How to assess trends in national publication output? Does international collaboration pay? And do US scholars overcite papers from their own country?

Finally, *Part 2.8* discusses new developments in the construction and application of bibliometric indicators. It primarily aims at illustrating how theoretical notions and assumptions are involved in their construction. This part also dedicates attention to the increasing importance of electronic publishing, and to recently developed new publication databases and search engines, particularly Elsevier's *Scopus* and Google's *Scholar*. It underlines the need to carry out systematic studies of the conditions under which citation analysis is actually used in research evaluation, and of its effects, and discusses the phenomenon that outcomes of citation analysis are often presented to the 'outside world' in the form of *rankings*.

Chapter 2

BASIC NOTIONS AND GENERAL CONCLUSIONS

2.1   Introduction

This chapter presents basic notions and assumptions, and general conclusions regarding the application of citation analysis in research evaluation and research policy. Section 2.2 states basic assumptions of the concept of scholarly research quality, and Section 2.3 highlights important aspects of rationality in evaluation and decision making processes. Section 2.4 formulates basic principles and criteria of appropriate use of citation analysis, or bibliometric indicators in general, in research evaluation. It builds upon an earlier paper on the uses and limits of the ISI Indexes (Moed, 2002a). The next three sections discuss the implications these principles have for the role of bibliometric investigators (Section 2.5), for scholars subjected to citation analysis (Section 2.6) and for evaluators and other users of its outcomes (Section 2.7). Finally, Section 2.8 focuses on the relationship between citation analysis and peer review.

2.2   About the nature of the concept of scholarly research quality

Any book about the use of citation analysis in the measurement of research performance should state explicitly its base assumptions about the nature of the concept of 'research quality'. On the one hand, research quality is not merely a social construct. It does not coincide with what scholars define or decide upon as quality, even if they have reached a consensus. It relates to a quality intrinsic to the research itself. On the other hand, the concept cannot be defined and measured in the same way as in physics or other areas of science. Research quality has a certain objectivity, but it is not a form of objectivity embodied in physics. Its objectivity can be illustrated by referring to an historical viewpoint. History will show which contributions to scholarly knowledge are valuable and enduring. The history of a scholarly contribution starts with reading and citing scholarly documents in which it is presented.

Citation analysis aims at obtaining indications of research quality from a particular form of social behaviour: referencing practices in scholarly publications. But there is no justification for the claim that "quality as measured by citation analysis is what quality is". This view can be denoted as *citationist*. There are very few if any practitioners in the field of citation analysis who accept its validity. The author of this book, however, shares with critics of citation analysis (e.g., Woolgar, 1991) their concern that its application on a large scale may narrow the notion of research quality, and reduce it to a one-dimensional, essentially quantitative concept. He believes that such a reduced concept is inadequate, and that its influence may be harmful for the development of science and scholarship.

But a relativistic account of scientific or scholarly activity, claiming that scholarly validity and truth are merely social constructs, or solely a matter of what scholars agree upon, is equally harmful. Citations or references can be conceived as social acts of members of the scholarly community. A sociology of science negating the existence of the intrinsic nature of research quality, but instead assuming that quality fully coincides with what scholars agree upon, opens the door wide to a *citationist* view.

2.3 Characteristics of research evaluation and policy processes

The domain of scholarship on the one hand and research policy – or more generally, the domain of politics in which it is embedded – on the other, represent two distinct spheres. Developing a view on what is 'good' research on the one hand, and formulating a 'good' policy, or making a 'good' policy decision on the other, are two distinct tasks. The criteria for what is 'good' and what is less so are fundamentally different in the two spheres. Although the research questions addressed in citation analysis may be derived from policy questions, the issue of validity and reliability of science indicators belongs to the domain of scholarship, and is addressed within scholarly theoretical frameworks, using appropriate scholarly research methodologies. On the other hand, applicability, policy relevance and usefulness are issues in the policy sphere.

A number of distinctions are useful to characterise the processes that make use of citation analysis or bibliometric indicators in general. These processes include both research evaluation procedures and the use of their outcomes within the framework of policy decision making processes in which evaluation processes are embedded. The characteristics relate to what can be denoted as 'rationality' embodied in such processes.

The first dimension relates to the basic perspective and the objectives of the evaluation. Assessing research quality of groups of scholars in a particular scholarly (sub)field can be carried out from two main evaluative perspectives, applying fundamentally different kinds of evaluation criteria. The first compares the performance of a group to that of other groups active in the same field. Such an assessment applies evaluation criteria that are denoted by Weinberg (1962) as internal. The second perspective assesses the scientific or scholarly merit of the field as a whole, and compares one field with another – within the same discipline, or even across disciplines.

Research assessments of groups of scholars may serve several kinds of objectives. They may primarily aim to provide departments subjected to evaluation with information that may enable them to improve their research performance. A second aim is to provide tools in decision making processes about the allocation of research funds. A third objective is to make research quality, particularly scientific excellence, manifest to the 'outside' world, i.e., for scholars from other disciplines, for potential external users of research results, and for the general public.

Another distinction is between *informal* and *formal* use of bibliometric indicators. In formal use, those subjected to the evaluation or decision making process are officially informed that such measures play a role as one of the sources of information. Their use may even be formally specified in a protocol of the evaluation process. Informal use of bibliometric indicators means that although such indicators are calculated and may play a role, evaluated entities are not aware of this, or at least not officially notified. Moreover, motivations of judgements or decisions do not explicitly refer to bibliometric analyses even when they have influenced the outcomes.

The degree of *openness towards scholars* whose performance is evaluated provides the next distinction. In an open way they have the opportunity to check the underlying data and to express their views on the outcomes. In a closed type of use, they have not seen the results or the underlying data.

The next three characteristics relate to the extent to which the users of bibliometric indicators – evaluators or decision makers – are *properly informed.* The first is whether or not the users are well informed about the *potentialities and limitations of bibliometric indicators* that were applied. Uninformed users may be confronted with sets of bibliometric indicators without knowing how these were constructed and how they should be interpreted. A second feature is the extent to which *expert knowledge of the cognitive and technical contents* of the works under evaluation is available in the process. A third characteristic regarding the extent to which users are informed is the availability of background knowledge of the *conditions* under which evaluated scholars carried out their activities, their *research objectives and strategies*.

Finally, two characteristics relate to the ways in which the final outcomes of the process are grounded and justified. The first is the extent to which the decision maker or evaluator *explicitly grounds a judgement* or decision by clarifying the criteria and considerations on which it is based and how it is related to the various sources of information available in the process. This particularly applies to the role of bibliometric indicators.

The second characteristic relates to whether the role the bibliometric outcomes play in the process is *enlightening* or *formulaic*. In the latter case, the outcome of the judgement or decision can be defined quantitatively or in categorical terms and is directly related to the outcomes of a bibliometric analysis through some kind of formula or algorithm. Bibliometric indicators play an enlightening role when they are used to contribute to insight, either by answering particular questions or by raising relevant issues during the process.

2.4   Use of bibliometric indicators in research evaluation and policy

In view of the distinctions regarding the concept of 'rationality' in decision-making or evaluation processes made in the previous section, this book further develops the following thesis with respect to the use of bibliometric indicators in a policy context. Their use at the level of individuals, groups and institutions is more appropriate the more it is:

(a) Formal – it is known beforehand to evaluators or decision makers and to scholars or institutions subjected to evaluation that indicators are used as one of the sources of information.

(b) Open – those subjected to the bibliometric analysis have the opportunity to examine the accuracy of underlying data, and to provide background information that in their view is relevant for a proper interpretation of the quantitative outcomes.

(c) Scholarly founded – the bibliometric investigators present their outcomes within a scholarly framework, discuss validity issues, explicitly state theoretical assumptions, and underline their potentialities and limits.

(d) Supplemented with expert and background knowledge about the substantive contents of the work under evaluation, the conditions under which evaluated scholars operated, and about their research objectives.

(e) Carried out in a clear policy context – i.e., applied in the framework of an evaluation procedure of which both the fundamental evaluative perspective and the objectives are clear to all participants.
(f) Stimulating users to explicitly state basic notions of scholarly quality, its dimensions and how they were operationalised and weighted.
(g) Enlightening rather than formulaic – the indicators are used to obtain insight in a particular aspect addressed in the process, rather than as inputs in formulas designed to algorithmically generate the process' outcomes.

In order to further elucidate this thesis, two ways of applying citation analysis can be compared with one another. In the first, a policy official engaged in a decision on hiring, promoting or tenuring a particular scholar, collects raw publication and citation data from the bibliographic ISI indexes available to him, or compiles the impact factors of the journals in which the scholar published, calculates simple statistics, sets some kind of threshold, and reaches a positive decision on whether the scholar's score exceeds it.

It is this type of use that was heavily criticised by many members of the scholarly community (e.g., MacRoberts and MacRoberts, 1987; 1996). The author of this book agrees that *this type* of use of evaluative citation analysis may better be excluded from the policy arena, for the following reasons. First, errors may easily be made in data collection. Secondly, simple statistics may be affected by strong biases that can be corrected by calculating more advanced ones. Valid reference values, enabling comparison of the scholar's activities to those of other colleagues from the same field are difficult to obtain through manual data collection of small data samples.

Next, a number of critical questions may be raised. To what extent is the significance of the scholar's work reflected in bibliometric scores? Are there special circumstances that must be taken into account? Bibliometric indicators are found to positively correlate with peer judgements in many fields, and Part 2.6 of this book presents more empirical case studies revealing such positive correlations, but is this also true for the field of the scholar under evaluation, and, if so, does this statistical correlation provide a sufficiently sound basis for drawing conclusions *about this particular case*? Moreover, assuming that the scholar is active in science, where collaboration and multiple authorships of papers is a common phenomenon, what is the precise contribution of the individual to the teamwork reported in the scholar's articles?

A second case relates to the development of a formal procedure for using bibliometric indicators in peer evaluations of research departments active in basic science at academic institutions in the Netherlands. The organisations involved on the user side are the Organisation of Universities in the Netherlands (VSNU) and the Netherlands Organisation for Scientific Research (NWO) and, on the side of the producer, the Leiden Centre for Science and Technology Studies.

Basic features of this procedure are that evaluated scholars are aware from the very beginning that peer review committees responsible for the evaluation will use bibliometric indicators. They have the opportunity to verify the underlying data. Each group receives the bibliometric outcomes related to its own activities. In addition, members of each group obtain an anonymous overview of the scores of all groups subjected to the analysis, enabling them to position their own group. A group has the opportunity to comment on the bibliometric outcomes, and its comments subsequently constitute a distinct source of information in the peer review process. Finally, bibliometric investigators have the opportunity to present their study to members of the review panel, to underline potentialities and limitations, and indicate possible pitfalls. All of these features constitute important steps towards an open, transparent, informed use of bibliometric indicators in research evaluation.

2.5   The role of bibliometric investigators

Whenever scholars communicate findings that will or may be 'used' in a policy environment, they have the obligation to properly inform the users about the limitations of their results, the framework in which these were obtained, the assumptions that were made, the uncertainties that are involved, and difficulties in interpretation that may emerge. This is particularly true for bibliometric investigators studying scholarly activity and developing bibliometric indicators used to address policy issues.

The aim of this book is precisely to provide information about citation analysis and bibliometric indicators, regarding both their 'technical' properties, such as their sensitivity to measurement errors, as well as their meaning and theoretical background. This information aims at enabling users of the indicators to properly value them, obtain insight in their potentialities and limitations, and use them in an informed, responsible way.

Scholars should not place themselves on the 'seats' of evaluators responsible for quality judgements, or policy officials responsible for policy decisions. Instead, they should acknowledge that the scholarly domain and the policy domain are distinct spheres, each embracing a proper form of rationality. As scholars, bibliometric analysts are experts in the first domain, and not in the second. It is their responsibility to contribute to the fulfilment of conditions under which evaluators or policy makers properly value their findings.

Bibliometric investigators empirically analyse and further operationalise the various manifestations of scholarly performance and examine their interrelationships. Moreover, they conduct empirical studies of the conditions under which research activities are carried out and identify from a physical, economic, sociological, historical or communication-scientific perspective various types of factors that may enhance or hamper scholarly performance. They critically examine peer review processes and the effects of policy measures. Parts 2.6 and 2.7 provide several examples of this type of study.

In research evaluation, however, it is the evaluator and *not* the bibliometric investigator who establishes what is valuable in scholarly activity and which dimensions of the concept of scholarly quality should have the greatest weight in formulating a quality judgement. *In this sense*, citation analysis itself does *not* evaluate. Bibliometric indicators can assist in building up insights into the quality of scholarly work under evaluation and in forming a judgement, and hence constitute a research evaluation *tool*.

2.6   The role of scholars subjected to citation analysis

Scholars confronted with citation analysis of their research publications based on the ISI Citation Indexes or with plans to carry out such an analysis, could consider addressing the following issues.

First, the extent which the database covers the written communication in their fields is a most important aspect. This book dedicates several chapters to it. In order to obtain at least some quantitative expression of the adequacy of coverage for their fields, scholars could analyse reference lists in their own papers and in those of a sample of their colleagues, along the lines presented in Part 2.2 of this book, and calculate indicators of the importance of journals in their fields and the extent to which they are covered by the ISI Citation Indexes.

The adequacy of ISI coverage in a field determines which role the ISI Indexes have to play in a bibliometric study of research performance of scholars in that field. In technical and applied sciences, social sciences and humanities there are alternative approaches to a standard analysis normally conducted in basic science fields such as physics or molecular biology. Part 2.3 of this book further illustrates these alternatives.

The next set of issues relates to the version of the ISI Citation Indexes that is used, according to which methods publication and citation data are collected, and how accurate their counts are. This information of a rather technical nature provides insight, for instance, into the extent to which important variations in author or institutional names are taken into account, and highly cited papers are properly identified. Part 2.4 of this book provides further details.

It is also crucial to obtain information about the time periods that are taken into account and on the basis of which grounds they are selected. Analyses may involve publications from a single year and thus provide a snapshot only, may relate to a time period of 8–10 years comprising two PhD generations, or to lifetime publication oeuvres. Citations may be counted during shorter or longer time periods. The outcomes of citation analysis depend upon which time windows are applied. As outlined in Part 2.1, each publication and citation time window has its proper interpretation and limits.

Another important issue is how the indicators deal with differences in publication and citation practices among scholarly disciplines. Absolute counts tend to be distorted by such differences, whereas normalised indicators can properly take them into account. This book illustrates that citation analysis is much more than merely counting absolute numbers of publications and citations.

Finally, scholars could request or even demand to have the opportunity to verify the publication and citation data that were collected regarding their own publication output, and to be able to comment on the outcomes, providing background information that is in their view indispensable for a proper interpretation of the quantitative outcomes. General notions of what citations measure, and the importance of properly valuing citation impact in an evaluative context, are extensively discussed in Part 2.5 of this book.

2.7   The role of evaluators

There is little systematic research about the actual use of bibliometric data or indicators in peer reviews of the past performance of scholars and research departments, either in the evaluation of grant proposals or in national or institutional research assessment exercises. The principal reason is that internal peer review processes are difficult to study, as they are normally carried without documentation of the bases for their conclusions. Statements about such internal processes cannot easily be tested and often have the status of informal or even anecdotal evidence.

In order to create more openness and transparency in an evaluation process, evaluators could seriously consider making the criteria they applied in forming their judgements more explicit. As far as the role of bibliometric indicators is concerned, this could be achieved by making general statements about their perceived value, what they essentially were assumed to measure, which distorting factors were identified and how other sources of information were used to neutralise these. In this way, a peer review committee's general view of scholarly quality may be brought into the open, and its judgements may be further evaluated and discussed within the context of that view.

2.8 Citation analysis and peer review

In view of the crucial importance of expert and background knowledge for a proper interpretation of bibliometric indicators, the conditions for their proper use at the level of individuals, groups or institutions are generally more readily satisfied in a peer review context than in a policy context. It can therefore be argued that bibliometric analysis at such lower aggregation levels normally best find their way to the policy arena through peer assessments.

But it does not follow that citation analysis is a tool within peer assessments only. Many empirical studies, some of which are summarised in Part 2.6 of this book, reveal the effects of biases of various sorts upon peer judgements. Citation analysis can be used as a tool to obtain relevant information from peers that they are not inclined to give away easily, by confronting them with particular bibliometric outcomes and explicitly asking for an explanation or interpretation. Moreover, it can be used to assess peer review procedures and indicate possible biases in peer judgements. Hence, citation analysis is also a tool for keeping this process honest. From the latter perspective, it is a tool for policy decision makers as well.

Generally, bibliometric analyses may be highly useful to policy decision makers when they are applied at higher levels of aggregation, aiming at providing insight in more general characteristics of scholarly activity, the conditions under which it is conducted and the procedures along which it is funded. They are particularly useful in addressing issues in which peers in principle are competent, but that are so complex and difficult to assess that normal peer review procedures cannot properly deal with them. Part 2.7 presents several studies addressing such issues.

Perhaps the most significant attribute of a scholar is his or her prestige. In a sense it is all that scholars have. Methodologies that claim to measure certain aspects of their performance should therefore be critically reviewed. This is true for citation analysis, but also for peer review and other methods assessing a quality as complex as the contribution to scholarly progress. Given the increasing importance of citation analysis in research evaluation and policy, an inaccurate or misinterpreted citation count can be as harmful as an invalid peer judgement.

Regarding the – either negative or positive – effects of the use of citation analysis or any other methodology in research evaluation, it is crucial to distinguish two points of view. One may focus on its consequences for an individual entity, such as an individual scholar, a research group or institution, or on the effects it has upon scholarly activity and progress in general. A methodology, even if it provides invalid outcomes in individual cases, may be beneficial to the scholarly system as a whole.

Each methodology has its strengths and limitations, and is associated with a certain risk of arriving at invalid outcomes. Although this book primarily deals with citation analysis, it presents evidence that this is also true for peer review. It is the task of members from the scholarly community and the domain of research policy, and not of this author to decide whether or not these risks of using citation analysis are acceptable and whether its benefits prevail. This book aims at providing information about the uses and limits of citation analysis that help scholars and policy makers to carry out such a delicate task.

Chapter 3

SYNOPSIS

Part 2.1   Assessing basic science research departments and scientific journals

Chapter 4   Citation analysis of basic science research departments

Chapter 4 deals with the use of citation analysis in the assessment of the past performance of academic research departments in *basic science*. It introduces advanced types of bibliometric indicators, particularly a normalised (or relative) citation impact indicator. The chapter critically discusses a number of statements and questions often raised by scientists and policy makers about the accuracy, validity and applicability of citation analysis in research evaluation. It presents problems and their solutions. It corrects misunderstandings, and highlights important factors that should be taken into account in a proper interpretation of the bibliometric outcomes. The chapter covers most of the issues discussed by Per Seglen in several publications (Seglen, 1997a; Seglen, 1997b). It also summarises many relevant outcomes and conclusions obtained in later chapters. The issues addressed in this chapter are briefly summarised in Table 3.1.

Table 3.1. Issues addressed in Chapter 4

Question/statement	*Reply*
Data collection and accuracy	
1. Is citation analysis (CA) easy to do because all data is in computerised literature databases?	No. Properly conducted CA requires a bibliometric database with special characteristics
2. How can one obtain accurate, complete publication data?	Publication lists verified by evaluated scientists constitute a proper starting point

Question/statement	Reply
3. Is it difficult to generate publication lists for authors or institutions?	No. Each scientist has a complete list in his or her CV and most institutions publish research reports
4. How can one collect accurate citation counts?	Citation data should and can be based on proper citation matching procedures
5. Does CA count citations to first authors only?	No. Citation statistics are not merely based on first author counts but include co-author counts
6. Can CA correct for author self-citations?	Yes. Author self-citations can be properly identified and excluded from the counts
7. Are senior scientists always co-author of papers by their research students?	Not always. Include 'missing' papers of senior scientists whenever appropriate; analyse groups rather than individuals

ISI Citation Indexes: coverage, biases

Question/statement	Reply
8. Why use the ISI Citation Indexes for CA?	It is the only database currently available covering for several decades all sciences, including for each paper all authors, their institutional affiliations and all cited references
9. How complete is the coverage of the ISI Indexes?	ISI covers about 7,500 of the most important journals mainly selected on the basis of their citation impact
10. Do the ISI Indexes cover mainly literature written in English?	Yes. But in science English is the dominant language on the international research front
11. How can one assess in an objective way the extent to which the ISI Citation Indexes cover for a group's subfield?	Determine from a group's and similar papers the extent to which they cite journals processed for the ISI Indexes
12. How well do the ISI Indexes cover the written communication in science disciplines?	It is excellent in most medical-biological sciences, physics and chemistry, and good in geosciences, mathematics, applied sciences and engineering
13. How well do the ISI Indexes cover the written communication in social sciences and humanities?	It is good in psychology, in other social sciences related to medicine, and in economics, and moderate in other social sciences and in humanities
14. How should one assess groups in science fields with good yet not excellent ISI coverage, particularly in applied sciences and engineering?	The target (=cited) and source (=citing) universe may be expanded with publications in proceedings, books and other important non-ISI sources
15. How should one assess research performance in fields with moderate coverage, particularly in social sciences and humanities?	It is proposed to give the ISI Citation Indexes a limited role or no role at all and to apply other types of techniques

Question/statement	Reply
General validity issues	
16. Scientists have many tasks and duties, and CA does not take into account all of these	Citation analysis assesses the contribution at the international research front, but it does not follow that other aspects are irrelevant
17. Authors cite from a variety of motives, some of which may have little to do with research 'quality'	CA does not capture motives of individuals but their consequences at an aggregate level
18. Do biases cancel out when analysed data samples are sufficiently large?	Individual vagaries in referencing behaviour cancel out but systematic biases must still taken into account
19. Has CA a US bias because US scientists excessively cite other US colleagues?	There is no conclusive evidence for this claim. A crucial issue is which norm one applies
20. Does CA provide an objective measure of research quality?	No. Citations measure impact rather than quality; measuring and valuing citation impact are analytically distinct
21. Is CA invalid because most papers are uncited?	Uncitedness depends upon type of paper, time window, discipline, and can be less than 10%
22. Does 'delayed recognition' or 'the Mendel effect' make CA invalid?	No. Delayed recognition occurs in exceptional cases. Changes in a research community's perceptions are reflected in citation impact
23. After some time, fundamental scientific work becomes decreasingly and then rarely cited (obliteration by incorporation)	This is not a problem if CA relates to citation impact generated on a shorter term (e.g., a 5–10 year period)
24. To what extent are citation counts affected by mutual citation arrangements?	This is difficult to assess. New indicators can relate citation impact to socio-cognitive distance between citing and cited paper
25. Are scientists in large fields cited more often than those in smaller ones?	Means tend not to depend on field size, but extremes of the citation distributions do
26. Does CA undervalue multi- or inter-disciplinary research?	New methodologies provide dedicated approaches to multi- or interdisciplinary research
27. Does CA overvalue methodological papers?	Methodological contributions play an important role in scientific research, and many are 'normally' cited
28. To what extent is CA affected by 'negative' citations?	Citation context studies found low shares of negative citations, but controversial papers may be highly cited. Hence, citation impact must be valued using expert knowledge
Indicators and their validity	
29. How does CA take into account differences in citation practices among disciplines?	A normalised citation impact indicator relates a group's citation impact to the world citation average in the subfields in which it is active

Question/statement	Reply
30. Can journal impact factors be used to assess publication strategies?	Normalised journal impact measures can be used to properly assess a group's journal packet
31. Is CA of individual papers unnecessary and the use of journal impact factors sufficient?	No. Journal impact is a performance aspect in its own right but cannot be used to predict actual citation impact
32. Does CA give only a static picture?	No. Application of appropriate publication and citation time windows provides informative impact trend data
33. Does CA give only a historical picture?	No. CA assesses past performance but may focus retrospectively on accountability of past activities and prospectively on future potential
34. Is CA biased in favour of older researchers with long scientific careers?	Not necessarily. 'Lifetime' citation counts tend to be biased but analysis may focus on performance during the more 'recent' past
35. Does CA give only a snapshot of a group's performance?	Not necessarily. A time period comprising two PhD student generations (8–10 years) is generally appropriate
36. Citation distributions are skewed	Highly cited papers are flags or symbols of research groups' ensembles and their programmes; other parameters of the citation distribution can be calculated as well
37. Are aggregate statistics useful?	Aggregate statistics are useful for an overview but breakdowns along various dimensions are essential
38. Outcomes of CA of science groups may be distorted by 'national' journals covered by ISI	This is true, although the number of 'national' science journals is limited. They can be removed from the analysis
39. Which data is indispensable for a proper interpretation of citation indicators?	A list with complete bibliographic information about a group's most frequently cited publications

General issues of interpretation and use

Question/statement	Reply
41. To what extent can CA assess the research performance of an individual scientist?	Performance of an individual and citation impact of the papers he or she (co-)authored relate to two distinct levels of aggregation
42. To what extent are outcomes of CA influenced by scientific collaboration among research groups?	Citation analysis should and can take into account scientific collaboration among individuals and among research groups
43. Is it appropriate to use CA as the principal tool in decisions about promotion or salaries of individuals?	No. This formulaic use of CA should be discouraged and discredits CA as a whole
44. Which are important criteria for proper use of CA in a policy context?	Use of CA is more appropriate the more it is formalised, open, scholarly founded, enlightening, and supported by background knowledge

Question/statement	Reply
45. Does CA make expert knowledge superfluous?	On the contrary. Interpretation of citation statistics requires expert knowledge
46. Can CA replace peer judgements?	No. CA can be a valuable additional tool in peer reviews of research performance
47. Is CA a tool for peers only?	No CA can also be used by policy makers to monitor and evaluate peer review processes
48. What is the role of CA in research evaluation?	CA itself does not evaluate. Evaluating agencies should express their notion of scientific quality

Chapter 5   Citation analysis of scientific journals

Chapter 5 deals with journal impact measures. The journal impact factor developed by Eugene Garfield and published by the Institute for Scientific Information in the Journal Citation Reports (JCR) is probably the most widely dispersed bibliometric construct. Chapter 5 starts with the definition of this impact factor. It measures the average citation impact in a particular year of one- and two-year-old documents published in a journal. Hence, it is a ratio with the number of citations as the numerator, and the number of citable documents as the denominator. It is determined by searching in a huge universe of millions of cited references in papers processed for the ISI Citation Indexes for references containing a particular cited journal title.

The chapter provides a technical and historical explanation of how ISI impact factors are calculated, and which problems are involved. In addition, it presents alternative journal impact measures. A basic notion underlying the chapter is that there is no single 'perfect' indicator of journal performance. The scholarly communication system is highly complex, citations constitute one of its representations – though a most valid and useful one – and journal performance is a multi-dimensional concept that cannot be expressed in any single measure. The adequacy of a journal impact measure is related to the type of use made of it, and the type of research question addressed. A particular indicator may be appropriate in one context, and less appropriate in another.

The following conclusions are drawn.

- The ISI impact factor published in ISI's JCR is a ratio of received citations (in its numerator) to published articles in a journal (in the denominator), and in this way corrects for differences among journals in the sizes of their annual volumes. It represents the mean of a skewed citation distribution.
- Citation counts to a journal are based on frequency counts per cited journal title. A positive effect is that discrepant citations indicating, for

instance, an erroneous volume or page number, are included in the counts. But a negative point is that important variations in cited journal titles may be overlooked.

- Publication counts in the JCR impact factor's denominator include citable items defined as normal articles, notes or reviews. To the extent that other types of document are cited, their citations do contribute to the numerator, but they are not included in the denominator, and thus may distort the ratio.
- The JCR impact factor measures the citation impact of articles in the second or third year after publication. It is therefore biased towards journals revealing a rapid maturing or decline in citation impact.
- Reference practices, particularly the number of references per article and their age distribution, vary considerably among subfields. Such differences distort impact factors to the extent that journals from different subfields cannot be directly compared with one another.
- A normalised journal impact indicator takes into account such differences in reference practices among subfields, by dividing a journal's impact by a citation 'average' in the subfields covered by the journal.
- Review journals tend to have higher citation rates than other journals. This can be taken into account by an advanced normalised impact indicator that disaggregates journal citation impact and subfield averages by type of document.
- Normalised citation impact measures vary according to the subfield classification system applied. In addition, they cannot easily be calculated for general or 'multi-disciplinary' journals covering several subfields rather than a single one.
- Moreover, the range of values such a measure obtains is typically between 0.0 and 5.0 and therefore rather different from that for JCR impact factors with which users are familiar.
- The distribution of citation impact among journals in a subfield varies among subfields. 'Top' journals in large subfields tend to have a higher citation impact than top journals in smaller ones. This is true both for JCR impact factors and for normalised measures.
- Prolific authors publish both in high impact and in lower impact journals. This underlines the importance of journals with a lower citation impact in the communication of research findings by both prolific and less prolific researchers.
- JCR journal impact factors are so widely dispersed and frequently used that, apart from technical, validity and availability issues, it seems difficult, at least in the short term, to have them replaced by generally accepted alternative measures.

Part 2.2   The ISI Citation Indexes

Chapter 6   *Basic principles, citation links and terminology*

In order to obtain a proper understanding of bibliometric performance measures derived from the *Science Citation Index* (SCI) and related ISI Citation Indexes, it is essential to have an insight into their coverage. Chapter 6 provides a concise introduction to the basic principles underlying a citation index. It highlights regularities in the global, multi-disciplinary scholarly communication system, captured by 'Garfield's Law of Concentration', stating that a comprehensive, multi-disciplinary index need not cover more than a few thousand journals.

It is argued in Chapter 6 that completeness and adequacy of coverage are distinct dimensions. Although ISI's *Web of Science* nowadays covers as many as 7,500 journals from all fields of scholarship, it does not claim to provide a complete coverage of all journals that are used in scholarly research. Instead, it claims to include the most important or useful ones. The total volume of journals included is determined on the basis of cost effectiveness. Their importance is assessed through a combination of an objective and truly unique internal monitor based on citation relationships among journals with assessments by experts from the various fields. One of the indicators applied in the internal monitor is nowadays known as the journal impact factor.

Chapter 6 explains why the ISI Indexes are unique and powerful tools, and why they constitute by far the most frequently used database in studies of the scholarly communication system and in research evaluation. It also presents definitions of a number of basic concepts in citation indexing, and defines three basic types of links between publications constituted by citations.

Chapter 7   *ISI coverage by discipline*

Chapter 7 presents an analysis of coverage of the ISI Citation Indexes. Adequacy of coverage is highly relevant today, particularly in view of the increasing importance of electronic publishing, and the fact that more and more research publications become freely available through the World Wide Web. If citation counts are to reflect anything like impact, importance or relevance, it is essential that the universe in which a citation analysis is carried out is carefully defined, and that the quality of its sources is continuously monitored. One would rather not count any citation that is electronically visible through the Internet, but rather focus on citations from peer reviewed sources meeting professional quality standards.

Eugene Garfield and others have published several studies that evaluate the adequacy of coverage of the *Science Citation Index* (SCI). Garfield analysed the extent to which the journals that were cited in ISI source articles were themselves included as source journals in the SCI. In this way, a quantitative analysis of cited sources provided insight into the structure of the scholarly communication system and the extent to which it is covered by ISI source journals, even though this view is *partial*, as it relates only to cited references in journal articles processed for the Indexes.

His analyses related to the SCI as a whole. They did not systematically examine differences among all science disciplines, nor did they present outcomes related to social sciences and humanities. Chapter 7 presents a thorough coverage analysis of the combined ISI Citation Indexes by discipline, conducted by the author. It applies a categorisation of science and scholarship into 15 main disciplines. A summary of the main outcomes is presented in Table 3.2.

Table 3.2. Adequacy of ISI coverage from the point of view of research evaluation

Excellent	*Good*	*Moderate*
Molecular biology and biochemistry	Applied physics and chemistry	Other social sciences
Biological sciences primarily related to humans	Biological sciences primarily related to animals and plants	Humanities and arts
Clinical medicine	Psychology & psychiatry	
Physics and astronomy	Other social sciences primarily related to medicine and health	
Chemistry	Geosciences	
	Mathematics	
	Engineering	
	Economics	

Biological sciences related to animals and plants includes amongst others plant sciences, ecology, biology and agriculture. Applied physics & chemistry includes amongst others the journal categories applied physics, materials science, chemical engineering, applied chemistry and instruments & instrumentation. Other social sciences related to medicine & health includes amongst others public environment and occupational health, nursing, and sport sciences. Other social sciences includes amongst others sociology, education, political sciences, and anthropology. Humanities include law.

Chapter 8   Implications for the use of the ISI Citation Indexes in research evaluation

Chapter 8 concludes that the ISI coverage of the literature is excellent or good in most disciplines. This positive outcome, obtained by an independent bibliometric investigator, provides a firm justification for the bibliometric use of the ISI Indexes in research evaluation in those disciplines. In fields with good coverage, communication media other than scientific journals were found to be important, particularly conference proceedings, reference works, handbooks and preprints.

ISI coverage was found to be moderate in certain parts of the social sciences – including sociology, education, political sciences, and anthropology – and particularly in the humanities, including law. In these fields, written communication tends to be dispersed among a large variety of sources, often with a national orientation, and these sources do not show a core – periphery structure as found in basic science. In addition, books are important sources.

A tentative classification of *four types of bibliometric studies* in function of the adequacy of ISI coverage of the field of inquiry is presented.

Table 3.3. Four types of research assessment studies and the role of the ISI Citation Indexes

Type of study	Cited/Target	Citing/Source	ISI coverage
1. Standard	ISI	ISI	Excellent – Good
2. Target expanded	ISI+non-ISI	ISI	Good
3. Source expanded	ISI+non-ISI	ISI+non-ISI	Good – Moderate
4. No ISI citation analysis			Moderate

Target articles are articles that are subjected to a citation analysis. Source articles are documents from which cited references are extracted. They constitute the citing universe.

– In fields with an *excellent* ISI coverage, it is generally appropriate in a citation impact analysis to take into account as target articles only those that are published in ISI source journals, and to use the total collection of cited references in ISI source journals as the citation universe. This type of analysis can be characterised as a standard ISI analysis. Chapter 4 in Part 2.1 presents typical outcomes of this type of study.
– If ISI coverage in a field is not excellent, but can nevertheless be qualified as *good*, the scheme suggests expanding the collection of target articles analysed in a standard ISI analysis by including target articles that are not published in ISI source journals. This approach is illustrated in Chapter 10 in Part 2.3.
– As coverage further decreases, it is proposed under certain conditions to expand the universe of citing sources with important sources, in order to obtain a more reliable expression of citation impact than a standard or target expanded analysis would provide. For instance, important books or proceedings of annual international conferences can be added to the citing universe.

– Finally, if ISI coverage in a field is *moderate*, it is questionable whether it is useful to conduct a citation analysis based on ISI data, even if the target or source universe is expanded. This is particularly true in fields that are fragmented into schools of thought or in which the communication is hampered by national or linguistic barriers. It is to be expected that in such fields alternative approaches, not based on citation data, are more fruitful than citation impact analyses. A case study is presented in Chapter 11 in Part 2.3.

Part 2.3   Assessing research performance in social sciences and humanities

Chapter 9   **Differences between science, social sciences and humanities**

Bibliometric indicators have been successfully applied in many sub-disciplines in basic science. Data from the SCI, produced by the ISI played an important role in analyses of research performance in these sub-disciplines. Thus far, social sciences and humanities have not often been subjected to such analyses. Those who are involved in the development of performance indicators for humanities and social sciences are confronted with the following situation.

– Policy makers have stressed the need to develop tools in social sciences and humanities to assist evaluation agencies in carrying out their tasks, in the same way as the current SCI-based methodologies provide supplementary research assessment tools in basic science.
– This methodology should take into account the characteristics of these domains of scholarship, their substantive contents and particularly the communication practices among their scholars and the structure of their communication system.

It was Derek de Solla Price who underlined that science on the one hand and humanities on the other are two distinct domains of scholarship with essentially different substantive contents, that ask for different "social apparatuses of information pooling and exchange". He found the differences among the two domains of scholarship reflected in the scholarly literature. Following this notion, Chapter 9 makes the following observations and suggestions.

– The social sciences constitute a broad and rather heterogeneous collection of disciplines. Chapters 7 and 8 revealed a good ISI coverage in *psychology and psychiatry, other social sciences related to medicine and health* and in *economics*. But *sociology, political science, educational sciences* and *anthropology* tend to show more resemblance to the humanities, where ISI coverage is moderate.

- In the latter fields books are important communication media. To a considerable extent the literature in these fields is dispersed among various language domains. References tend to be dispersed among a variety of cited sources, many of which have a national orientation. The basic principles of a citation index, outlined in Chapter 6, tend to be less appropriate in these fields than they are in basic science.
- Even within a single subfield, different approaches or paradigms may be adopted, revealing different publication and referencing characteristics, for instance, in 'quantitative' compared to 'qualitative' sociology.
- It can be argued that outcomes of genuine scholarly research, even those primarily related to national aspects, deserve to be communicated – in an appropriate form – to a wider international scholarly audience. But the findings regarding the ISI Citation Indexes suggest that they cover substantial proportions of social science and humanities journals that have a national rather than an international orientation.

These considerations lead to the conclusion that one should be cautious in using the ISI Citation Indexes in the assessment of research performance in social sciences and humanities, particularly in subfields that have a qualitative rather than a quantitative orientation.

Chapter 10   Expanded citation analysis: A case study in economics

In Chapter 8 it was suggested carrying out a target expanded citation analysis in a field with a good, yet not excellent ISI coverage. Whereas a standard citation analysis takes into account only citations to target articles that were published in journals processed for the ISI Citation Index, a target expanded analysis also determines the citation impact of documents published in media not covered by ISI, such as books and conference proceedings.

Chapter 10 describes the main lines of a methodology for such a target expanded citation analysis. A case study is presented, assessing academic research departments in the field of *economics*. It was assumed that, although the collection of ISI source or citing documents shows a good yet not excellent coverage in this field, their cited references may still provide valid citation impact estimates, to the extent that the ISI source articles constitute a representative sample of a wider population of citing sources.

The analysis presented in Chapter 10 investigated the extent to which the outcomes of a standard citation analysis differ from those obtained from a target expanded analysis. A ranking of departments according to the citation impact of their ISI-covered papers differs significantly from that based on the citation impact of their non-ISI-covered documents. Hence, for several departments, the impression of their citation impact substantially changes if that of non-ISI documents is taken into account. It is expected that this methodology can be fruitfully applied in the applied sciences and engineering as well.

Chapter 11   *A case study of research performance in law*

Chapter 11 presents a case study of scholarly output in the field of *law*. Its basic assumptions were:

- Important contributions to scholarly progress are sooner or later communicated in scholarly publications. This is considered to be a universal characteristic in all domains of scholarship.
- The concepts of research performance and research quality do have a meaning in all fields of scholarship, particularly in social sciences and humanities.
- A principal aim of the development and application of bibliometric indicators is to stimulate a debate among scholars in the field under investigation on the nature of scholarly quality, its dimensions and operationalisations.

The main elements of the methodology can be summarised as follows.

- As a starting point documents were analysed containing statements of scholars in the field under study about how an assessment of research performance should be conducted. The analysis identified the main aspects of research quality involved, issues that were raised, and problems that remained unsolved. Earlier reports of peer review committees constituted a fruitful basis for such an inventory.
- Scholars from the field under study were involved in all stages of the study. They were stimulated to develop classification systems, and to structure their own research output accordingly.
- Quantitative analysis of publication output was used as a mirror, reflecting how scholars structured their activities and their research output. This structure was examined empirically from the point of view of its consistency and the degree of consensus among scholars.
- The need was recognised to develop adequate classification systems for scholarly activities and research output prior to any comparative measurement of scholarly performance.
- The interaction process between bibliometric investigators and scholars involved did not lead to a full consensus among all participants.

Therefore, on the basis of their professional competence, the bibliometric investigators presented to the scholarly community what they considered to be the most appropriate approach for structuring and measuring research performance. They exercise a sufficient degree of *openness* in their presentation, both towards the scholars and to policy makers.

– If the extent to which research findings reach beyond a purely national or local viewpoint and are exposed to criticisms from a wide international scholarly audience is considered as a relevant criterion of research quality in social sciences and humanities, a major task would be to develop for the various subfields valid indicators of this aspect of research performance.

– But it is argued that it cannot be taken for granted that the ISI Citation Indexes provide valid indicators in all subfields of these domains of scholarship. A challenge would be to systematically explore alternative data sources and methodologies. The expertise and perceptions of scholars active in the various subfields should play an important role in such an exploration.

Part 2.4   Accuracy issues

Chapter 12   *Introductory notes on accuracy issues*

Bibliometric analyses of the scholarly system relate to various entities, at various levels of aggregation. The basic entity is the individual research publication. From an institutional or geographical perspective, publications may be aggregated at the level of individual scholars, research groups, departments, institutions, nations, and even supra-national entities such as the European Union. From the viewpoint of their substantive contents, they may be arranged by research topic, scholarly subfield or discipline.

At first sight it may seem rather a simple task to collect publication data on an individual scholar or institution, by searching for their names in the database's author field or corporate address field, or to determine accurate citation counts to a given set of papers. However, Chapters 13 and 14 illustrate that such a task is not as simple as it may seem. These chapters describe a number of problems of a more technical nature, and present their solutions. An overview of these problems is given in Table 3.4. The chapters warn against assuming a one-to-one correspondence between data stored in the database on the one hand and 'real' entities in the scholarly system on the other. Chapter 12 starts with a number of important comments on these issues by Eugene Garfield that serve as a useful background for a proper interpretation of the next chapters in this part of this book.

Table 3.4. Technical problems and their solutions presented in Part 2.4

Problem	Solution
Individual paper	
Citation counts may be inaccurate	Apply advanced citation matching procedures coping with major discrepancies
Authors	
Homonym/synonym problem	Use verified bibliographies; let scholars check selected publications
Institutions	
Variations in institutional names in address data	Use verified bibliographies; de-duplicate names but let institutions check results
Institutions may be difficult to define	Use background information on institutions' structure
Institutions and countries	
In social sciences and humanities many articles do not contain addresses at all	Be careful in those disciplines drawing conclusions from address data
Fields, disciplines	
Subfield classification system based on journal categories may be less appropriate	Use additional clustering on a paper-by-paper basis, particularly for papers in multi- or inter-disciplinary journals

Chapter 13   Accuracy of citation counts

Chapter 13 deals with to the accuracy of citation counts. A basic problem in any citation analysis is: how does one collect sufficiently accurate citation counts of target articles, and how does one cope with errors or discrepancies in cited references? Discrepancies may occur, for instance, when a scholar citing a particular target article has indicated an erroneous starting page number, or has misspelled the cited author's name in his or her reference list. Another example relates to target articles published by 'consortia' of many authors. Scientists citing such papers may indicate either the formal first author or the name of the consortium. Although a knowledgeable retriever is aware of this and can properly deal with such a discrepancy, a less advanced, computerised citation analysis may easily generate inaccurate citation counts for those papers.

A huge analysis of over 22 million cited references matched to 18 million target articles extracted from the ISI Citation Indexes reached the following conclusions.

– When citation data are derived from 'simple' citation matching procedures that do not take into account discrepancies as those indicated above, citation counts at the level of individuals or groups of scholars may be particularly affected by characteristics of their names, the journals in which they publish, the type of scientific collaboration they employ and their country of origin.

– The overall number of discrepant cited references is around 7 per cent of the number of citations obtained in a simple matching procedure ignoring important errors or variations in reference lists. Most importantly, discrepant references were found to be skewly distributed among individual target articles, authors, journals and countries.

– It is concluded that citation data collection procedures must be sound and accurate. Therefore, advanced citation data handling procedures must be applied, taking into account inaccurate, sloppy referencing, editorial characteristics of scientific journals, referencing conventions in scholarly subfields, language problems, author identification problems, unfamiliarity with foreign author names, and data capturing conventions.

Chapter 14   Problems with the names of authors and institutions, and with the delimitation of subfields

Chapter 14 discusses problems in the use of author names in ISI's author field. It also discusses the use of information on institutional affiliations in the 'corporate address field' of ISI source publications. The following conclusions are drawn.

– Any proper use of such names must deal with homonyms and synonyms. The latter relates to the problem that one person may appear under several name variations in the author field, and the former to the phenomenon that different persons may have the same name.

– On the one hand, a substantial number of scholars do show a one-to-one correspondence with a particular author name in the database. For those scholars, articles can be easily extracted by searching for their names in the author field. But other scholars' names may be dispersed in the database, or relate to several persons.

– The crucial problem is that for a given scholar it is often difficult if not impossible to know a priori to which class he or she belongs. It is therefore concluded that, prior to any further use of bibliometric indicators in research evaluation, publication data collected on individual scholars or groups of scholars needs to be verified by the scholars themselves.

– ISI de-duplicates names of main institutions to some extent, particularly those of institutions located in the USA. But in this de-duplication process errors are sometimes made.

- In numerous cases it is extremely difficult if not impossible to capture all variations under which an institution's name may appear in addresses in scientific publications. Authors do not always give full information on their affiliations, and may even indicate these inconsistently. There may also be conceptual problems as to how an organisation should be properly institutionally defined.
- Bibliometric assessments of individual research organisations tend to be politically highly sensitive, as the institutions' prestige is at stake. Hence, an appropriate identification scheme of an organisation's publication output must involve detailed background knowledge provided, or at least thoroughly verified, by representatives of the organisations themselves.
- Not all source articles included in the ISI database contain data on the institutional affiliations of their authors. The percentage of ISI source articles without an address is about 20 per cent in the SSCI and around 50 per cent in the A&HCI. This also has important consequences for the accuracy of publication counts by country using the authors' geographical locations from the corporate address field.

A classification often applied in bibliometric analysis is that of *journal categories*, based on a grouping of journals into scholarly subfields. The number of journal categories is in the order of magnitude of 150. One of the major problems is the positioning of 'multidisciplinary' journals that cover a broad variety of subfields. Typical examples are the journals *Nature* and *Science*. Moreover, the journal category system contains categories representing distinct levels of aggregation.

It is a proper instrument for providing a first, rough breakdown of scholarly activities by discipline or sub-discipline. But if more precise field delimitations are needed, for instance at the level of narrow research specialties, or if an analysis focuses on new emerging, multi-disciplinary fields, it is more appropriate – and technically feasible – to use alternative methods for clustering papers according to their substantive contents.

Part 2.5   Theoretical aspects

Chapter 15   *What do references and citations measure?*

What do citation counts measure? Citations are manifestations of complex processes that may be studied from various disciplinary perspectives. In order to understand what citations indicate, and to relate citation counts to common concepts in evaluative bibliometrics such as 'research performance', 'scholarly quality', 'influence' or 'impact', insight is needed into the nature of such processes. Their theoretical understanding contributes to what is often denoted as a 'theory of citation'.

Table 3.5. Views on what references and citations measure

Author	References conceived as	Citations measure
Garfield, Salton	Descriptors of document content	
Garfield	Manifestations of scholarly information flows	Utility (quantity of formal information use)
Small	Elements in a symbol making process	Highly cited items as concept symbols
Merton, Zuckerman	Registrations of intellectual property and peer recognition	Intellectual influence
Cole and Cole		Socially defined quality
Gilbert	Tools of persuasion	Authoritativeness
Cronin	The character and composition of reference lists reflect authors' personalities and professional milieux	It is unclear what citations measure; the interplay between institutional norms and personal considerations must be studied first
Martin and Irvine	References reflect both influence, social and political pressures, and awareness	Differences in citation rates among carefully selected matched groups (partially) indicate differences in actual influence
Zuckerman	Referencing motives and their consequences are analytically distinct	Citations are proxies of more direct measurements of intellectual influence
Cozzens	References are at the intersect of the reward, rhetorical and communication system but rhetorics comes first	Recognition, persuasiveness and awareness each generate a certain portion of variation in citation counts
White	Inter-textual relationships mainly reflect straightforward acknowledgement of related documents	Co-citation maps provide an aerial view and measure a historical consensus as to important authors and works
van Raan	References are partly particularistic but in large ensembles biases cancel out	The upper part of the distribution of a 'thermodynamic' ensemble of many citers measures 'top' research
Wouters	The reference is the product of the scientist	The citation is the product of the indexer. Validity of citations cannot be grounded merely in reference behaviour

Chapter 15 depicts the field of quantitative science as a multi-disciplinary research activity. This research further develops, tests, and interprets bibliometric indicators in various disciplinary research contexts, using methodologies and theoretical notions from the physical sciences, social sciences and humanities.

Characterising the variety of approaches on the basis of the scholarly disciplines from which they originated and to which they show the greatest affinity, Chapter 15 identifies physical, sociological, psychological, historical, and information- or communication-scientific approaches. It illustrates that in each of these disciplinary approaches distinct 'paradigms' exist. It clarifies theoretical positions of a number of authors who have contributed to a deeper understanding of what citation-based indicators measure. These authors and some of the key notions from their theoretical work are listed in Table 3.5.

Chapter 16   Towards a theory of citation: Some building blocks

Chapter 16 critically discusses the notions of the various authors presented in Table 3.5. This discussion is essentially open, as it does not assume the primacy of any existing citation theory, but aims to contribute to the further development of a framework in which each approach eventually finds its proper place. The reflections presented in this chapter primarily relate to 'science', or, more generally, to subfields with a quantitative substantive content and strongly developed international social and communication networks. The following observations and propositions were made.

– If quantitative science studies is a multi-disciplinary research field, the quest for a comprehensive theory of citation can be conceived as the difficult task to transform a *multi-disciplinary* activity into an *interdisciplinary* one. The existence of distinct paradigms within a single disciplinary viewpoint makes this task even more difficult.

– The development of science indicators in a scholarly, disciplinary context has thus far not resulted in a broad *consensus* among its practitioners upon what such indicators reflect. But it is invalid to assume that whenever various, competing theoretical positions exist, it follows that there is no theoretical foundation at all.

– Both a 'citation analytical' and a 'social constructive' viewpoint are valuable, but extreme positions denoted as a 'citationist' or 'constructivist' viewpoint tend to have a negative impact upon the quest for a scholarly foundation of citation analysis.

– Reference lists have a limited length and authors have to be selective in including cited sources. Reference lists are *unique* in the sense that very few papers have identical lists, but they contain at the same time more *commonly used* cited references. Hence, the distribution of citations amongst citable papers in any field is skewed. The crucial issue at stake is how this skewness can be related to research performance.

– Citation analysis applied in an evaluative context does not aim at capturing motives of individuals but rather their consequences at an aggregate level. It embodies a fundamental shift in perspective from that of the psychology of individual citers towards what scientists jointly express sociologically in their referencing behaviour about the structures and performances of scholarly activity.

– When applied to an individual entity (e.g., an individual scholar or research department), its special circumstances and characteristics may distort the outcomes of citation analysis. Enlarging data samples does not necessarily rule out all sorts of bias. Random errors tend to cancel out, but systematic biases may still affect the outcomes.

– It is proposed to conceive research articles as elements from coherent publication ensembles of research groups carrying out a research programme. Citing authors acknowledging a research group's works do not distribute their citations evenly among all papers emerging from its programme, but rather cite particular papers that have become symbols or 'flags' of such a programme. This tendency accounts for *a part* of the skewness observed in citation distributions of individual papers.

– It is proposed to conceive a cited reference list as a distinct part of a research paper, with proper functions related to the use of references bibliographically in citation indexing and bibliometrically in research evaluation. Citing authors tend to ensure that important groups and their programmes are represented in the *reference list* of their papers. Including works in a reference list can be interpreted in terms of intellectual influence, but its expression *in the citing text* may be vague or implicit.

Chapter 17   *Implications for the use of citation analysis in research evaluation*

Chapter 17 further discusses the implications of the observations and notions outlined in Chapters 15 and 16 for the use of citation analysis in research evaluation. The following propositions are made.

– Each of the perspectives or 'paradigms' discussed in Chapters 15 and 16 is valid and illuminates referencing practices. It is therefore extremely difficult if not impossible to express what citations measure in a single theoretical concept that comprises all the interpretations covered by the various approaches. In order to characterise what citations measure, the term *citation impact* rather than impact should be used, as it expresses the methodology along which impact is measured.

– Citation impact is basically a quantitative concept that can be operationalised in elementary or in more sophisticated ways – for instance, through crude citation counts or an advanced, normalised measure. Intellectual influence and other evaluative concepts are theoretical concepts of a basically qualitative nature, and can be assessed only by taking into account the cognitive contents of the work under evaluation.

– The issue at stake is whether citation analysis can be used in research evaluation. Therefore, the relationships between citation impact on the one hand, and evaluative concepts such as 'intellectual influence' and 'contribution to scholarly progress' need to be clarified.

– In principle it is valid to interpret citations in terms of intellectual influence. But the concepts of citation impact and intellectual influence do not coincide. Whether or not citation impact properly reflects intellectual influence depends upon how the latter concept is defined.

– If one disregards the permanence of the intellectual influence, its cognitive direction and longer term implications, this concept becomes more similar to that of citation impact. On the other hand, if an evaluator considers these aspects of intellectual influence as important attributes in an assessment, discrepancies between a work's citation impact and the evaluator's assessment of its intellectual influence are apt to rise.

– Outcomes of citation analysis must be *valued* in terms of a qualitative, evaluative framework that takes into account the substantive contents of the works under evaluation. An important implication is that *evaluators* should make their evaluation criteria sufficiently clear in advance.

– Citation impact may be affected by factors that have no apparent relationship to the intellectual influence or any other evaluative concepts intended to be measured, and that hence throw obstacles in properly interpreting the former in terms of the latter. The interpretation of citation impact thus involves a quest for possible biases or distortions.

– From this perspective, it is crucial at which level of aggregation citation analysis is carried out. If the evaluation concerns an individual 'entity' such as an individual scholar or a research department, the individual characteristics and circumstances of each evaluated entity may easily distort the outcomes of a citation analysis and should therefore be taken into account.

– If the evaluation relates to an aggregate of entities rather than an individual unit, the effects of special characteristics and circumstances of individual entities to some extent cancel out. But it must be underlined that systematic biases as regards the aggregate as a whole may still occur and should be taken into account.

Part 2.6   Citation analysis and peer review

Chapter 18   Peer review and the use and validity of citation analysis

The scholarly community has developed many institutionalised forms of internal evaluation, in which peers assess manifestations of scholarly work. The aim of a peer review process is not to settle scholarly debate, but rather to contribute to the fulfilment of conditions under which it meets professional standards. According to Robert K. Merton, the 'ethos of science' demands that scholarly work is judged on the basis of 'purely' scholarly criteria. Judgements should not depend upon the personal or social attributes of the authors of the work to be reviewed. Peer reviewers therefore should manifest disinterestedness and maintain a professional distance not only with respect to their own activities, but also regarding the work being evaluated.

But it has been argued that peer judgements are influenced by factors other than the scholarly merits of the research under evaluation. Peer evaluators may be influenced by political and social pressures within the scientific community, tend to evaluate in terms of their own research interests and activities, and may conform to conventionally accepted patterns of belief. Several empirical studies found low degrees of agreement among reviewers, and identified various kinds of bias, including the evaluated scholars' academic status and gender, institutional and cognitive bias.

Citation analysis and peer review can be related to one another in the following three ways. Chapter 18 dedicates attention to each of these.

- *Bibliometric indicators are applied as tools for monitoring and studying peer review processes*. Chapter 18 presents a brief overview of a number of important studies analysing peer review processes of submitted journal manuscripts, grant proposals, and of the past performance of individual scholars and research departments. Two case studies are presented in Chapters 19 and 20.
- *Bibliometric indicators are applied as supplementary tools in peer review processes*. It is argued that peer review processes are normally carried out without documentation of the bases for conclusions. It is therefore difficult to assess the extent to which citation and publication data are used in peer review. When citation analysis does not constitute an official source of information in a peer review process, it does *not* follow that citation or publication data do not play a role at all.

– *The outcomes of peer reviews are used as a validation instrument of bibliometric indicators.* During the past 50 years numerous studies have been examined from the point of view of validation of bibliometric indicators statistical correlations between peer judgements about the research performance of individual scholars or research departments on the one hand, and the outcomes of citation analysis on the other. Chapter 18 summarises some interesting examples.

Chapter 19   Analysis of peer assessments of research departments

Chapter 19 presents four empirical case studies conducted by the author, analysing statistical correlations between peer ratings and citation impact indicators. These studies relate to an assessment of the past performance of academic, basic *research departments* in the natural and life sciences. Three reviews were conducted within the framework of national research assessment exercises in the Netherlands, evaluating academic research in *biology*, *physics* and *chemistry*, respectively. A fourth study involved a peer review of basic science research departments in a larger Western-European university. In the three Dutch exercises peer review committees consisted of around 8 members. Bibliometric indicators were actually provided to the peers during the review process. In the university review, they were not. All four reviews applied the same criteria and rating system. Peers categorised departments into 5 classes, denoted as 'excellent', 'good', 'satisfactory', 'unsatisfactory' and 'poor'. The following results were obtained.

– The Spearman rank correlation coefficient between citation impact and peer rating was around 0.5 in all studies, and was only slightly higher in procedures formally using the outcomes of a bibliometric study in the review in which indicators did not play a formal role.

– The distribution of peer ratings among departments was about the same in all studies (for instance, the percentage of departments rated excellent was about the same in all studies), whereas the overall citation impact level of evaluated departments varied substantially from one study to another.

– If those responsible for the evaluation of the three Dutch disciplines had not conducted a peer review at all, but had solely commissioned a bibliometric study, the outcomes of the latter would correctly predict a peer rating in terms of good or excellent versus satisfactory, unsatisfactory or poor, in 8 out of 10 cases.

– The peer qualification 'excellent' discriminated very well between departments with a citation impact below world average and those that were above that average, but it discriminated less well in the latter set

between departments with a very high and those with a less high citation impact.
- Similarly, a very high citation impact discriminated very well between departments rated excellent or good and those receiving lower peer ratings, but it did not discriminate properly between good and excellent departments in the perception of the peers.

The outcomes of these case studies suggest the following.

- A peer rating system tends to generate a distribution of ratings among departments that depends upon the rating system itself, and that is to some extent independent of the overall performance level of evaluated departments.
- Citation analysis is a good predictor of how peers discriminated between a 'valuable' and a 'less valuable' past performance, but does not properly predict within the class of 'valuable' performances peers' perception of 'genuine excellence'.
- If one assumes that applied citation impact indicators reflect excellence adequately, it follows that peer review committees tended to be able to identify 'good' or 'valuable' research meeting minimum quality standards, but that they were only partially successful in spotting excellence or 'top' research. This finding is in agreement with outcomes of earlier studies on peer judgements of journal manuscripts and grant proposals.
- This underlines the need for policy makers who organise research assessment exercises at a national level to thoroughly reflect upon the objectives of such exercises. If the principal objective is to indicate excellence in the top of the quality distribution, one may ask how the review process should be organised in order to provide proper conditions to meet that objective.

Chapter 20   Analysis of a national research council

Chapter 20 presents a study analysing the evaluation and funding procedures carried out by a National Research Council from a smaller Western-European country, in which grant proposals were evaluated by some 25 expert committees, each covering a (sub-)discipline. The study was commissioned by the country's minister responsible for research. It examined statistical relationships between peer ratings of grant proposals, grant decisions made by the Council, and the citation impact of the applicants, the trans-disciplinary nature of their research, and their proximity relationship with the expert committees evaluating their proposals.

The latter three factors were analysed because government representatives wished to assess whether the Council's procedures rewarded researchers of high international research quality, whether trans-disciplinary research was hampered, and whether proximity relationships between applicants and evaluating committees made the outcomes of the procedure inequitable. Impact and trans-disciplinarity were measured through citation analysis. Important outcomes were:

- The granting decision followed the rating made by the expert committees fairly strictly. But the applicants whose proposals were granted jointly received only half of the total budget requested.
- All committees showed more or less the same rejection rate in terms of the total budget requested in submitted applications. Citation impact of national researchers in a (sub-)discipline did not influence this ratio in a statistically significant way.
- Applications submitted by applicants who were members of the evaluating committee showed a much higher probability of being granted than those submitted by scientists who have never been a member of any committee.
- Applications submitted by researchers whose publications generated a high citation impact had a significantly higher probability of being granted than those submitted by researchers with a low citation impact.
- No differences were found in applicants' citation impact between applications rated by the expert committees as 'very good' and those qualified as 'good'.
- There was no correlation between an application's probability of being granted and the degree of trans-disciplinary of the research carried out by its applicants.

Questions raised in a public report presenting the outcomes of the study were:

- To what extent is the budget allocated to a granted application sufficient to carry out the research activities described in the proposal?
- To what extent should the distribution of funds among disciplines be influenced by the overall level of national performance of scientists active in those disciplines?
- Is it necessary to adjust the procedures for handling applications submitted by expert committee members in order to make the procedures more equitable?
- Is there a need for expert committees to discriminate more rigorously between 'very good' and 'good' applications?

- Is there a need to develop ways to stimulate more strongly trans-disciplinary research?
- Is it appropriate that expert committees evaluate applications, decide on granting and fix budgets at the same time?

The study played a role in the negotiations between the research council and the minister responsible for research. It illustrates how quantitative, bibliometric methods can fruitfully contribute to an *internal* debate within funding agencies about funding procedures and evaluation criteria, and to a *public* debate between a funding agency and the national science policy sphere.

Part 2.7 Macro studies

Citation analysis is often used to obtain from a comparative perspective indications of the performance of particular entities in the scholarly community, such as individuals, departments, or institutions. An essential characteristic of this type of study is that the name of an entity under evaluation is crucial. The analysis aims at making statements about a particular entity, and the bibliometric outcomes have a meaning only if its name is attached to them.

But citation analysis is also a most powerful tool to analyse general, structural aspects of the scholarly system. Individual entities are conceived as 'cases', and certain properties or regularities among them are analysed. The entities' names are irrelevant. These can be used as intermediary variables enabling collection of specific types of information about the entities, and can be deleted once this information is collected. Bibliometric indicators, then, are only indirectly linked to entities through the additional information on them included in the analysis, and they are used to analyse general patterns or statistical correlations between variables rather than individual performances. In Part 2.7 four studies of this type will be presented. Each study deals with issues that have a high policy relevance and that can be denoted as 'classical' in the field of quantitative science studies.

- Did scientists' global publication productivity increase during the 1980s and 1990s (Chapter 21)?
- How to measure trends in national publication output (Chapter 22)?
- Does international scientific collaboration pay (Chapter 23)?
- Do US scientists overcite papers from their own country (Chapter 24)?

Chapter 21   Did global scientific publication productivity increase during the 1980s and 1990s?

A first study, presented in Chapter 21, relates to publication practices of scholars in the various scholarly disciplines. In this study, the level of accuracy of the underlying bibliometric data does not have to be as high as that needed in an assessment of an individual, provided that errors are more or less randomly distributed among the various data samples analysed.

It analyses patterns in scientists' *publication productivity*, defined as 'the number of published papers per scientist', but operationalised in several ways. In view of the vital importance of basic research and the various policy measures imposed on it during the past decades, it is relevant to examine trends in this type of productivity during the 1980s and 1990s. Did it decrease, as several bibliometric investigators suggested in earlier studies? Or did it increase, as one might expect in view of the various policy measures aimed at enhancing research performance? And if not, why not? The following results were obtained.

– An 'average' scientist can justly claim that he or she published more research articles over the years, in the sense that the number of papers added annually to his or her personal publication lists increased during the time period considered.
– But from a global perspective, the overall publication productivity, defined as the total number of articles published by all authors in a year divided by the number of scientists active in that year, remained approximately constant during the past two decades.
– This paradox is explained by the phenomenon that scientists collaborated with one another more intensively in recent years than they did in the past, so that the sizes of the teams authoring papers gradually increased.
– At the level of disciplines, however, basic and applied physics and chemistry tend to show an increase in overall publication productivity over the years, and medical and biological sciences a decline.

The outcomes are discussed from two points of view.

– *Possible effects of the use of various types of bibliometric indicators in research evaluation upon scholars' publication practices*: Scholars successfully increased their individual publication output through more collaboration and authorship inflation, possibly stimulated by the use of 'crude' publication counts in research evaluation. However, there is no evidence for an overall increase in 'salami' publishing. In basic and applied physics and chemistry the 'quantity of publication' strategy has been dominant – possibly as a compensation for a relative decline in funding – whereas in medical and biological sciences, scientists may have been more restrictive in what they published – perhaps under the influence of the emphasis in research evaluation upon publications in 'top' journals using journal impact factors.

– *Possible effects upon the scholarly system of recent policies, aiming to enhance its productivity, intensity of collaboration economic relevance*: Major trends in basic research funding have stimulated collaboration but have not resulted in a higher overall publication productivity, at least in the medical and biological sciences. Increase in efficiency and productivity, a higher economic relevance and more globalisation are to some extent conflicting policy objectives for basic science. The amount of energy and resources absorbed by collaborative work and globalisation may be so substantial that it held overall publication productivity back from an increase.

Chapter 22 Measuring trends in national publication output

Interpreting bibliometric indicators at the macro level is by no means an easy task. Some indicators are based on absolute numbers, and others on simple percentages or more sophisticated 'relative' measures. Some reflect pure 'output', whereas others either implicitly or explicitly relate 'output' to 'input'. In addition, the various producers of macro indicators do not apply one and the same methodology. They found different solutions to a number of major methodological problems.

Not infrequently, the various indicators and methodologies seem to lead to different conclusions. Even when bibliometric investigators use the same methodology and find the same quantitative pattern, their interpretations of that pattern may differ from one another. This makes bibliometric indicators vulnerable to selective use and manipulation. The principal remedy bibliometric investigators have against misinterpretation or selective use of their indicators is to explain as accurately as possible how these indicators were constructed. The aim of this chapter is to provide such information as regards the construction and interpretation of publication based macro indicators.

One of the most crucial problems is how to handle papers reporting on collaborative work, published by authors affiliated with institutions from different countries. Chapter 22 illustrates how the outcomes of trend analyses of national publication output and their interpretation in terms of the 'state' of a country's science system depend upon how these problems were solved.

A starting point of the analysis is the observation that in many Western countries during the time period 1998–2002 the total number of papers to which they contributed – using an 'integer' counting scheme – increased, whereas publication counts accounting for increasing international collaboration – applying a 'fractional counting scheme'– showed a decline. Chapter 22 seeks an explanation of this pattern

For 20 major countries, eleven macro indicators were calculated and compared with one another. The analysis represents the first macro study that takes into account the country in which each individual *author* is active (i.e., the country in which an author's institution is located), enabling one from the perspective of a particular country's papers to distinguish foreign from domestic authors.

Focusing on the papers to which a 'scientifically established' country contributed, and analysing the teams authoring such papers, one of the key findings is that the number of *foreign* authors in those teams increased, whereas their number of *domestic* authors remained constant. As a result, in 2002, there were *relatively* more foreign authors in papers from established countries than there were in 1998. This is what one would expect to find as globalisation and international collaboration increase. Many established countries showed this pattern, but apparently not all of them. Scientifically emerging countries tended to show a different pattern. These countries not only published more papers, but the number – and in most cases even the proportion – of domestic scientists in the teams producing them increased as well.

Chapter 22 draws the following general conclusions.

– In order to assess the trend in a single country's publication output, an analysis *per publishing author* explored in this chapter is most useful. Informative indicators are the absolute number of publishing domestic authors (i.e., authors working in institutions located in the country itself) and the average number of published papers per domestic author.

– Assuming that the ISI Citation Indexes provide a valid reflection of global scientific activity, these two indicators give an answer to the following questions: did the country's scientific workforce expand or shrink, and did the number of papers in which it participated per (unique publishing) domestic author increase or decline?

– Regardless of the indicators one uses, it is sensible to compare countries from an appropriate comparator group with one another. Focusing on a single country only makes it much more difficult to properly interpret trends in indicators for that country alone.

– It is essential to calculate a *series* of indicators and to provide them with a consistent interpretation. None of the indicators is perfect and each one indicates a proper, distinct aspect of publication output. Isolating one single measure from the others may distort the results and lead to biased conclusions.

Chapter 23 *Does international scientific collaboration pay?*

The benefits of international scientific collaboration are heavily debated among scientists and science policy makers, and constitute an important research topic in the field of quantitative science and technology studies. Funding agencies such as the European Commission stimulate collaboration within the European Union by using it as a funding criterion. The issue examined in Chapter 23 is: how does the citation impact of internationally co-authored papers relate to that of papers in which no international collaboration is involved, denoted as 'purely domestic' papers?

Research articles were categorised according to the number of countries involved in the collaboration. About 85 per cent of internationally co-authored papers had authors from two countries and reflect bi-lateral international collaboration. The remaining 15 per cent reflect multi-lateral collaborations involving authors from 3 or more countries. A more detailed analysis focused on bi-lateral international collaboration. Countries were grouped according to the citation impact of their 'purely domestic' papers into those with a high and those with a low citation impact. The following general conclusions are drawn.

– In all science disciplines, internationally co-authored papers had on average higher citation rates than papers with authors from a single country. But this outcome itself is of limited relevance, as established countries with a high overall citation impact are over-represented in the set of internationally co-authored papers.
– When scientifically advanced countries collaborated with one another, they profited in about 7 out of 10 cases from bi-lateral collaboration, in the sense that they *both* raised their citation impact compared to that of their purely domestic publication output.
– But when advanced countries contributed in bi-lateral international collaboration to the development of scientifically less advanced countries – and thus to the advancement of science on a somewhat longer term than the time horizon normally adopted in research evaluation – this collaboration tended to negatively affect their short-term citation rates, particularly when their role in the collaboration was secondary.
– Research evaluators may consider conceiving short-term impact at the research front and longer term development of scientifically less advanced countries as distinct aspects in their own right, and bibliometric investigators could develop special indicators enabling them to do so.

Chapter 24 Do US scientists overcite papers from their own country?

In the debate on the validity of citation analysis in research evaluation, national biases or self-preoccupation in scientists' reference practices constitute an important issue. It has particularly been claimed that US authors excessively or disproportionately cite other US colleagues, and that this distorts the outcomes of citation analysis. Chapter 24 presents first results of a study aimed at empirically examining this claim. It is argued that it is all a matter of perspective, of how precisely the concepts 'excessively' or 'disproportionally' are defined.

A simple measure of the degree of country self-citation can be defined as the proportion of references in a country's papers to other papers published from that country, denoted as its domestic papers. Among the many factors that may influence country self-citation, Chapter 24 takes into account the following three.

- The size of a country's publication output. A country with a large publication output tends to show a higher self-citation rate than one with a small output, because the former has more domestic papers to cite than the latter.
- The degree of integration of research activities at a national level. Countries with strongly developed national networks tend to show more intra-national citation links than ones in which national scientific networks are poorly developed.
- The significance of a country's domestic papers. Countries publishing papers of high significance tend to cite their own papers more frequently because they are more significant.

The research question can be formulated as follows: Does a country's observed self-citation rate deviate from an expected rate that takes into account the size of the country's output, its strength of national networks, and the significance of its papers? The analysis compares the USA to other major individual countries, and to an aggregate of Western European countries, conceiving Western Europe as one single (supra-)national entity. It applies several advanced measures of country self-citation. The study found *no* conclusive evidence that US scientists excessively cite their own papers. More specifically, the following conclusions were drawn.

- *All* countries overcite themselves, relative to what one would expect on the basis of the size of their publication output. The US self-citation rate is similar to that of Japan, somewhat higher than that for major Western-European countries, but lower than that for Western-European countries with smaller publication outputs. Thus, at the level of individual countries there is *no* empirical basis for the general claim that US scientists overcite papers from their own country more than scientists from Western-European countries overcite their domestic papers.

– But US scientists overcite US papers to a much stronger degree than Western European scientists overcite the total collection of Western European papers. If the rate at which Western European authors cite themselves constitutes the norm, it follows that US scientists excessively cite themselves. But if one adopts the degree of integration of national research activities within the USA as a norm, it follows that Western-European scientists *undercite* each other and that their research activities are not yet sufficiently integrated, notwithstanding the realisation of a level of co-authorship similar to that within the USA.

– Authors from countries other than the USA and Western Europe cite US papers on average more frequently than they cite Western European papers. This outcome may evidently be affected by biases in references practices of authors from the various other countries, biases that do not necessarily cancel out. But it at least illustrates that differences in significance of US papers compared to Western-European ones constitute a factor that should not be overlooked in further studies on country self-citation.

Part 2.8   New developments

Chapter 25   *Development of new indicators*

In Chapter 2 its was argued that in research evaluation it is not the bibliometric investigator but rather the evaluator who establishes what is valuable in scholarly activity and which dimensions of scholarly quality should have the greatest weight. Now that full bibliometric versions of the ISI Citation Indexes are available, bibliometric indicators can become more fine-tuned, and more focused towards issues addressed by policy makers and evaluators.

At the same time, this development draws attention more explicitly to theoretical assumptions underlying the various types of indicators, and to the question of which aspects of research performance they actually measure. Discussions about indicators may at first glance seem technical, but normally there are theoretical notions involved that need to be highlighted and further clarified. From this perspective, Chapter 25 presents notes on the further development of citation based indicators. The list of suggestions for new indicators is far from exhaustive, and primarily aims at illustrating how theoretical notions are involved in their construction, and how they depend upon what one aims to measure.

It addresses ways to deal with differences in 'size' or publication volume; benchmarking; indicators of highly citedness; how to deal with co-publications; indicators of breadth, persistence, coherence and depth of a knowledge base; productivity measures relating output to input; indicators of the contribution to the training of new scientists; 'qualitative' citation analysis; the further development of 'weighted' or 'recurrent' citation measures; and historical indicators research.

Chapter 26   Electronic publishing, new databases and search engines

During the past few decades more and more scholarly documents have become available in electronic form. In the last few years publishers of scholarly information have made their journals and articles available through the Internet to universities, corporations and government institutes. At the same time, scholars are more and more encouraged to self-archive their documents and deposit them in publicly accessible websites. Chapter 26 discusses some major trends in electronic publishing and archiving, and their potentialities for developing new methodologies that can be applied in the assessment of research performance.

It dedicates attention to the recently introduced search engine *Google Scholar* that enables users to find scholarly information available across the web, and to Elsevier's *Scopus*, an online search engine covering abstracts and cited references from around 14,000 scientific journals covering all science. Similar to the ISI Citation Indexes, *Scopus* covers the primary, serial, peer reviewed literature.

In an electronic archive downloads of articles can be monitored, by collecting and analysing data on document downloads captured by a web-server. A key issue is how the number of times a document is downloaded in full text format from an electronic archive statistically relates to the number of times it is cited in sources included in the archive, or in journals processed for the ISI Citation Indexes. Chapter 26 discusses some recent studies addressing this issue for particular journals, fields and electronic archives.

It is argued that electronic publishing, and the electronic availability and indexing of scholarly documents have an enormous positive influence upon scholarly communication, and hence scholarly progress in general. As more and more scholarly documents become available in electronic form through the Internet, their use as sources in bibliometric or citation analysis is expected to increase in the near future.

But from the perspective of research evaluation it is essential to make clear that including in a citation analysis more sources does not necessarily lead to more valid assessments of the contributions scholars make to the advancement of scholarly knowledge. In assessing the contribution to scholarly progress, the importance of (citing) sources in a field, and the extent to which the contents of their documents contain new knowledge and meet professional quality standards are crucial criteria. A combination of peer review and citation analysis can be fruitfully used to assess these issues, following the lines developed by Eugene Garfield when he created the *Science Citation Index*.

Chapter 27   Further research

Chapter 27 highlights two important issues of a more general nature as regards the use of citation analysis in research evaluation, that need to be further studied in future research. The first is the need to carry out systematic studies of the conditions under which citation analysis is actually used in research evaluation, and of the effects of its use upon the scholarly community, its evaluators and the policy arena. It underlines that insights obtained from such studies could play an important role in the development of new indicators.

An important topic is the effects of formulaic use of bibliometric indicators in the allocation of research funds upon scientists' publication practices. Studies of these effects are most illuminating, but the crucial issue at stake is not whether scholars' publication practices change under the influence of the use of bibliometric indicators, but rather whether or not the application of such measures as a research evaluation tool enhances research performance and scholarly progress in general.

A second issue discussed in Chapter 27 is the phenomenon that outcomes of citation analysis are often presented to the 'outside world' in the form of *rankings* of entities such as individual scholars, research departments or institutions. This may also occur with outcomes of peer reviews, such as those carried out in the framework of national research assessment exercises.

Such rankings are readily conceived as a tool showing research policy makers and administrators which entities need additional support, and for which entities support should be reduced or even abandoned. Moreover, it becomes a tool for those who are themselves not members of the scholarly community, but who are about to enter the scholarly system, to identify their best entry point, This is the case, for instance, for students choosing an academic institution for their further training, or for managers of firms in search of particular scholarly knowledge.

It is argued that the need of policy makers and the wider public to obtain insight into the scholarly quality of the various groups is legitimate, but that scholarly quality is not as straightforwardly measured as performance in many other societal domains. Moreover, rankings disregard the relationships among entities and how these relationships influence an individual entity's performance.

Bibliometric investigators should look for means to express these notions in the outcomes they produce. This is a matter both of developing new indicators, and of proper presentation of their outcomes.

PART 2.1

ASSESSING BASIC SCIENCE RESEARCH
DEPARTMENTS AND SCIENTIFIC JOURNALS

Chapter 4

CITATION ANALYSIS OF BASIC SCIENCE RESEARCH DEPARTMENTS

4.1   Introduction

The use of citation analysis in the assessment of the past research performance of individual scholars, research groups, departments and institutions is one of the most important topics in evaluative bibliometrics. During the past decades numerous bibliometric assessments of individuals or research departments were carried out. The outcomes were used in an evaluative or policy context. However, many of these studies were never made public, let alone that they were published in the scientific literature. Therefore, it is impossible to estimate how frequently this type of use of citation analysis has taken place in the various countries.

This chapter exclusively deals with methodologies and types of use that were described and openly discussed in the public literature. Many authors from various countries contributed to their further development. This introduction section highlights a number of key contributions. Some important macro studies assessing national scholarly systems, and their producers, are discussed in Chapter 22.

In the USA, Francis Narin (1976) was one of the first who applied citation analysis in a systematic way to the assessment of research departments and institutions, using a standardised methodology. Eugene Garfield illustrated in several articles the potentialities of citation analysis in the evaluation of research faculty (e.g, Garfield, 1983a; 1983b). The US National Research Council carried out several large scale citation analyses assessing PhD programs at universities in the USA (e.g., Goldberger, 1995). These studies are further discussed in Chapter 18. A paper by Hicks et al. (2004) presents an overview of the use of bibliometric methods by the US federal government during the past decade.

Hicks et al. (2004) noted that in the USA *companies* such as Thomson/ISI and CHI Research were the main contributors to evaluative bibliometric methodologies, whereas in Europe and Australia these were mainly further developed in *academic* research departments. "This may have underpinned a certain reluctance by American academics to accept bibliometric as a methodology, let alone as an area in which foreign academics and US firms lead" (Hicks et al., 2004, p. 79).

During the past three decades many important contributions to the use of citation analysis in the assessment of research groups and departments were made in European academic institutions. Ben Martin and John Irvine at *SPRU, University of Sussex* (UK), conducted in the early 1980s an important study on the performance of research departments in the field of radio astronomy (Martin and Irvine, 1983). *The Centre for Science and Technology Studies* at *Leiden University* (the Netherlands) developed a series of new bibliometric methodologies. Anthony van Raan (1996; 2004a) presents reviews of these developments. In Australia, Linda Butler and Paul Bourke at the *Australian National University* carried out several bibliometric studies of research departments in Australian academic institutions (e.g., Bourke and Butler, 1998; Butler, 2004).

During the past two decades, the Leiden Centre for Science and Technology Studies has conducted dozens of citation analyses of scientific institutions, research departments, research groups and individual scientists. The outcomes were used as additional information in an evaluation of their research performance. These studies were carried out along the following main lines.

- In a first step the time period of analysis was fixed, and a list was compiled of the scientists who were active in the entities to be evaluated.
- Their names were matched with a publication database containing all source articles processed for the ISI Citation Indexes, and for each name a preliminary list of publications was compiled.
- Preliminary lists were sent to scientists involved for verification. Missing articles were added, and incorrectly assigned papers were deleted.
- Verified lists were subjected to a citation analysis. Both simple and sophisticated bibliometric indicators were calculated, and special analyses were carried out within the framework of particular policy issues addressed in the study.
- The outcomes of the citation analyses were sent to the scientists subjected to the analysis for comments, enabling them to provide background information that was in their view indispensable for a proper interpretation of the results.

- The bibliometric results, the scientists' comments, and 'tentative' conclusions by the analysts were included in a final report. This report was sent to the agency undertaking the evaluation.
- In most studies a public report was written, presenting the main outcomes and conclusions, at a high level of aggregation. Smaller entities subjected to the analysis such as research departments were anonymous.

Overviews of the methodology applied in these studies and of significant outcomes can be found in van Raan (1996), Van Den Berghe et al. (1998), and van Raan (2004a). A typical outcome of the citation analyses is presented in Figure 4.1. It relates to research departments active in the field of chemistry in universities located in the Netherlands. It provides an overview of the number of articles published by a department during a time period of ten years, and their normalised citation impact, i.e., the average citation impact of the department's papers compared to the world citation average in the subfields in which the department is active.

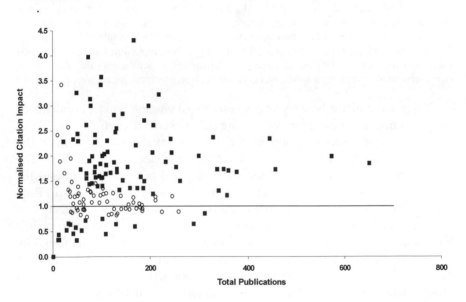

Figure 4.1. Number of articles published and their normalised citation impact for 159 research departments active in the field of chemistry at Dutch Universities. (Source: van Leeuwen et al., 2002).

Articles and their citations are counted during the ten-year time period 1991–2000. Black squares above (below) the horizontal reference line represent departments for which the citation impact is significantly above (below) the world average in the subfields in which a department is active. The horizontal reference line represents the world citation average in the subfields in which a department is active.

Table 4.1. Example of the calculation of a department's normalised citation impact

| Document type | Department | | Subfield |
	Papers	Citations per paper	Citations per paper
Article	10	5.0	4.0
Review	2	10.0	8.0

Normalised citation impact= (10*5.0 +2*10.0) / (10*4.0+2*8.0) = 70/56=1.25

In this example a department has published 10 articles and 2 reviews in a particular subfield. Their average citation rates are 5.0 and 10.0, respectively. The total actual number of citations collected by the department's papers amounts to 10*5.0+2*10.0=70. In the entire subfield in which the department is active, articles and reviews are assumed to be cited on average 4.0 and 8.0 times, respectively. The expected number of citations received by the department's papers can be calculated as 10*4.0+2*8.0=56. The normalised citation impact is defined as the ratio of actual and expected number of citations, and in this example amounts to 1.25. When a department has published papers in two subfields, a similar type of weighting scheme is applied, the weights being determined by the number of papers in each subfield. For more technical details the reader is referred to Moed et al., 1995. The notion that actual citation rates of departments or journals must in some way be related to citation characteristics or averages for the fields in which they are active, can be found in several publications (e.g., Narin, 1976; Vinkler, 1986; Braun et al., 1988). The method applied in Figure 4.1 not only takes into account the subfield in which the department is active, but also the type of documents the department published, and even the years in which the papers were published.

Table 4.1 explains how a group's normalised citation impact is calculated by presenting a simple example. Figure 4.2 presents a cognitive profile of the work of a research group in the field of medicinal chemistry. The horizontal axis denotes the share of articles published in a subfield. The vertical axis gives the names of the subfields, and between parentheses the normalised citation impact of the papers published in a subfield. Both publications and citation relate to the ten-year time period 1993–2002.

This chapter discusses a large number of comments, criticisms, claims and questions raised by scientists subjected to citation analyses, by evaluators using bibliometric indicators as supplementary tools, and by policy makers commissioning bibliometric studies. It focuses on the use of citation analysis in basic science, but addresses several issues regarding the applied and technical sciences, social sciences and humanities as well. It covers most of the issues raised by Per Seglen in several publications (e.g., Seglen, 1997a; Seglen, 1997b), and by scientists subjected to citation analyses that were conducted during the past two decades by members of the Leiden Centre for Science and Technology Studies (CWTS).

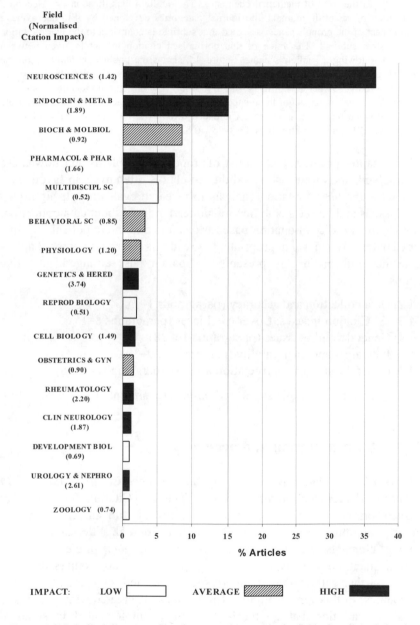

Figure 4.2. Sub-disciplinary profile of a research group in the field of medicinal chemistry.
(For legend see next page)

Legend of Figure 4.2 on previous page:

Figure 4.2 presents a breakdown into research subfields of the publication output of a research group active in the field of medicinal chemistry. The subfield classification is based on a categorisation of scientific journals into journal categories developed by ISI. The average citation impact of the group's papers assigned to a subfield is compared to the world citation average in that subfield. The value of this normalised citation impact is given between parentheses following a subfield's name. Figure 4.2 shows the publication activity (on the horizontal axis) and citation impact per subfield. It shows for instance that the group has published more than 35 per cent of its papers in journals covering the subfield neurosciences. The normalised citation impact of these papers amounts to 1.42. Black coloured bars indicate subfields in which the normalised citation impact exceeds 1.2. For grey bars this ratio lies between 0.8 and 1.2, and for white bars it is below 0.8.

This chapter provides a checklist of important problems and how these can be solved, and discusses the validity of claims often made in favour of – or against – the use of citation analysis in research evaluation. It highlights crucial issues and corrects common misunderstandings about data collection, accuracy and validity of citation based indicators and their applicability in a policy context. Whenever appropriate, the reader is referred to other chapters for further information. It presents 48 paragraphs, arranged into five sections:

- 4.2: Data collection and accuracy (paragraphs 1–7).
- 4.3: ISI Citation indexes: Coverage, biases (paragraphs 8–15)
- 4.4: General validity issues (paragraphs 16–28).
- 4.5: Indicators and their validity (paragraphs 29–39).
- 4.6: General issues of interpretation and use (paragraphs 40–48).

Brief summaries of all issues addressed are presented in Table 3.1 in Chapter 3.

4.2   Data collection and accuracy

1. Is citation analysis (CA) easy to do because all data are in computerised literature databases? No. The ISI Citation Indexes were designed primarily for the purpose of retrieval and dissemination of scholarly literature. Such use of the author, journal, title, and citation indexing elements can be denoted as *bibliographic. Bibliometric* use involves quantitative analysis of bibliographic data, and requires that raw data are further reformatted, standardised, quantified, and linked to other data sources. In this way, a bibliometric database is created with search and analysis capabilities that go far beyond those implemented in standard literature retrieval software.

2 How can one obtain accurate, complete publication data? A crucial first step in any performance analysis is to obtain complete, *verified* publication lists of scientists or institutions to be evaluated. Only in this way can problems related to inconsistent foreign language spelling of author names, synonymy and homonymy and variations in institutional addresses be solved. These problems are further discussed in Chapter 14.

3. Is it difficult to generate publication lists for authors or institutions? Nowadays most if not all scientists have their publication lists in computer-readable form, and many institutions publish annual research reports with their publication output. In order to use these lists they should be reformatted and accurately linked on a 'paper-by-paper basis' to a bibliometric database described in Paragraph 1 above. If an institution is unable to provide lists of scientists appointed rather than publications lists, a list can be generated by linking scientists' names to the author index in the database. But such lists are preliminary and need further verification.

4. How can one collect accurate citation counts? Citation statistics of individuals or groups of scientists may be inaccurate when they are based on improper citation matching procedures, and may be affected by factors such as sloppy referencing, editorial characteristics of journals, author identification problems, referencing conventions in particular subfields, language problems, unfamiliarity with foreign author names and ISI data capturing conventions. However the main problems can be overcome by applying sophisticated citation matching methods. This point is further discussed in Chapters 12 and 13.

5. Does CA count citations to first authors only? The Citation Index of the printed or CD-ROM version of the SCI gives the first author of cited papers only. Therefore, several studies conducted in the past were based on first author counts only. But in the first step of the data collection process in an advanced citation analysis all articles published by a scientist are retrieved, regardless of whether he or she is a first author or a co-author. In a next step, citation counts are collected for each article. Thus, citation statistics for a scientist are not merely based on first author counts, but also include citations to articles of which he or she is a co-author.

6. Can CA correct for author self-citations? Impact on research activities outside the own group constitutes the primary interest in performance assessments. Thus, the methodology should allow the possibility of excluding author self-citations, occurring when the citing and cited document have at least one author in common. This is technically feasible and has provided accurate estimates in many current studies. A necessary condition is that all authors of a cited and a citing paper are known.

7. Are senior scientists always co-authors of papers by their research students? Authorship conventions vary among disciplines and institutions. In many science institutions it is a rule that each published paper is co-authored by a senior scientist, but in some the latter may only be mentioned in an acknowledgement. Such papers can be included whenever necessary. But it is more appropriate to analyse research groups rather than individuals, and to collect papers published both by senior and by junior group members.

4.3   ISI Citation Indexes: coverage, biases

8. Why use the ISI Citation Indexes for CA? The ISI Citation Indexes are unique. They constitute the only currently available database that covers *one century* for all sciences, and that includes for each document all authors, their institutional affiliations and all cited references. They include for a processed source all the items published in it ('cover to cover' processing). Data fields are to a considerable extent standardised by ISI's internal data capturing and formatting procedures. The ISI Indexes are further described in Chapter 6.

9. How complete is the coverage of the ISI Indexes? Although ISI's *Web of Science* nowadays covers as many as 7,500 journals from all fields of scholarship, it does not claim to provide a complete coverage of all journals that are used in scholarly research. Instead, it claims to include the most important or useful ones. Completeness and adequacy of coverage are distinct concepts. The total volume of journals included is determined on the basis of cost-effectiveness. Their importance is assessed through a combination of an objective and a unique internal monitor based on citation relationships among journals, and assessments by experts from the various fields. The reader is referred to Chapter 6 for more details.

10. Do the ISI Indexes cover mainly literature written in English? In science, English is the dominant language on the international research front. Hence, the major number of articles in journals processed for the ISI Indexes is written in English. Papers published in other languages tend to have less impact on the research front, although their impact at the national level, for instance in the medical sciences upon medical practitioners, may be considerable. A large percentage of articles in English in the ISI Indexes thus reflects the international research front.

11. How can one assess in an objective way the extent to which a group's field is covered by the ISI Citation Indexes? In order to assess adequacy of coverage in a field in which a group is active, one may determine from a group's papers the extent to which they cite journals processed for the ISI Indexes. Since a group's papers may not constitute a representative sample of the field as a whole, cited references in other papers in the group's (sub-)discipline should be analysed as well. The fraction of references to journal items indicates the importance of journals in the field's written communication system, and – within the set of references to journals

– the fraction of references to ISI-covered journals indicates the extent to which the ISI indexes cover the journal communication system.

12. How well do the ISI Indexes cover the written communication in science disciplines? Chapter 8 concludes that it is excellent in molecular biology & biochemistry, biological sciences related to humans, clinical medicine, physics & astronomy and chemistry, and good yet not excellent in applied physics & chemistry, biological sciences related to animals and plants (including agriculture), engineering, geosciences and mathematics. But for several subfields, particularly in engineering, coverage is moderate. In applied and technical sciences, proceedings volumes and reference works play an important role.

13. How well do the ISI Indexes cover the written communication in social sciences and humanities? In social sciences and humanities ISI coverage of the communication system is good in psychology and psychiatry, and in other social sciences related to medicine and health, including amongst others public environment and occupational health, nursing, and geriatrics. It is also good in economics, but moderate in sociology, education, political sciences, and anthropology, and particularly in arts & humanities. In these fields, books and national journals play an important role. Differences between science, social sciences and humanities are further discussed in Chapter 9.

14. How should one assess groups in science fields with good yet not excellent ISI coverage, particularly in applied sciences and engineering? In fields with good yet not excellent ISI coverage, the universe of ISI sources can be expanded in two ways. First, one can expand the set of a group's target (cited) publications subjected to a citation analysis with publications in media not covered by the ISI Citation Indexes. Secondly, one can expand the universe of source (citing) publications in which the citation analysis takes place, by adding important journals not covered by ISI, proceedings volumes of important international conferences, or books. Expanded citation analysis is particularly useful in applied sciences and engineering, and in economics. Chapter 10 gives an example of this type of analysis.

15. How should one assess research performance in fields with moderate coverage, particularly in social sciences and humanities? In fields with moderate coverage, particularly in social sciences and humanities, it is proposed to give the ISI Citation Indexes in research performance assessments a limited role or no role at all, and to focus on the development of indicators applying other types of techniques. Chapter 11 presents further details and a case study in the field of law.

4.4   General validity issues

16. Scientists have many tasks and duties, and CA does not take into account all of these. Citation analysis assesses the contribution at the international research front. Academic researchers normally have research, teaching and social services, including patient care duties for medical researchers. In their research and development work medical researchers have two main tasks: contributing to scientific and technical progress at the international research front, and communicating important findings and practical applications to a wide national and international audience of medical professionals and practitioners. Bibliometric methods focus on the contribution to the research front, regardless of how important the other aspects may be in a full performance assessment.

17. Authors cite from a variety of motives, some of which may have little to do with research 'quality'. A crucial distinction in the debate on what citations measure is that between motives and consequences. It may be true that authors cite from a variety of motives, but citation analysis does not aim at capturing motives of individuals, but rather their consequences at an aggregate level. It embodies a fundamental shift in perspective from that of the psychology of individual citers towards what scientists jointly express sociologically in their referencing behaviour. This issue is further discussed in Chapters 15 and 16.

18. Do biases cancel out when analysed data samples are sufficiently large? Chapter 16 argues that random errors can be expected to cancel out when analysed data samples are sufficiently large, but systematic biases may remain. Hence, individual vagaries in referencing behaviour cancel out, but the results of CA must still be analysed for systematic biases. In addition, biases may not only be caused by the 'citing side', but also by the 'cited side'. Hence, when citation analysis is used to draw conclusions about the performance of a particular entity such as an individual scientist or research group, its outcomes may be affected by 'distorting' factors that are specific for that entity.

19. Has CA a US bias because US scientists excessively cite other US colleagues? A detailed analysis presented in Chapter 24 found no empirical evidence supporting the claim that US scientists overcite papers from their own country more than scientists from Western-European countries overcite papers from their countries. All countries overcite themselves, relative to what one would expect on the basis of their shares of citable papers in the database. The US self-citation rate is somewhat higher than that for major Western-European countries, but smaller than that for smaller Western-European countries. More details are presented in Chapter 24.

20. Does CA provide an objective measure of research quality?
Citations measure impact rather than quality. Citation impact can be conceived as an aspect of research quality, but it does not fully capture the latter concept. It is hypothesised in Chapter 17 that, regardless of what particular motives authors may have to cite, citations to research groups' publication ensembles reflect that their work cannot be ignored and should be mentioned. Citations can be interpreted in terms of intellectual influence, although its expression in the citing text may be vague or implicit. Measuring citation impact on the one hand, and interpreting and valuing citation impact in terms of a qualitative, evaluative framework on the other, are two distinct perspectives.

21. Is CA invalid because most papers are uncited? It has been claimed that large percentages of papers are never cited, and that this would make citation analysis invalid. But thorough empirical studies show that uncitedness depends upon type of paper, time window and discipline, and can be less than 10 per cent. It is true that meeting abstracts are rarely cited. As a rule of thumb, for a journal with an impact factor of 1.0, roughly speaking some 50 per cent of one- and two-year-old papers is uncited in a particular year, and for those with an impact factor of 2, about 25 per cent is uncited. Citation windows applied in journal impact factors are relatively short (see Chapter 5). Enlarging them, uncitedness percentages drop substantially. Glänzel et al. (2003) found that 21 per cent of SCI papers published in 1980 were uncited during a 20-year period

22. Does 'delayed recognition' or 'the Mendel effect' make CA invalid?
These terms refer to the phenomenon that articles that were not cited during the first years after publication may only after some time be recognised as important and become highly cited. Studies by van Raan (2004b) on 'sleeping beauties', Glänzel et al. (2003) and Garfield (1980) showed that delayed recognition is a rare event occurring in exceptional cases only. Glänzel et al. found that only 0.3 per cent of papers published in 1980 and not cited during the first 5 years after publication received more than 15 citations before the year 2000. The exceptional cases illustrate that a scientific community's perception of what are promising approaches may change over time, and that CA conducted over longer time periods reflects such changes.

23. After some time, fundamental scientific work becomes decreasingly and then rarely cited. This phenomenon is termed 'obliteration by incorporation' and has been observed in several studies. But to the extent that citation analysis focuses on the citation impact of papers made in the short term, typically during the first 5 to 10 years of a publication's lifetime, this factor is less likely to distort the analysis.

24. To what extent are citation counts affected by mutual citation arrangements? Empirical research related to the claim that citation counts are affected by mutual citation arrangements is confronted with the difficulty of distinguishing this type of citation behaviour from 'normal' citation practices of a small number of groups working in narrow specialties. Experts are in principle able to identify excessive mutual citation. Citation analysis would be enhanced if citation impact could be assessed in a systematic, quantitative way as a function of the socio-cognitive 'distance' between citing and cited papers (see Chapter 25).

25. Are scientists in large fields cited more frequently than those active in smaller fields? In large fields there is indeed a larger universe of citing papers, but at the same time a larger volume of citable papers competing for citations. The average number of references per paper does influence the average level of received citations per paper, but its relationship to the size of a field is unclear. But it can expected on statistical grounds – and is empirically shown for journal impact in Chapter 5 – that in larger fields the extremes of the citation distribution (the most frequently cited papers) tend to have higher values than those in smaller fields (e.g., Seglen, 1992; Garfield, 1998).

26. Does CA undervalue multi- or interdisciplinary research? Multi- or interdisciplinary research generally requires a dedicated approach. Assessing this type of research has become one of the important topics in bibliometrics, and more and more methodologies become available for analysing it (.e.g., van Raan and van Leeuwen, 2002; Bordons et al., 2004). Chapter 20 presents a good example. These methodologies mark a shift in perspective, from merely counting citations towards characterising the sources or origins of the citations, for instance, by analysing the cognitive contents of citing papers.

27. Does CA overvalue methodological papers? Whether or not methodological contributions are more frequently cited than, for instance, theoretical contributions, needs to be examined in more detail. Many scientists tend to value the latter type of contribution more highly than the first. But it must be emphasised that new methods, techniques and instruments play an important, often crucial role in the advancement of scientific knowledge. Nobel Prizes have recognised several methodological breakthroughs. The well-known methodological paper by Lowry on protein determination is indeed extremely highly cited, but this can be viewed as a statistical anomaly. Methods journals do not receive extraordinary impact (Garfield, 1996).

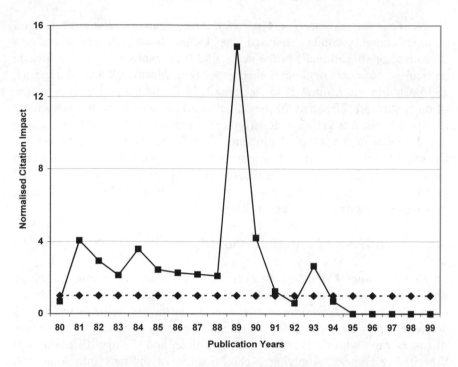

Figure 4.3. Citation analysis of papers by Fleischmann and Pons

This analysis comprises the articles published during the period 1980–2003 by S. Pons and/or M. Fleischmann containing 'Univ Utah' or 'Univ Southampton' in their corporate address. Data were collected using background knowledge obtained from various sources through the internet, but were not verified by the two authors themselves. A total of 196 articles was identified, authored by at least one of them. The total number of citations to all these articles during 1980–2003 was about 6,000. During 1980–1982 they had on average 6 articles per year, and during 1984–1989 about 20 per year. As from 1990, the number of articles decreased from 9 in 1990 to 0 in 1995 and later years. The broken line represents the world citation average in the subfields in which the authors were active. The horizontal lines show the normalised citation impact of the papers published in the various years, measured during the first four years after publication. The peak in 1989 reflects the publication of a controversial article about 'cold fusion' (Fleischmann, M. and Pons, S. 'Electrochemically induced nuclear fusion of deuterium' *Journal of Electroanalytical Chemistry and Interfacial Electrochemistry*, vol. 261, pp.301–308, 1989). This article was cited 711 times until 2003, 490 of which were during the first four years after publication. It claimed that the process of nuclear fusion had been done at room temperature in an electrolytic cell. Attempts to repeat the work by major, reputable laboratories, were unsuccessful. It is interesting to note that the citation impact of the authors' work prior to 1989 was substantially above world average. Three papers collected over 150 citations during their lifetime. The controversial paper generated a very high citation impact, probably also due to the fact that the authors had an excellent past performance when the paper was published. This case illustrates that citation impact on the one hand and research 'quality' or contribution to scientific progress on the other, are distinct concepts.

28. To what extent is CA affected by 'negative' citations? Several citation context studies analysed the extent to which references are 'negative' or 'negational', in the sense that they explicitly reject or negate particular statements made in a cited paper (e.g, Moravcsik and Murugesan, 1975; Chubin and Moitra, 1975; see Small, 1982 and Liu, 1993 for a review of more studies). The share of 'negative' citations was found to vary among disciplines, but was generally low (typically, around 10 per cent), but studies noted several methodological problems in defining 'negative' citations. On the other hand, the controversial papers by Fleischmann and Pons on cold fusion were highly cited. This is illustrated in Figure 4.3. Hence, it is argued in Chapter 17 that citation impact must be valued within a qualitative, evaluative framework using expert knowledge.

4.5   Indicators and their validity

29. How does CA take into account differences in citation practices among disciplines? A normalised citation impact indicator relates a group's citation impact to the world citation average in the subfields in which it is active. Citation practices differ considerably among subfields, both in terms of the average number of references per article, and the age distribution of the cited references. Applying a classification of journals into some 150 subfields, a normalised citation impact indicator of a group calculates the ratio of the average number of citations per article published by the group and the world citation average in the subfields in which the group is active. This indicator also takes into account document type (e.g., whether it is a normal research article or a review) and its age. If a group is active in several subfields, a weighted average is calculated, the weights being equal to the fraction of articles published in each subfield. Groups with a citation impact equal to the world average in their subfields obtain a score of 1.0. For an example the reader is referred to Table 4.1.

30. Can journal impact factors be used to assess publication strategies? A normalised journal impact measure can be used to properly assess a group's journal packet. This indicator takes into account the subfield covered by the journal, and the type and age distribution of documents published in it. Thus, a number of methodological problems related to the journal impact factors published in ISI's Journal Citation Reports (JCR) can be solved (see Chapter 5). A group normally publishes articles in a set of journals, denoted as a journal packet. For such a packet a weighted, normalised journal impact measure can be calculated, the weights being determined by the number of papers in each journal.

31. Is CA of individual papers unnecessary and the use of journal impact factors sufficient? Journal impact is a performance aspect in its own right, but cannot be used to predict actual citation rates. The extent to which groups of scientists publish their output in the more prestigious, or even the 'top' journals in their fields, is often viewed as an important aspect of scientific research performance. The indicator of the impact of a group's journal packet described above can be validly used to assess this aspect. However, these journal measures cannot be used to predict 'actual' citation rates and therefore are no valid surrogates of the actual citation impact of a group's publications (Seglen, 1992; Seglen, 1994; Garfield, 1996; see also Section 5.4 of this book).

32. Does CA give only a static picture? No. Application of appropriate publication and citation time windows provides informative citation impact trend data. On the one hand, the time horizon applied in assessing the citation impact of publications should not be too short, as it takes some time for a contribution to demonstrate its importance and gain citation impact. On the other hand, application of longer periods may reduce policy relevance when articles published in the distant past are analysed. Moreover, citations to important contributions may decline over the years as their findings become established. Depending upon the field, application of a citation window of 3 to 5 years following the year of publication has proven to yield the most informative trend data.

33. Does CA give only a historical picture? No. One approach focuses on an assessment of the past performance of an entity (e.g., group, institution) from a perspective of accountability of research funds allocated to it during a particular time period. In this case it is appropriate to take into account only articles emerging from that entity's institution as reflected in authors' institutional affiliations. A second approach is directed more towards the future and focuses on the performance of the scientists who are currently active in an entity, regardless of whether they worked in that entity during the entire time period of analysis. It provides a view on the past performance of those who have the task of shaping the future of this institution. Past performance is a good predictor of future performance (e.g., van Raan, 1996).

34. Is CA biased in favour of older researchers with long scientific careers? When 'lifetime' citation counts are collected, citation analysis tends to be biased in favour of older researchers with long scientific careers. Lifetime citation counts include citations to a scientist's total publication record, and tend to increase with the duration of the career. But citation analysis can focus on the citation impact of papers published during the more 'recent' past, for instance, during the past 8 to 10 years.

35. Does CA give only a snapshot of a group's performance? No. A group's publication output, and particularly its citation impact, may vary considerably from year to year. Thus, snapshots based on articles published in a single year do not normally provide stable results and are practically useless. In addition, a group's state of development cannot be assessed on the basis of only one year. A time period including at least two PhD student generations (8–10 years) is needed to obtain a valid picture of a group's performance and its development (van Raan, 1996).

36. Citation distributions are skewed. This is true both for papers of leading groups and for those of less prominent groups, and for papers in high and for those in low impact journals. Chapter 16 hypothesises that highly cited papers represent 'flags' of research groups' publication ensembles or symbols of their research programmes. Flag papers and normal articles both constitute indispensable elements of a group's work. In this sense, citations to highly cited papers are citations to the entire ensemble. The distribution of citations among articles published by a group can be properly characterised by the sum of citations to the entire ensemble; the corresponding mean citation rate, often denoted as citation per publication ratio, corrects for differences in size of the publication ensemble. But other parameters of the distribution are also informative, particularly the percentage of uncited papers, the maximum score, and the median and the 90th percentile or other percentiles of the citation distribution.

37. Are aggregate statistics useful? Aggregate statistics are useful for an overview, but breakdowns in various ways are essential. Statistics at the level of a large entity during a longer time period provide rough though useful indications of its international orientation and citation impact. However, more detailed analyses by group, (sub-)discipline or type of scientific collaboration are indispensable for a more complete bibliometric picture. In addition, an analysis per year gives insight into developments over time. Characteristics of the sources of the citations, e.g., citing journals or institutions and their country of origin, provide useful additional information.

38. Outcomes of CA of science groups may be distorted by 'national' journals covered by ISI. Zitt et al. (2003) found that 'national oriented' journals have a negative influence upon a country's citation impact figures in international benchmarking studies. Van Leeuwen et al. (2000; 2001) found that when German and French papers in national language journals included in the ISI database were removed, the normalised citation impact of the articles from these countries tended to *increase*. However, as argued in Chapter 7 the number of 'national' journals included in the ISI Indexes is limited. One should distinguish between a national and an international point of view. In order to assess research performance from a national perspective, it is appropriate to take national journals into account. In assessments from an international perspective, it is proposed to exclude these journals from the analysis (see for instance Moed, 2002b, analysing research performance of China).

39. What data is indispensable for a proper interpretation of citation indicators? Browsing through a group's list of most frequently cited articles is indispensable for proper interpretation of statistics at any level of aggregation. It is hypothesised in Chapter 16 that these papers constitute the flags of the publication ensembles subjected to a citation analysis. Statistically, their citation impact may to a large extent determine a group's total and average citation rates. This list does not necessarily coincide with a list of the best papers in the perception of the evaluated scientists themselves.

4.6 General issues of interpretation and use

40. What is the most appropriate level of aggregation in CA in science? In science, the research group is the natural 'business' unit and therefore constitutes the most useful aggregation level in a citation analysis. Scientific research is the result of team work. A research group consists of a group leader, other senior scientists, postdoctoral researchers and PhD students. Senior scientists may divide tasks among each other. To the extent that their activities are integrated, it is more appropriate to analyse their joint performance rather than focusing on a single individual.

41. To what extent can CA assess the research performance of an individual scientist? Performance of an individual and citation impact of the papers he or she (co-)authored relate to two distinct levels of aggregation. In science, the publications (co-)authored by an individual researcher are often, if not always, the result of research to which other scientists have contributed as well, sometimes even dozens of them. The crucial issue is how one should relate the citation impact of a team's papers to the performance of an individual working in that team. This can be done properly only on the basis of sufficient background knowledge of the particular role of the scientist in the research presented in his/her publication ensemble, for instance, whether this role has been leading, instrumental, or technical.

42. To what extent are outcomes of CA influenced by scientific collaboration among groups? Citation analysis should take into account scientific collaboration among research groups. Groups tend more and more to collaborate with other groups from their own institution, from their country or from abroad. The intensity and nature of collaboration, and its effect upon individual groups' citation impact should and can be carefully assessed by applying appropriate indicators. Chapter 23 presents outcomes of analyses at an aggregate level and assesses from a bibliometric viewpoint the extent to which participants in bi-lateral international collaboration profit from this type of collaboration in terms of raising their citation impact.

43. Is it appropriate to use CA as the principal tool in decisions about promotion or salaries of individuals? In formulaic use, the outcome of a quality judgement or policy decision is defined in categorical terms ('promoted or funded') or even quantitatively ('level of salary or funding budget') and is directly related to the value of bibliometric indicators through some kind of formula or algorithm. It is argued in Chapter 2 that bibliometric indicators are inappropriate for this type of use. Formulaic use of CA should be firmly discouraged and discredits CA as a whole.

44. Which are important criteria for proper use of CA in a policy context? In Chapter 2 it is argued that in the policy domain, the use of citation analysis is more appropriate the more it is carried out openly according to transparent procedures with clear objectives; subjected entities are able to verify data and comment on results; potentialities and limitations, technical and validity issues are explicitly stated; its outcomes contribute to insight, or pose problems or address particular questions that participants in the process seek to answer; and the process ensures the availability of expert knowledge on the entities involved and the fields in which they are active.

45. Does CA make expert knowledge superfluous? No, on the contrary. Interpretation of citation statistics requires additional expert knowledge. Citation impact must be valued in a wider evaluative framework. Generally, the 'special' characteristics of the entity to be evaluated must be taken into account, and proper knowledge is indispensable as regards the substantive content of the entity's work and the field in which it is active. For instance, controversial or erroneous research findings may gain a high citation impact at least in the short term (see paragraph 28 and Figure 4.3 above).

46. Can CA replace peer judgements? No. Citation analysis is a valuable, *additional tool* in peer reviews of research performance. It provides in a quantitative framework a condensed representation of citation patterns in an entire field's literature from a range of years, and can be used as such to sharpen or even correct a peer's own impression of an entity's research quality. In science, peers often find citation data relevant, and they may collect such data themselves from the ISI Citation Indexes. Chapter 2 denotes this type of use as informal, and the extent to which it takes place can barely be determined empirically.

47. Is CA only a tool for peers? No. On the one hand Chapter 2 argues that, in view of the importance of expert and background knowledge, bibliometric analysis at the level of individual scholars, research departments and institutions normally best finds its way to the policy arena through peer assessments. But it does not follow that citation analysis is a tool to be used by peers only. Chapters 19 and 20 illustrate that citation analysis can also be used to monitor or evaluate peer review processes and to keep peer review honest. Used in this way, it is a tool for policy decision makers as well.

48. What is the role of CA in research evaluation? Scientific quality is a multi-dimensional concept that is not fully captured by citation impact. It is argued in Chapter 2 that peer review committees or other evaluating agencies using citation analysis should specify in advance the dimensions to be taken into account in an assessment, and their relative weights. Alternative quality concepts may be developed and applied. Discussions about methodology and outcomes of citation analysis often manifest themselves as 'technical' but are essentially about underlying notions of research quality. As a quantitative-empirical science, citation analysis should maintain a 'neutral' position with respect to the various quality concepts and give their validity a hypothetical status. In this sense citation analysis itself does not evaluate, but its outcomes may help to make explicit and further develop such concepts.

Chapter 5

CITATION ANALYSIS OF SCIENTIFIC JOURNALS

5.1   Introduction

Eugene Garfield's creative work on journal impact measures served more than one function. As outlined in Chapter 1, these measures were originally designed and applied to monitor the journal coverage of the *Science Citation Index*. They constituted a tool to identify on a permanent basis the most important journals in the scientific communication system, and to highlight candidates to be included or dropped in view of the need to establish a cost-effective Citation Index. Garfield emphasised, however, that journal citation analysis could also be used to study the scientific-scholarly communication system, and could contribute to its better functioning, and hence to a better science.

> As a communication system, the network of journals that play a paramount role in the exchange of scientific and technical information is little understood (Garfield, 1972, p 471). Using the SCI data base to map the journal communications network may contribute to more efficient science (ibid., p. 477).

Ever since, Garfield has published numerous citation analyses of the journal network, and other investigators in the field of library and information science and in almost every branch of the natural and social sciences have carried out hundreds of studies. The journal impact measure most widely spread among the scientific community is the journal impact factor. Nowadays it is used as a direct reflection of a journal's prestige or quality. Journal editors and publishers communicate the values of impact factors of their journals to reading audiences. Impact factors are not only used to rank journals, but also to evaluate individual scholars and research groups or departments according to the journals they select for publication, even in decisions about salaries or promotion. This chapter aims to provide technical information about the impact factor of which potential users should be aware.

The impact factor of a journal J in year T is defined as follows:

> The number of citations received in year T by all documents published in J in the years T-1 and T-2
>
> ÷
>
> The number of citable documents published in J in the years T-1 and T-2

It is a *ratio*, with the number of citations in the numerator, and the number of citable documents (research articles and reviews) in the denominator. It thus represents the arithmetic mean of the distribution of citations amongst documents published in a journal. For a particular year it takes into account citations to documents published in the two preceding years only. In other words, it reflects the average citation impact of one- and two-year-old documents. In the denominator, only 'citable' documents are counted. This term is explained below.

Section 5.2 presents a critical methodological discussion of the journal impact factor published in ISI's Annual Journal Citation Reports (JCR), and highlights the basic assumptions that underlie it. It does not discuss data on journal citation impact from other ISI information products, such as its 'Journal Performance Indicators'. Section 5.3 presents a normalised or relative journal citation impact indicator as an alternative measure. Finally, Section 5.4 discusses further issues regarding journal impact measures, outlines new developments, and makes concluding remarks.

5.2   Issues regarding ISI/JCR impact factor

Why calculate a ratio (citations per article)?

Journals show substantial differences with respect to the number of documents they publish in a year. This is clearly illustrated in Table 5.1 which presents key statistics on the number of articles, pages and issues per journal processed for the SCI. Garfield argued that the citation frequency of a journal is a function not only of the scientific significance of the material it publishes, but also of the number of articles it publishes annually.

In view of the relation between size and citation frequency, it would seem desirable to discount the effect of size when using citation data to assess a journal's importance ... We have attempted to do this by calculating a relative impact factor – that is, by dividing the number of times a journal has been cited by the number of articles it has published during some specific period of time. The journal impact factor will thus reflect an average citation rate per published article" (Garfield, 1972, p. 477).

Table 5.1. Statistics on articles, pages and issues in SCI source journals

Indicator	Mean	P25	Median	P75
Articles/Journal	210	50	97	204
Issues/Journal	9.6	5	8	12
Articles/Issue	22.0	9	14	22
Pages/Article	6.2	1.5	5.5	8.5
Cited Refs/Article	23.4	5	19	33

Data relates to 3,700 journals processed for the SCI in the year 2001. P25, P75: 25th and 75th percentile of the distribution. The table shows, for instance, that 25% of journals have less than 50 articles per year and another 25% more than 204 articles. The median number of issues per journal is 8, and the median number of articles per issue is 14. Median values are lower than means, reflecting that distributions are skewed to the right.

However, the impact factor represents the mean value of a skewed citation distribution. This is illustrated in Figure 5.1 and Table 5.2 which compare the distributions of citations among documents published in two journals: *Analytica Chimica Acta* and *Analytical Chemistry*. Many, if not all journals show skewed citation patterns such as those presented in Figure 5.1.

Table 5.2. Parameters of the citation distributions for two journals plotted in Figure 5.1

	AC Analytical Chemistry	ACA Analytica Chimica Acta
No. documents	1,932	1,466
Mean citation rate	4.5	1.9
Skewness	2.8	1.9
Uncited documents (%)	12.4	27.8
90th Percentile	10	5

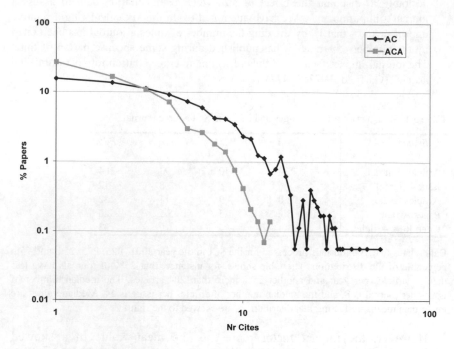

Figure 5.1. Distribution of citations among documents for two journals

AC: *Analytical Chemistry*. ACA: *Analytica Chimica Acta*. Citation counts relate to the year 2002; cited papers were published in 2000 and 2001.

Why count citations to 1–2 year-old articles?

Some journals have a long history, whereas others were founded recently. The former may be cited more frequently in a particular year than the latter because they have a large number of citable back volumes. Moreover, the citation impact of a journal's older volumes may not properly reflect its current status. In view of this, a measure was constructed that expresses the citation impact of one- and two-year-old annual volumes.

> In selecting an items-published base for each journal, I have been guided by the chronological distribution of cited items in each annual edition of the SCI. An analysis of this distribution has shown that the typical cited article is most heavily cited during the 2 years after its year of publication ... Therefore, since my sample consists of references made in 1969, I have taken as the items-published base for each journal the number of items it published during 1967 and 1968 (Garfield, 1972, p. 472).

But the age distributions of cited references vary significantly among disciplines. This is shown in Figure 5.2 which presents age distributions for the total ISI database and for two research fields (journal categories): biochemistry & molecular biology and mathematics. It shows that for the total ISI database the average cited article is most heavily cited when it is two years old.

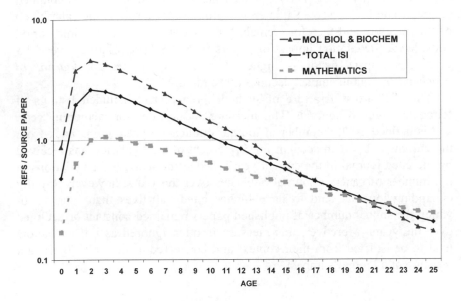

Figure 5.2. Age distributions of cited references in two disciplines and in the total ISI database

In mathematics, however, this maximum is reached one year later. The figure also shows that an average article in mathematics cites one- or two-year-old papers less frequently than do articles in biochemistry & molecular biology. To be precise, in the former field a paper contains on average 1.6 references to one- or two-year-old articles, whereas in the latter it is 8.4 references.

That is why impact factors of journals in the former field are generally so much lower than those for journals covering the latter. Garfield was very well aware of such differences, and emphasised in many publications that one should not directly compare journals from different disciplines with one another.

Although the age distributions are to some extent affected by changes in the annual number of articles published in the various fields, the figure reveals that in mathematics the citation impact of papers declines much more slowly with their age than in biochemistry & molecular biology. In other words, older papers tend to be more relevant in the former field than they are in the latter.

But citation impact decline rates vary even among journals covering the same discipline. This phenomenon is illustrated in Figure 5.3. It compares four journals covering biochemistry & molecular biology on the basis of the average citation rate of articles as a function of their age. Details are given in the legend of this figure. The ISI impact factor is based on the rates obtained at ages 1 and 2. The scores at later ages do not play a role in the calculation of this measure and therefore remain 'out of sight'. During the time period considered, the citation impact of papers in *FEBS Letters* halves every 4.5 years. Its impact factor is higher than that of *European Journal of Biochemistry*, but its impact declines more rapidly.

The JCR are well aware of such differences and included listings of 'cited half lives' of journals. This measure is calculated for each citing year, and is defined as "the number of journal publication years going back from the current year which account for 50 percent of the total citations received by the cited journal in the current year". It does not correct for variations in the number of papers a journal publishes over the years, however. Rapidly expanding journals tend to have higher cited half-lives than journals of which the annual number of published papers remained constant or declined over the years. Moreover, this measure is often ignored as impact factors tend to be isolated from their context and conceived as the only significant measure of a journal's impact.

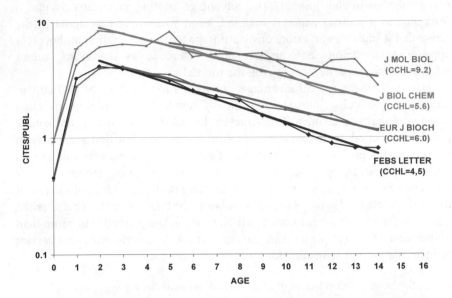

Figure 5.3. Citation impact as a function of age of cited documents for four journals

FEBS LETTER: *FEBS Letters*; J BIOL CHEM: *Journal of Biological Chemistry*; EUR J BIOCH: *European Journal of Biochemistry*; J MOL BIOL: *Journal of Molecular Biology*.
Data are extracted from an earlier study (Moed et al., 1998) and relate to citations in a single year (1995) to citable papers published during the 14 previous years. The plot gives the average citation rate (Cites/Publ on a logarithmic scale) of papers as a function of their age. Age 0 refers to citations to papers published in the same year as the citing year. The citation rates for ages 1 and 2 are those that constitute the JCR journal impact factor. Decline was modelled as an exponential decay process. Straight lines in the plot are regression lines resulting from fitting data points from the age at which the citation rate reaches its maximum value onwards. From the regression coefficient the decay constant was determined, defined as the (estimated) time period in which the average citation impact is reduced by a factor of two. Since the calculation of this decline constant corrects for differences in the numbers of documents published per year, it is denoted as the Corrected Citation Half-Life (CCHL). For instance, for *FEBS Letters* a CCHL of 4.5 was obtained. Thus, during the time period between age 3 and 14, the average citation impact halves every 4.5 years. J MOL BIOL shows a much slower decline with a CCHL of 9.2.

Why use cited journal titles from reference lists?

ISI's JCR provide detailed citation data on all journals covered by the ISI Citation Indexes and constitute the most frequently used information product on journal impact factors. They contain amongst others listings of journals ranked by impact factor and arranged by category – groupings of journals covering the same (sub)discipline. The impact factor's numerator is determined by counting in the total database cited references containing the name of a particular journal. The advantage of this procedure is that a reference to a journal paper is counted, even when it is inaccurate in the sense that it indicates an erroneous starting page number or first author. It is appropriate to count such an erroneous reference as the citing author intended to cite a particular paper in the journal.

However, there are disadvantages as well. First, it may be difficult to identify a particular journal in a file of hundreds of millions of cited references that use at most 20 characters to indicate the title of the source publishing a cited document. Not all journals may be identified accurately in this way. This problem is illustrated in Table 5.3. It presents for the journal *Astronomy and Astrophysics* the title variants used by citing authors in their reference lists when they cite a paper published in it. It is rather obvious that the title variant *Astron Astrophys* relates to this journal. This variant accounts for almost 80 per cent of all citations to the journal: but more than 20 per cent of references indicate the acronym A A. Overlooking this variant reduces the journal impact factor by some 20 per cent.

Table 5.3. Variants of cited journal titles: the journal *Astronomy and Astrophysics*

Cited journal title variant	Citations N	%	Citations/Article
Astron Astrophys	7,566	79	2.3
A A	2,047	21	0.6
All other	15	0	0.0
Total	9,628	100	2.9

Data relate to the year 2002, and are extracted from the bibliometric version of the ISI Citation Indexes on CD-ROM created at the Centre for Science and Technology Studies at Leiden University (the Netherlands). Seventy-nine per cent of references to the journal indicate the journal title *Astron Astrophys*. However, authors citing this journal also indicate in 2,047 cases (21 per cent) its acronym *A A*. Ignoring these references would reduce the journal's impact factor from 2.95 to 2.31. This issue was raised by Sandqvist (2004). The outcomes presented in Table 5.3 apparently diverge from figures presented by Sandqvist, This is probably due to differences in methodology and in versions of ISI Indexes used (CD-ROM versus Web of Science version). Abt (2004) reported that the JCR impact factor of this journal (and several other astronomical journals) was incorrect for the years 1998–2001, due to changes in a computer program used by ISI to calculate impact factors, but that as from 2002, ISI corrected its program and included the '*A A*' variant in the counts for this journal. However, the decline in its impact factor in 1998 compared to 1997 and particularly its increase in 2002 compared to 2001 reported by Abt is larger than the 20 per cent for the variant '*A A*' presented in Table 5.3.

A second disadvantage relates to the concept of "citable" document in the definition of the impact factor. Source articles in the ISI Citation Indexes are categorised by type. Important types are normal research articles, review articles, notes (prior to 1996), letters, editorials, news items, corrections and meeting abstracts. As a rule, the JCR includes as citable items in the impact factor's denominator the number of normal articles, notes and reviews. But many journals contain other types of documents as well. When these other types are cited, the citations do contribute to the impact factor's numerator, but the cited papers are not included in the denominator. In a sense, these citations are 'for free' (Moed and van Leeuwen, 1996). Table 5.4 illustrates this problem for one particular journal: *the Lancet.*

Table 5.4. Free citations: *Lancet* (2002)

Type of document	No. Docs	Cites	Cites/Doc
Articles, reviews	1,544 (a)	13,106	8.5
Other types	4,899	2,564	0.5
Total	6,443	15,670 (b)	2.4
JCR-like (reconstructed) impact factor = (b) / (a)			10.2

Data relate to the year 2002, and were extracted from the bibliometric version of the ISI Citation Indexes on CD-ROM created at the Centre for Science and Technology Studies at Leiden University (the Netherlands). In 2000 and 2001, this journal has published 1,544 documents (articles and reviews) denoted by the JCR as citable. These documents are counted in the impact factor's denominator. There are 4,899 other types of documents, mainly letters, editorials and news items published in the journal. Although these are in JCR terms conceived as non-citable, they are cited a total of 2,564 times. These citations are included in the total citation count of 15,670 that constitutes the impact factor's numerator. The 'JCR-like', reconstructed impact factor is the ratio of total citations and citable items, and amounts to 10.2. If the numerator included only citations to those document types that are counted in the denominator, the impact factor would be 8.5, which is 16 per cent lower than that based on citations to all types of documents. The value of 10.2 found for the JCR-like (reconstructed) impact factor is somewhat lower than that given in the JCR, because the set of journals used by ISI to calculate its JCR is somewhat broader than that of the CD-ROM version. Therefore, it is termed in this table the JCR-like or reconstructed impact factor.

Both the problem of journal title variants and that of 'free citations' to non-citable documents can in principle be solved by linking cited references to a journal on a 'paper-by-paper' basis and determining citation counts for each individual paper in a journal. However, this solution requires that the linking matching process is carried out carefully, and takes into account numerous variations or errors in cited references. This issue is further discussed in Chapter 13.

5.3   Normalised journal impact measures

Several authors have suggested alternative journal impact measures that account for differences in referencing practices among scientific disciplines. These are denoted as normalised or relative measures, and in principle enable cross-comparisons of journals among disciplines. An overview is presented in Glänzel and Moed (2002).

Knowledgeable users of JCR data are aware that review journals tend to have higher impact factors than ordinary journals. In fact, in many disciplines review journals are in the top of the journal rankings. The printed edition of the JCR contained listings giving for each journal the share of review articles published in it. A normalised measure developed at the Leiden Centre for Science and Technology Studies (CWTS) does not only take into account differences in referencing practices among disciplines, but also the type of cited document and its age relative to the year of citation.

Table 5.5. Example of the calculation of a normalised journal impact measure

Aggregate	Articles		Reviews	
	No. Docs	*Cites/Doc*	*No. Docs*	*Cites/Doc*
Discipline	15,000	3.0	1000	5.0
Journal	500	4.0	100	6.0

Normalised impact = (500*4.0 + 100*6.0) / (500*3.0+100*5.0)=2,600/2,000=1.3

The numerical example presented in this table takes into account only the journal's discipline and the type of cited document it published. The method can easily be expanded with the factor age of cited documents. The crucial point is that a journal's papers of a particular age are compared to other papers of the same age. The normalised impact measure can be conceived as a ratio of the actual and expected number of received citations. Within a discipline, each type of document has its own expected citation rate. In the example, this rate is 3.0 for articles and 5.0 for reviews. Since the journal publishes 500 articles and 100 reviews, the expected number of citations is 500*3.0 + 100*5.0=2,000. The actual number is 500*4.0+100*6.0=2,600, so that the ratio of actual and expected citations is 1.3. In calculating mean citation rates in a discipline, the method takes into account all papers in all journals covering that discipline. Alternative methods proposed by Sen (1992) and Marshakova-Shaikevich (1996) apply a normalisation factor that is based only upon documents in a discipline's journal with the highest citation impact or in the 5 journals with the highest citation impact, respectively. Contrary to the methodology outlined in Table 5.5, these methods use journal impact factors obtained from ISI's JCR, and do not take into account the type of document or the document's publication year within the impact factor's publication window. An alternative approach is a ranking procedure similar to percentile ranking, generating rank-normalised impact factors (e.g., Pudovkin and Garfield, 2004).

It can be calculated for a series of citing years rather than one single year, and for cited documents of any age, particularly for those that are older than one or two years as selected in the JCR impact factor. A simple numerical example in Table 5.5 illustrates how this measure is calculated. The normalised impact measure can be conceived as a ratio of the actual and expected number of received citations. A ratio of 1 indicates that a journal's impact is 'as expected' given the discipline it covers, the type of documents it publishes and the age distribution of its cited papers.

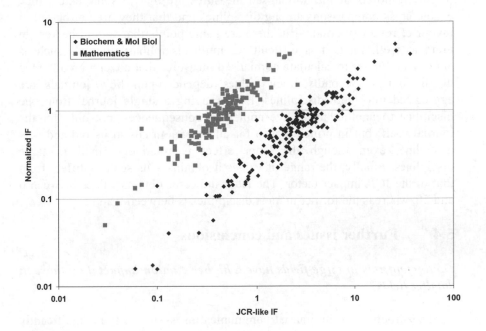

Figure 5.4. Normalised versus JCR-like impact measures in two disciplines

The JCR-like impact factors relate to the citing year 2003. They are termed 'JCR-like' because they are not obtained from the JCR, but were reconstructed from data included in the combined ISI Citation Indexes on CD-ROM. The normalised impact measure relates to citations given in the years 1999–2003 to documents published during the same time period, but the application of different citation windows, particularly the ISI impact factor window, provides similar outcomes. For more comparisons between ISI impact factor and normalised journal impact measures, see van Leeuwen (2004a).

Figure 5.4 compares the JCR-like impact factors to the normalised measures for all journals in two disciplines; mathematics and biochemistry & molecular biology. JCR impact factors in the former are mostly between 0.1 and 1.0, whereas in the latter they are between 1 and 10. But the normalised measures in the two disciplines have very similar ranges of values. Figure 5.4 also shows that even within a discipline the positions of journals may very among the two rankings. For instance, the journal in biochemistry & molecular biology with the highest JCR-like impact factor ranks third according to its normalised citation impact. This is a review journal.

Strong points of the normalised measures are that to some extent they enable cross-comparisons among disciplines and that they are not biased in favour of review journals. But there are some points that should be kept in mind as well. First, it is difficult for multi-disciplinary journals such as *Science* or *Nature* to calculate normalised measures that cover a broad range of disciplines. Secondly, their values depend upon how journals are aggregated into (sub-)disciplines. Even moving a single journal from one discipline to another may have numerical consequences, not only for the journal itself, but in principle also for all other journals in its old and new discipline, even though the latter effect is relatively small in large disciplines. Finally, the range of values it obtains – its scale – differs from that of the JCR impact factor. The latter indicator obtains values between 0 and 50, whereas the former in most disciplines is between 0 and 5.

5.4   Further issues and conclusions

Do top journals in large fields have a higher citation impact than those in smaller fields?

The structure of the journal communication system differs significantly from one discipline to another, in the sense that the distribution of citation impact among journals in a discipline varies among disciplines. Figure 5.5 shows that 'top' journals in large disciplines tend to have a higher citation impact than top journals in smaller ones. This phenomenon should be taken into account in any use of journal impact indicators, regardless of whether one applies normalised measures or those published in the JCR. The analysis presented in Figure 5.5 underlines the usefulness particularly of field-normalised journal impact indicators in comparative studies of disciplinary journal communication systems.

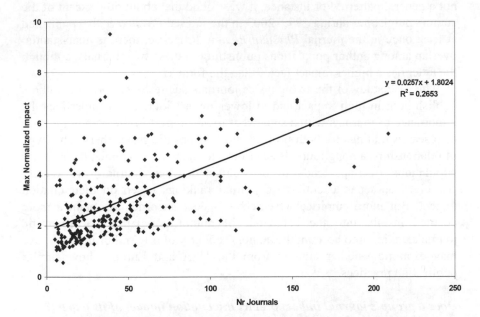

Figure 5.5. Number of journals covering a discipline versus the citation impact of its highest impact journal

Data are extracted from the CWTS database of ISI Citation Indexes on CD-ROM. The normalised impact measure relates to citations given in the years 1999–2003 to documents published during the same time period. Figure 5.5 shows that large disciplines in terms of numbers of journals published have higher extreme citation impact values than smaller ones. From a linear regression follows the result that the size of a discipline accounts for 27 per cent of the variance in the normalised impact of a discipline's most frequently cited journal. The regression line is plotted in the graph. The categorisation of journals into sub-disciplines is derived from the system of journal categories developed by the Institute for Scientific Information.

Do top groups publish in top journals only and less prominent groups merely in lower impact journals?

A claim often made about journal impact factors and journal performance in general is that the most prolific authors publish only in the most prestigious journals, whereas less prolific authors publish their papers in journals with a lower status. If this were true, one would expect that in a particular field a journal with a high impact factor and one with a lower impact would have distinct sets of publishing authors.

Empirical analysis of author populations by journal revealed that this is not a general pattern. For instance, it was found that about 50 per cent of the authors publishing during 1999–2003 in the journal *Physica B* also published at least once in the journal *Physical Review B*. Hence, there is a substantial overlap among author populations publishing in these two journals, although the latter has a higher impact factor than the former.

The case study of the two physics journals suggests that prolific authors publish both in high impact and in lower impact journals. It underlines the importance of journals with a somewhat lower impact in the communication of research findings by both prolific and less prolific researchers. This type of relationships among journals according to the extent to which their author populations overlap, tends to be neglected when journals are merely conceived as separate entities in journal rankings based on their citation impact. But more empirical research is needed in order to obtain a more detailed insight into the behaviour of author populations of scientific journals, taking into account the authors' country of origin. For instance, one may examine whether authors from the USA and Europe show similar publication practices.

Does a group's journal impact predict the citation impact of its papers?

Journal impact factors are quite often used to assess the research performance of individual scientists or departments. Although the status of the journals in which a group publishes is an aspect of research performance in its own right, journal impact factors should not be used as surrogates of citation impact of a group's publications. This point was emphasised by Garfield (1996), Seglen (1994), van Raan (2004a), and many others.

A secondary analysis of the outcomes of four bibliometric studies of a large number of research departments undertaken at CWTS and presented in Chapter 19 found that the normalised impact of the journals in which the papers were published explains between only 20 and 40 per cent of the variance in the normalised citation impact of a department's papers, described in Chapter 4. Specifically, in the studies on Dutch departments in biology, chemistry and physics, and the study on the anonymous university presented in Chapter 19, the explained variance was 0.43, 0.18, 0.26 and 0.39, respectively.

New developments

A future task would be to develop a field-normalised journal impact indicator that is less sensitive to changes in journal (sub-)disciplinary classification systems; that can be computed for multi-disciplinary journals;

and that has a scale more comparable to that of the JCR impact factor. But it would not be wise to concentrate too strongly upon developing the single, 'perfect' measure. Journal performance is a multi-dimensional concept, and a journal's position in the scientific journal communication system has many aspects. It is questionable whether all dimensions can be properly expressed in one single index.

A more productive approach is to develop and present a *series* of indicators for the various dimensions, and highlight their significance and limitations. In addition, it must be noted that JCR journal impact factor is nowadays so widely dispersed and so frequently used that it seems difficult if not impossible to have it replaced by a single alternative measure, especially in the near future.

Pinski and Narin (1976) developed an important methodology for determining citation based influence measures of scientific journals and (sub-)disciplines. They calculated a measure termed "*influence weight of a journal*", and described as "a size independent measure of the weighted number of citations a journal receives from other journals, normalised by the number of references it gives to other journals" (p. 298). One of the methodology's key elements is that it assigns a higher weight to citations from a prestigious journal than to a citation from a less prestigious or peripheral journal. The authors showed how this notion can be incorporated in a "self consistent 'bootstrap' set of relations, in which each unit plays a role in determining the weights of every other unit" (Pinski and Narin, 1976, p. 300). Their notions may play an important role in the further development of journal impact measures. This point is further discussed in Chapter 25.

PART 2.2

THE ISI CITATION INDEXES

Chapter 6

BASIC PRINCIPLES, CITATION LINKS AND TERMINOLOGY

6.1 Introduction

Throughout this book the term 'ISI Citation Indexes' is used to denote a series of information products based on citation indexing of scientific literature and produced during the past 50 years by the Institute for Scientific Information (currently Thomson Scientific, Inc.). An overview of the various versions is presented in Table 6.1. One may distinguish between the printed, CD-ROM, online and internet version of the Indexes. In recent years the *Web of Science* is by far the most frequently used version and has the largest journal coverage.

In order to obtain a proper understanding of bibliometric performance measures derived from the *Science Citation Index* and related Citation Indexes, it is essential to have an insight into their coverage. A crucial issue, therefore, is how sources are selected, which selection criteria are applied, and how these criteria are founded in an understanding of the scholarly communication process. This chapter provides information on these issues.

Section 6.2 outlines the basic principles underlying the ISI indexes, developed by Eugene Garfield. Garfield's 'Law of Concentration' of sources in a multi-disciplinary index, and an 'internal' coverage monitor based on citation relationships, plays a key role. It explains why the ISI Indexes are unique and powerful tools, and why they constitute by far the most frequently used database in studies of the scholarly communication system and in research evaluation. Section 6.3 explains the various types of citation relationships. This technical discussion provides a background for properly understanding basic features of citation indexes and their adequacy of coverage.

Table 6.1. Versions of the ISI Citation Indexes

Version	Acronym	Full name	Field coverage
Printed	SCI	Science Citation Index	Science
	SSCI	Social Science Citation Index	Social Sciences
	A&HCI	Arts & Humanities Citation Index	Arts and Humanities
CD-ROM	SCI	Science Citation Index	Science
	SSCI	Social Science Citation Index	Social Sciences
	A&HCI	Arts & Humanities Citation Index	Arts and Humanities
		5 Specialty CD-ROMS	Biochemistry, Biotechnology, Chemistry, Neurosciences, Materials Science
		Compumath Citation Index	Mathematics & Computer Science
Online		SCISEARCH online	Above indexes and selected journals from ISI's Current Contents
Internet	WoS	Web of Science	Combines all indexes and includes *SCI-Expanded* covering additional science journals

6.2   Basic principles

Publication behaviour of scholarly authors and the importance of the sources in which they publish has been a major research topic in the field of information science for many decades. In 1953, one of the pioneers, S.C. Bradford, in an empirical analysis of the literature in the field electrical engineering, made the following observation.

> Articles of interest to a specialist must not only occur in the periodicals specializing in his subject, but also, from time to time, in other periodicals, which grow in number as the relation of their fields to that of the subject lessens, and the number of articles on his subject in each periodical diminishes (Bradford, 1953).

He formalised this observation into what has later been termed *"Bradford's Law of Dispersion or Scattering"*, describing how the relevant documents in a subject are statistically distributed among publishing sources. In the information science literature, this law has received much attention ever since. From it, Garfield and other information scientists developed a simple rule stating that somewhere between 500 and 1,000 different journals are required to obtain 95 per cent of the significant literature published in a field.

Applying this rule to a database covering all fields of scholarship, it would seem that the number of journals to be included would be as large as 500 to 1,000, multiplied by the number of disciplines involved. But this is not the case, as is reflected in *Garfield's Law of Concentration*. Garfield has shown in numerous studies that there is a considerable overlap among journal sets covering the various disciplines.

> This type of evidence makes it possible to move from Bradford's law of dispersion to Garfield's law of concentration, which states that the tail of the literature of one discipline consists, in a large part, of the cores of the literature of other disciplines. So large is the overlap between disciplines, in fact, that the core literature for all scientific disciplines involves a group of no more than 1000 journals, and may involve as few as 500 (Garfield, 1979, p. 23).

Garfield summarised the outcomes of one of his studies, which was based on SCI journals covered in the year 1969, as follows:

> One study of the SCI data base shows that 75% of the references identify fewer than 1000 journals, and that 84 of them are to just 2000 journals. […] The same study also showed that 500 journals accounted for 70% of the material indexed in SCI in 1969 and that almost half of the 3.85 million references published in SCI in that year come from only 250 journals (ibid., p. 20).

If a comprehensive, multi-disciplinary citation index does not need cover more than a few thousand journals, how should these journals be selected? A key concept is *cost effectiveness*.

> Because the problem of coverage is one of practical economics, the criterion for what is covered is cost effectiveness. The cost-effective objective of an index is to minimize the cost per useful item identified, and to maximize the probability of finding any useful item that has been published. […] A cost-effective index must restrict its coverage, as nearly as possible, to only those items that people are likely to find useful (ibid., p 20).

Garfield argued that in each field of scholarship its practitioners can easily identify the most important journals publishing the highest quality materials. The real problem is to "make the coverage as complete as possible by expanding it beyond the core of journals whose importance to a given field is obvious" (ibid., p 20).

How then is this core expanded and new journals selected for inclusion in the database? Garfield developed a powerful and unique criterion: the frequency at which journals are cited in those sources that are already included in the index. The basic assumption underlying this criterion is that the number of times a journal's items are cited is an expression of its importance or utility as a medium for communicating research findings.

As the number of times a journal is cited depends upon the number of items it publishes in a year, and as some journals were founded recently whereas others may have existed for many decades, the total number of citations to a journal needs to be corrected for the size of its annual volume, and for its age. Thus, instead of taking into account in a particular year all citations to a journal regardless of the age of the cited materials, Garfield developed a measure based on citations to items published in the two previous years only. As a size correction, this amount was divided by the number of items the journal has published in those two years.

This measure is now called 'journal impact factor' and is further discussed in Chapter 5. The journal impact factor – and several related measures – are used both to monitor journals that are already being covered in the index, and to identify journals that are not yet covered but that merit serious consideration. These statistics are used in combination with peer assessments conducted by ISI's editorial board.

In order to make a reliable estimate of the number of scholarly and scientific journals published worldwide, it would be necessary to have a proper definition of what a scholarly journal is. Garfield argued that there is no agreement on what constitutes a journal. In 1979, he estimated that there were an order of magnitude of 10,000 scientific journals (Garfield, 1979). Price suggested the total number of journals in 1980 to be about 40,000 (Price, 1980a). Mabe and Amin (2001) and Mabe (2003) analysed *Ulrich's International Journal Directory*. For the year 2001 they found the number of active, refereed, scholarly journals to be about 14,700. It increased during the past two centuries with a mean annual growth rate of about 3.5 per cent. They also assumed that the set of source journals processed for the ISI Citation Indexes represents about 95 per cent of all journal citations found in the ISI database, and concluded that over 16,000 titles would cover 100 per cent.

Completeness and *adequacy* of coverage are distinct dimensions. Although ISI's *Web of Science* nowadays covers as many as 7,500 journals from all fields of scholarship, it does not claim to provide a complete coverage of all journals that are used in scholarly research. Instead, it claims to include the most important or useful ones. The total volume of journals included is determined on the basis of cost effectiveness. Their importance is assessed through a combination of a unique internal monitor based on citation relationships among journals with assessments by experts from the various fields.

An important issue is the extent to which the journals processed for the ISI Citation Indexes can be denoted as '*international*'. There are several ways to measure a journal's internationality. Zitt and Bassecoulard (1998; 2004) calculated 'relative internationalisation measures' of individual SCI journals, by comparing the geographical distribution of authors publishing in a journal to that for the specialty or discipline covered by the journal. A journal is termed 'international' if its distribution is similar to that for the specialty as a whole.

Their analysis of journals processed for the SCI or SCI-Expanded revealed a mix of two journal populations: a great majority of journals could be denoted as international, whereas a small minority was nationally oriented, but also showed a steady overall trend towards internationalisation. They attributed the inclusion of nationally oriented journals to several factors, including an ISI policy towards emerging countries to process their promising journals, even when they still show little internationalisation.

Several studies found that the SCI covers journals from developing or rapidly emerging countries that publish articles mainly written by authors from those countries and that have the function to communicate their research findings to a wider, international audience (e.g., Moed, 2002b, and Jin and Rousseau, 2004, related to China). But even some journals from Western, established countries with mainly national authors are included when their citation impact is sufficiently high. A more detailed analysis of journal internationality is presented in Chapter 7.6.

Although many scholarly literature databases are available, the *Science Citation Index* and its related indexes are beyond any doubt the most frequently used in the study of scholarly activity. The principal reason is that they have a number of important characteristics that jointly make them unique and highly appropriate for this type of use.

- The ISI Citation Indexes constitute a comprehensive, *multi-disciplinary* database nowadays covering around 7,500 international scholarly journals. The multi-disciplinary nature of the database provides unique possibilities to study multi- or interdisciplinary research activities.
- The Indexes include all *cited references* in documents from all journals processed. In the scholarly literature itself, the cited references are ordered by the document they are contained in. In a *citation index*, they are ordered alphabetically, and for each individual reference a listing is compiled of source documents citing it.
- ISI processes journals *'cover to cover'*. This means that in principle all items published in a journal are included in the database. Editorial materials, news items, corrections, and letters are included whenever they are published in processed journals.
- ISI extracts from its source documents information on *all contributing authors* and *all their institutional affiliations or 'addresses'*. ISI

processes several millions of address entries per year, and dedicates a substantial effort to re-formatting, correcting and unifying the raw data extracted from the original documents.

– ISI Indexes include the titles of all documents, as well as their abstracts and author and indexer assigned key words whenever available. The opportunities these data offer to information retrieval and studies of scholarly activity, particularly those unravelling the structure of scholarly disciplines and identifying research topics, are briefly discussed in Chapter 14.3.

6.3   Citation links and terminology

Table 6.2 explains a number of technical terms that are used throughout this book. Regarding the use of the terms 'reference' and 'citation', it adopts a distinction proposed by Derek de Solla Price:

> It seems to me a great pity to waste a good technical term by using the words *citation* and *reference* interchangeably. I therefore propose and adopt the convention that if Paper R contains a bibliographic footnote using and describing Paper C, then R contains a *reference* to C, and C has a *citation* from R. The number of references a paper has is measured by the number of items in its bibliography as endnotes and footnotes, etc., while the number of citations a paper has is found by looking it up on some sort of citation index and seeing how many other papers mention it (Price, 1970, p. 3).

Although a number of book series is processed for the ISI Citation Indexes, scholarly journals constitute the overwhelming part of its sources. It is essential to make clear, however, that the *cited material* in the index is not restricted to journals. Articles in journals processed for the Citation Indexes may cite documents published in multi-author books or proceedings volumes, technical reports, patents, and so on, and all such cited references are included in the index.

In Table 6.3 the total collection of scholarly sources is schematically subdivided into two complementary domains: sources (mainly journals) that are processed for the ISI indexes, and those that are not ('non-ISI covered sources'). These two domains of the scholarly literature give rise to four types of citation relationships. In articles published in ISI covered sources everything an author cites is included in the index, regardless of whether the cited document is published in ISI source journals ('*internal*' ISI citations) or not ('*external*' ISI citations).

Table 6.2. Terminology

Term	Explanation
Reference/ Citation	If R contains a footnote describing item C, R contains a reference to C, or R cites C, and C has a citation from R, or is cited by R. C is a (cited) reference contained in R. R is the source of the reference.
ISI source item or document	Article, chapter or other entity published in a journal or book series processed by ISI
ISI source journal	A journal that is processed by ISI, extracting full bibliographic information of all its items
Cited item or document	An article, chapter or other entity referenced in – or cited from – an ISI source item
Paper, item	Neutral terms indicating a document
Source	(1) General: A communication medium in which an item is published (e.g. journal, book). (2) In relation to ISI data it often refers to ISI source journals, i.e. sources of cited references.
Target article	An article for which the citation frequency is to be determined in a citation/impact analysis
Communication media	All types of written communication media or sources of publications including journals, proceedings volumes, monographs, multi-author books, reports

The right-hand column of Table 6.3 represents references in sources that are not covered by the ISI indexes. These references may cite either ISI covered or non-ISI covered journals, but both types are by definition not recorded in the ISI indexes.

Table 6.3. Citation relationships between ISI covered and non-ISI covered sources

Sources of cited documents	Sources of citing documents	
	ISI covered	Non-ISI covered
ISI covered	'Internal' ISI citations	Not recorded in ISI Indexes
Non-ISI covered	'External' ISI citations	

A distinction should be made between a Source Index and a Citation Index. The *Source Index* contains bibliographic information on all the documents in journals processed for the ISI Citation Indexes, denoted as ISI source journals. It includes the full title of each document, all contributing authors and their institutional affiliations, the source journal title, publication year, volume number, and starting and ending page number. ISI also processes the cited references from the source articles, by extracting the name of the first author of the cited document, the source or medium (e.g., journal, book) in which is was published, the publication year, the volume number and the starting page number (if applicable). These data are included in the *Citation Index*, keeping a link to the source article containing the cited reference.

In the original documents, cited references are ordered by the source articles containing them. But in a Citation Index, source articles are ordered by the references they cite. This index lists for each cited reference the source articles citing it. This is achieved by sorting the cited references into alphabetical order. Although this information on cited references is limited, it is in most cases sufficient for an informed user to identify citations to a particular work. The technicalities of this matching process are further discussed in Chapter 13.

Table 6.4. Citation links between source articles in the Web of Science

	Description	*Symbolic*
1	Article R1 is an ISI source article, i.e., it is published in a journal processed by ISI	R1
2	Full bibliographic information of R1 is available, including the cited references it contains, all authors, institutional affiliations, title, etc.	
3	Let C be one of R1's cited references. The bibliographic description of C is limited: only first author, source title, publication year, volume and page number (if any)	R1 cites C
4	Assume that C is published in a journal processed by ISI (an ISI source journal) at least in the year in which C was published	
5	Then there must be another source article in the Index, R2, that is identical to C. C and R2 are different representations of one and the same document	C=R2
6	Thus C constitutes a citation/reference link between R1 and R2.	R1 cites R2

If a cited document is published in a journal processed for the Index, it appears in *two* different representations. First, it appears as a cited reference in an ISI source article. As such, it is included in the Citation Index and is defined by the limited information described above. But this document is also included in the Source Index as an ISI source article, and full bibliographic information on it is available.

In the Index a marker can be inserted indicating that the two forms are different representations of one and the same document. Thus, the cited reference constitutes a *link between two source articles*, one of which cites the other. And this is precisely what is achieved in the *Web of Science*. This superb feature enables a user to walk ('click') along citation paths back and forth in time from one source article to another. Table 6.4 summarises the main steps leading to such links.

The links between ISI source articles discussed here should be distinguished from other types of links that are frequently applied both in bibliographic and in bibliometric use of the ISI indexes: those established through bibliographic coupling and so-called co-citation links. These links are defined in Table 6.5.

Table 6.5. Bibliographic coupling and co-citation links

Type	Description	Symbolic
Bibliographic coupling	Based on the number of cited references two source articles have in common	R1 cites C and R2 cites C ➔ R1 and R2 are bibliographically coupled
Co-citation	Based on the number of times two cited references are cited in the same source article	R cites C1 and C2 ➔ C1 and C2 are co-cited

The physical implementation of links between source articles based on citation relations is a unique characteristic of ISI's *Web of Science*, and is by technical necessity not implemented in earlier CD-ROM versions of the ISI Indexes. The latter include source articles from a single year. Since citations in documents published in a particular year are normally given to items published in earlier years, there would be very few citation links between source articles included in the same annual volume.

The creation of citation links between ISI source articles not only establishes a unique *bibliographic* search tool in ISI's *Web of Science*. It also constitutes an enormous step forward in *bibliometric* citation analyses *from the perspective of research evaluation*, as complete bibliographic information is available of both citing and cited documents.

In the Centre for Science and Technology Studies at Leiden University, a large bibliometric database was created from the CD-ROM versions of the ISI Citation Indexes (see Table 6.1), covering the time span 1980–2004. This database includes links between source articles based on citation relations of the type specified in Table 6.4. These links are analysed in more detail in the next chapter, in order to obtain more insight into the coverage of the ISI Indexes. There are some differences in journal coverage between this CWTS database and ISI's *Web of Science*, but these will hardly influence the results.

Chapter 7

ISI COVERAGE BY DISCIPLINE

7.1 Introduction

This chapter evaluates the coverage of the ISI Citation Indexes by analysing reference patterns in ISI source journals, i.e., journals processed for the ISI Indexes. It builds upon earlier studies, presented in Section 7.2, carried out by Price, Narin, and particularly by Garfield. Following the lines developed by Garfield, cited reference patterns are used to study the scholarly written communication system in the various domains of scholarship, and to assess the extent to which it is covered by the ISI Citation Indexes.

Throughout this book the concept of ISI coverage relates to the extent to which the *sources* processed by ISI for its Citation Indexes (mainly scholarly journals) cover the written scholarly literature in a field. As argued in Chapter 6, articles published in ISI source journals may cite documents published in other sources than those processed for the Indexes. For instance, they may cite monographs, book chapters, reports, proceedings articles, and journals not processed for the Citation Indexes. The total collection of cited documents thus constitutes a publication universe that is broader – and, as shown below, in some disciplines much broader – than the universe of ISI sources from which the cited references themselves are drawn. Coverage relates to the ISI source universe, and *not* to that of all cited documents. In Chapter 7 the ISI coverage of the source universe is evaluated – in what is termed a *database internal* approach – by comparing this source universe to the universe of cited documents.

It is essential to make clear, however, that such an approach provides a *partial* view of the communication system. Since the analysis deals with cited references in ISI source articles only, it disregards those given in sources that were not processed for the ISI indexes, including non-ISI covered journals, books, proceedings volumes, reports, patents, and so on. It provides a view of the scholarly communication system seen 'through ISI glasses'. The implications are further discussed in Section 7.7.

If a database internal, partial coverage analysis for some field finds a moderate ISI coverage, this outcome may be further evaluated from two perspectives. On the one hand, it reveals that the ISI source universe for that field is substantially less broad than its cited document universe. On the other hand, it also points to the *potentialities* to use the cited references in ISI source articles to obtain an indication of the citation impact of all types of publications, not merely articles in ISI source journals, but also other documents, such as book chapters, monographs and proceedings articles. The crucial issue is whether or not the ISI sources, and the cited references therein, are a representative sample of the total – or at least a much broader – population of documents in a field.

Section 7.3 defines three indicators of coverage and discusses their interpretation. In Section 7.4 the outcomes are presented at the aggregate level of all ISI Citation Indexes, whereas Section 7.5 presents results by discipline. Section 7.6 presents an analysis of journal internationality by discipline. Finally, Section 7.7 discusses the various outcomes and draws conclusions.

7.2   Some earlier studies of ISI coverage

In numerous studies Garfield analysed the extent to which journals processed for the *Science Citation Index* covered written communication in the various scientific disciplines. He focused on the items that were referenced in SCI source articles. One study, already mentioned in Section 6.2, related to the SCI for the year 1969 and reported that "75 % of the references identify fewer than 1000 journals, and that 84 of them are to just 2000 journals" (Garfield, 1979, p. 21).

In other studies, he hypothesised that "non-journal citation is useful in distinguishing 'pure' and 'applied' research". He found that on average about 20 per cent of the references in science journals cite books and other non-journal items. From a sample of journals in basic chemistry it was 9.6 per cent, whereas in applied chemistry it was 45 per cent (Garfield, 1974; 1976). From an analysis of references in 382 journals identified as engineering/applied science, he concluded:

> A complete listing of items cited ten or more times would show a definite preponderance of books at the top of the list, with journal articles becoming more prevalent towards the end ... Most of the books referred to in the engineering sciences are standard texts or handbooks used by engineers in their fieldwork. In the engineering sciences this finding suggests that there exists a

strong link between engineering scientists and practicing engineers, both of whom regard the text- or handbook as an indispensable authority for basic knowledge of the field (Garfield, 1976).

In 1981, Carpenter and Narin analysed adequacy of SCI coverage on the basis of journal-to-journal citation relationships of the type published by ISI in its Journal Citation Reports. They argued that if in a field a journal from some country frequently cites journals that are not covered by the SCI and that are apparently from the same country, there is an implied lack of SCI coverage for that country in that field (Carpenter and Narin, 1981).

For nine main fields they analysed 5 journals from major countries. They determined for each journal the percentage of references to journals covered by the SCI, and identified highly ranked cited journals that were not covered by this database. As outlined in Section 6.2, this is precisely what ISI has done for many years in monitoring the contents of their databases. Their analysis related to the SCI sources processed in 1974. For that year, they concluded that the SCI is representative of scientific publishing activities for most major countries and most fields.

The analyses presented in the next chapter build upon the earlier work by Carpenter and Narin. However, there are some important differences. They relate to the source year 2002. Instead of grouping its cited references per citing journal on the basis of cited journal titles and determining whether or not a cited journal is covered by ISI, the approach presented in Chapter 7 is based on matching cited references in all 2002 ISI source articles on a paper-to-paper basis to ISI source articles published in earlier years, going back as far as 1980. Moreover, cited sources not covered by ISI are roughly classified into journals and non-journals.

In his well-known paper "The Citation Cycle", Derek de Solla Price quantitatively addressed the coverage of the *Science Citation Index* (SCI). In fact, his tour of the citation cycle started with the selection of source journals processed for the SCI. He stated:

> If ISI were perfectly successful, as no doubt they are not quite, in skimming only cream, they would get as sources just those source journals which are the most cited. In that case, one can apply the powerful principle of Bradford's approximation to the distribution law of cumulative advantage in journals; cumulating citations from the most-cited journals downwards, the total of citations is proportional to the logarithm of the number of journals included (Price, 1980a)

For the year 1977 setting the number of SCI journals to 2,700 and the total number of journals published worldwide to 40,000, he estimated from Bradford's law that the SCI included $\log(2,700)/\log(40,000) = 0.75$ or 75 per cent of all cited papers. He concluded: "Thus although it is derived from only 1/15 of the source papers, it includes 3/4 of the cited literature". It must be assumed that in the last part of this phrase Price meant the cited journal literature. It should be noted that his results relate to the SCI rather than to the total collection of ISI source journals.

The number of source journals, source items and references he analysed were obtained from the SCI Source Index, whereas statistics on cited works were extracted from the Citation Index, but the two indexes were not linked in the way established in the *Web of Science*. As shown in the next section, the availability of links between source articles on the basis of citation relations provides an opportunity of estimating coverage parameters directly.

The studies described above analysed coverage of the ISI Indexes from a database internal point of view. Many other studies adopted a database-external viewpoint, and compared ISI coverage to that of other scholarly literature databases and bibliographies, and determined their degree of overlap. For instance, analyses of publication lists of scholars and institutions determined the percentage share of publications published in journals that were processed for the ISI Citation Indexes.

7.3   Coverage indicators and their interpretation

Under the assumption that references in ISI source journals adequately reflect the importance of written communication media, the following three indicators were calculated:

– The importance of journals in a field's written communication system.
– ISI coverage of the journal literature in a field.
– The overall ISI coverage of a field. The latter indicator is the numerical product of the former two.

Technical details are presented in Table 7.1. Instead of using a cited reference as the unit to be counted, one can also identify and count unique cited items. Thus, an item that is cited 100 times would contribute 100 cited references in the former, but only one cited item in the latter counting procedure. Numbers and percentages of cited items represent what Price termed as the 'cited corpus'. They are less sensitive to highly citedness of cited items, and can be used as supplementary to those derived from cited references.

All cited references were analysed in ISI source items processed in the year 2002 for the various ISI indexes on CD-ROM. For each cited item it was determined whether or not it was included as a source article in the database, and hence published in an ISI source journal. The methodology for matching cited references and source articles is described in Chapter 13. It is rather difficult to identify cited items that are not published in ISI covered journals, since the information on such items available in the ISI is limited. Consequently, indicators based on cited items are rough estimates. Those based on cited references, however, can be measured quite accurately.

Table 7.1. Definition and interpretation of coverage indicators

Symbol	Description	Interpretation
	Based on cited references	
1a	% References to documents published in journals, relative to total references	Importance of journals as communication media in a field
1b	% References to documents published in ISI source journals, relative to total references to journals	ISI coverage of the journal literature in a field
1a*1b	% References to articles published in ISI source journals, relative to total references	Overall ISI coverage of a field
	Based on unique cited items	
2a	% Cited items published in journals, relative to total cited items	As above, but less sensitive to highly cited items. Figures are rough estimates
2b	% Cited items published in ISI source journals, relative to total cited items published in journals	
2a*2b	% Cited items published in ISI source journals, relative to total cited items	

Cited documents not published in ISI source journals – and therefore not included as source articles in the ISI – were roughly classified into two classes: journal items and non-journal items. This classification was carried out automatically. Journal items are normally characterised by a volume number and a starting page number, whereas for cited items in other types of sources at least one of these fields is normally missing. Therefore, cited items characterised by a volume and starting page number were categorised as journal items, and all other items as non-journal items. A limited number of journals does not use a volume numbering system, whereas book or proceedings series may use volume numbers. But when applied to large data samples, it provides the best estimate currently available of the fraction of journal and non-journal items in ISI's cited references from a field.

7.4   Results at an aggregate level

Results for the combined ISI Citation Indexes on CD-ROM and for source year 2002 are presented in Table 7.2. In order to obtain an insight into the most important index, the *Science Citation Index*, studied separately by Narin and Price, Table 7.2 also presents indicators for the SCI only.

Focusing on the analysis of cited references in the upper half of Table 7.2, it follows that the percentage of cited references to items published in journals – measuring the importance of the journal literature, seen through 'ISI journal glasses' – amounts to 84 per cent for the combined ISI Citation Indexes and 88 per cent for the SCI. The ISI overage of the journal literature is about 90 per cent in both collections of source papers. Around 9 out of 10 cited references to journal items are given to journals processed for the Indexes.

Table 7.2. Coverage indicators for combined ISI Citation Indexes and for SCI only

Symbol	Description	Combined ISI Indexes (%)	SCI only (%)
	Based on cited references		
1a	Importance of journals as communication media	84	88
1b	ISI coverage of the journal literature	90	91
1a*1b	Overall ISI coverage	75	81
	Based on unique cited items		
2a	Importance of journals as communication media	76	83
2b	ISI coverage of the journal literature	80	83
2a*2b	Overall ISI coverage	61	69

Data relate to around 21 million references in articles, letters and reviews in 2002 ISI source journals processed for the combined Citation Indexes on CD-ROM, to 8.4 million cited items published during the time period 1980–2002.

Definition of the indicators: *Importance of journals as communication media*: % References to documents published in journals, relative to total references. *ISI coverage of the journal literature:* % References to documents published in ISI source journals, relative to total references to journals. *Overall ISI coverage*: % References to articles published in ISI source journals, relative to total references. The latter indicator is the numerical product of the first two indicators. Data for SCI only are included to enable comparisons with earlier findings by Price. Row 1b of the table can be interpreted as follows. Considering an average reference list in a 2002 ISI source paper, disregarding cited items published prior to 1980, and taking into account only cited items published in journals, about 9 out of 10 of such references are to ISI source items. The percentages calculated for SCI source articles only are generally higher than those for the combined ISI indexes since the latter include the Social Science and the Arts & Humanities Citation Index for which coverage percentages are generally lower.

Multiplying the two indicators per ISI source journal collection, it is found for the combined indexes that about 3 out of 4 cited references are published in ISI source journals. For the SCI this fraction is even higher: about 4 out of 5. Analysing unique cited items, all percentages are generally somewhat lower than those for cited references. This reflects that ISI covered articles are on average more frequently cited than items published in other sources.

7.5   Results per discipline

Using a classification system of journals into about 150 categories developed by ISI, journal categories were aggregated into 15 disciplines. This disciplinary classification is further explained in Chapter 14. Table 7.5 at the end of this section presents ISI coverage indicators per *subfield (journal category)*, for the major journal categories in each discipline.

Table 7.3 presents coverage indicators per discipline. For all science disciplines except mathematics and engineering the percentage of references to journal items – measuring the importance of journals – is at least 75 per cent. This is also true for psychology & psychiatry, and for other social sciences related to medicine & health. For other social sciences and humanities & arts the importance of journals in the scholarly communication system is considerably less than it is in other main fields.

Focusing on the extent to which the combined Citation Indexes on CD-ROM cover the journal literature (column 1b in Table 7.3), it follows that all disciplines show a coverage percentage up to or above 80 per cent, except mathematics, engineering, other social sciences and humanities & arts. For five disciplines – molecular biology & biochemistry, biological sciences related to humans, chemistry, clinical medicine and physics & astronomy – this percentage is near to or even above 90 per cent.

It can be observed from Table 7.3 that the indicator reflecting the importance of journals as communication media and that measuring the extent to which the ISI indexes cover those media, positively correlate with one another. In fact, the Pearson correlation coefficient amounts to 0.92.

The overall ISI coverage ranges between 92 per cent in molecular biology & biochemistry to 17 per cent in humanities & arts. It is above 80 per cent in molecular biology & biochemistry, biological sciences related to humans, chemistry, clinical medicine and physics & astronomy. These outcomes aggregate publications authored by scholars from all over the world. A breakdown of articles by country of origin provides insight into the variability among the 20 countries with the highest number of publications in 2002.

The results of this analysis are presented in Figure 7.1. It shows that the relative standard deviations in the overall ISI coverage of the 20 countries are higher in social sciences and humanities disciplines than they are in science disciplines. In the latter group, authors from the various countries show a remarkable uniformity in their referencing behaviour.

For instance, in molecular biology & biochemistry, the coverage percentage ranges between 81 and 94 per cent. In humanities & arts and other social sciences, however, there is much more variability among countries. In the former field, overall ISI coverage percentages vary between 5 and 24 per cent, and in the latter between 20 and 43 per cent.

Table 7.3. ISI coverage indicators per discipline

Discipline	1a Importance of journals (%)	1b ISI coverage of journal literature (%)	1a*1b Overall ISI coverage (%)
Molecular biology & biochemistry	96	97	92
Biological sciences related to humans	95	95	90
Chemistry	90	93	84
Clinical medicine	93	90	84
Physics & astronomy	89	94	83
* Total ISI *	84	90	75
Applied physics & chemistry	83	89	73
Biological sciences ~ animals and plants	81	84	69
Psychology & psychiatry	75	88	66
Geosciences	77	81	62
Other social sciences ~ medicine & health	75	80	60
Mathematics	71	74	53
Economics	59	80	47
Engineering	60	77	46
Other social sciences	41	72	29
Humanities & arts	34	50	17

Disciplines are ranked by descending overall ISI coverage (last column).
Definition of the indicators:
Importance of journals as communication media: % References to documents published in journals, relative to total references.
ISI coverage of the journal literature: % References to documents published in ISI source journals, relative to total references to journals.
Overall ISI coverage: % References to articles published in ISI source journals, relative to total references. The latter indicator is the numerical product of the first two indicators.

Applied physics & chemistry includes amongst others the journal categories applied physics, materials science, optics, chemical engineering, mechanics, applied chemistry, acoustics, and instruments & instrumentation. Other social sciences related to medicine & health includes amongst others public environment and occupational health, nursing, sport sciences. Other social sciences includes a.o. sociology, education, political sciences, and anthropology. Humanities include law.

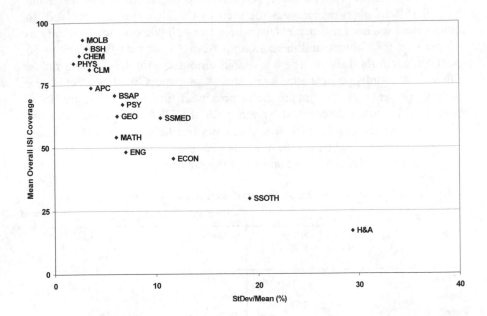

Figure 7.1. Analysis of overall ISI coverage by country

For each of the 20 countries with the highest total publication output in 2002 the percentage of references to ISI source items was determined per discipline. Next, per discipline the mean value and the standard deviation was calculated of the distribution of this percentage among countries. The vertical axis plots this mean and the horizontal axis the standard deviation expressed as a percentage relative to the mean. Papers by authors from more than one country (resulting from international collaboration) are not included. Mean values of disciplines displayed on the vertical axis of Figure 7.1 differ slightly from those presented in Table 7.3, not only because the data relate to 20 countries only, but particularly because Figure 7.1 shows averages of coverage percentages among countries, whereas Table 7.3 presents 'globalised' percentages (see Egghe and Rousseau (1996) for a further explanation of differences between 'averaged' and 'globalised' bibliometric quotients).

Abbreviations: H&A: humanities & arts; APC: applied physics & chemistry. BSAP: biological sciences related to animals and plants. BSH: biological sciences related to humans. CHEM: chemistry. CLM: clinical medicine. ECON: economics; ENG: engineering. GEO: geosciences. MATH: mathematics. MOLB: molecular biology & biochemistry. PHYS: physics & astronomy; SSOTH: other social sciences; PSY: psychology & psychiatry; SSMED: other social sciences related to medicine & health.

Table 7.4 shows for two social science fields presented in Figure 7.1 the overall ISI coverage percentages for each of the 20 countries involved. In other social sciences this percentage varies from 20 per cent for Germany to 43 per cent for Taiwan, and in economics from 37 per cent for Brazil to 56 per cent, again for Taiwan. The USA ranks among the top five in both fields. Since this country contributes large shares of papers in these fields, the overall percentages per main field presented in Table 7.3 are to a considerable extent determined by those for the USA. The table does *not* reveal a tendency that English speaking countries have higher ISI coverage percentages than countries from other language domains. UK and Australia are in both main fields near the bottom of the ranking.

Table 7.4. ISI Coverage per country for two social sciences fields shown in Figure 7.1

Other social sciences		*Economics*	
Country	*Overall ISI Coverage (%)*	*Country*	*Overall ISI Coverage (%)*
Taiwan	43	Taiwan	56
Japan	38	Spain	53
Spain	37	South Korea	52
China	34	USA	52
USA	33	Japan	52
Israel	32	Israel	50
South Korea	32	China	48
Netherlands	31	Canada	47
Belgium	31	Belgium	45
Sweden	30	Netherlands	45
Brazil	29	Italy	44
India	29	Switzerland	44
Canada	28	India	43
Finland	28	Germany	43
Italy	26	Finland	42
Switzerland	25	France	42
Australia	24	Sweden	41
United Kingdom	24	Australia	39
France	22	United Kingdom	39
Germany	20	Brazil	37

Table 7.5 presents coverage indicators per subfield (journal category) for the major journal categories, arranged by main field.

Table 7.5. Overall ISI coverage for major journal categories per discipline

Journal Category	*Imp Jnl*	*Cov Jnl*	*Ovl Cov*	*Journal Category*	*Imp Jnl*	*Cov Jnl*	*Ovl Cov*
Applied Physics and Chemistry				***Biological sciences ~ animals and plants***			
Acoustics	77	84	65	Agriculture, dairy & anim	80	85	69
Chemical engineering	77	87	66	Agriculture, Soil science	74	83	61
Chemistry, Applied	83	85	71	Ecology	77	84	64
Instruments & instrum	72	86	63	Food science & technology	82	85	69
Materials Sci, Multidisc	83	89	74	Marine & fresh water biol	81	80	65
Mechanics	75	84	63	Plant sciences	87	88	77
Optics	86	91	78	Veterinary sciences	84	84	70
Physics, Applied	87	93	81	Zoology	81	83	67
Biological sciences ~ humans				***Chemistry***			
Endocrinol & metabol	95	95	91	Chemistry	91	93	84
Hematology	96	95	92	Chemistry, Analytical	89	92	82
Immunology	97	96	93	Chemistry, Inorg & nucl	89	94	84
Microbiology	93	94	88	Chemistry, Organic	93	95	88
Neurosciences	95	96	91	Chemistry, Physical	89	95	85
Pharmacol & pharmacy	93	93	87	Electrochemistry	87	91	79
Physiology	94	96	90	Polymer science	87	91	79
Virology	96	97	93				
Clinical medicine				***Economics***			
Cardiac & cardiovasc s	96	93	89	Business	64	78	50
Clinical neurology	92	91	84	Business, Finance	66	83	55
Gastroenterol & hepatol	95	92	88	Economics	56	83	47
Genetics and heredity	93	96	89	Management	59	76	45
Medicine, Gen & intern	88	88	77				
Oncology	95	94	89				
Radiology & nucl med	92	88	81				
Surgery	94	84	79				
Engineering				***Geosciences***			
Computer sci, Artif int	53	77	41	Environmental sciences	73	85	62
Computer sci, Theory	45	70	31	Geochem & geophysics	82	83	68
Eng, Civil	51	71	36	Geology	79	70	55
Eng, Electr & electron	65	83	54	Geosciences, Multidisc	77	76	58
Eng, Mechanical	67	76	51	Meteorology & atmos sci	81	88	72
Nuclear sci & technpol	69	85	58	Mineralogy	83	81	67
Robotics	49	67	33	Oceanography	82	85	70
Transportation	37	57	21				

Journal Category	Imp Jnl	Cov Jnl	Ovl Cov	Journal Category	Imp Jnl	Cov Jnl	Ovl Cov
Humanities & arts				**Mathematics**			
Archeology	41	50	20	Mathematics	72	68	49
History	19	48	9	Mathematics, Applied	70	77	54
Humanities, Multidisc	20	55	11	Statistics & probability	69	79	55
Language and linguist	30	53	16				
Law	61	40	24				
Literature	19	58	11				
Literature, American	19	66	13				
Literature, German,							
Netherl, Scandinav	17	40	7				
Philosophy	28	68	19				
Molecular biology & biochem				**Other social sciences**			
Biochem res methods	92	95	88	Anthropology	42	71	30
Biochem & molec boil	96	97	94	Educational sciences	42	65	27
Biotechnology	90	93	84	Geography	42	73	31
Cell biology	97	97	94	Information & library sci	47	71	33
Developmental biology	96	97	94	Internal relations	33	67	22
				Political sciences	32	74	24
				Social sci, Interdiscipl	42	75	31
				Sociology	37	74	27
Other social sciences ~ medicine & health				**Physics & astronomy**			
Family studies	60	79	47	Astronomy & astrophysics	88	93	82
Health care science	72	79	57	Phys, Atom, molec, chem.	90	96	87
Health policy & service	66	80	53	Phys, Condensed matter	91	96	87
Nursing	69	65	45	Phys, Fluids & plasmas	86	93	80
Public environment & occupational health	81	85	69	Phys, Mathematical	82	92	76
Rehabilitation	67	76	51	Phys, Multidisciplinary	87	93	81
Sport sciences	87	78	67	Phys, Nuclear	89	93	83
Substance abuse	71	85	60	Phys, Particles & fields	90	92	83
Psychology & psychiatry				**Psychology & psychiatry**			
Behavioral sciences	87	93	81	Psychol, Developmental	71	86	61
Psychiatry	87	92	80	Psychol, Experimental	78	91	71
Psychol, Biological	86	93	81	Psychol, General	81	91	73
Psychol, Clinical	74	87	64	Psychol, Social	69	86	60

Legend for Table 7.5:
Imp Jnl: Importance of journals as communication media: % References to documents published in journals, relative to total references.
Jnl Cov: ISI coverage of the journal literature: % References to documents published in ISI source journals, relative to total references to journals.
Ovl Cov: Overall ISI coverage: % References to articles published in ISI source journals, relative to total references. The latter indicator is the numerical product of the first two indicators.
The table includes per main field at most 8 major journal categories in terms of number of ISI source papers covered. They are listed in alphabetical order.

7.6   Journal internationality by discipline

Internationality is an important property of a journal. There are many ways to bibliometrically measure a journal's international or national orientation (e.g., Zitt and Bassecoulard, 1998). This chapter focuses on the country of origin of the authors publishing in a journal.

Table 7.6. National orientation of journals by discipline

Discipline	No. Journals	Median INO	% Journals with INO>90%
Chemistry	440	33	12
Applied physics & chemistry	723	36	10
Mathematics	390	37	2
Physics & astronomy	260	37	10
Engineering	1,061	41	9
Molecular biology & biochemistry	530	41	4
Biol sci related to humans	856	43	5
Geosciences	437	44	14
Biol sci related to animals and plants	879	48	16
Clinical medicine	1,459	50	12
Economics	299	62	15
Psychology & psychiatry	557	68	18
Social sci related to medicine	449	69	22
Humanities & arts	1,110	71	24
Other social sciences	879	72	22

INO: Indicator of a journal's national orientation, defined as the share of the papers from the country most frequently publishing in a journal, relative to the total number of papers published in the journal. A purely national journal would have an INO value of 100 per cent. Disciplines are ranked by median INO.

For each journal processed for the ISI Citation Indexes in the year 2002 the geographical distribution of its publishing authors was determined. The country that contributed the largest number of papers to a journal was identified, and the share of its papers was calculated, relative to the total number of papers published in the journal. This share represents a first, rough indicator of national orientation (INO) of a journal. Thus, for purely national journals this share would be 100 per cent.

In the next step, journals were grouped per discipline, applying the classification presented in Table 14.2 in Chapter 14. Per discipline, the distribution of the indicator of a journal's national orientation among all journals was analysed. Of these distributions Table 7.6 presents the number of journals included, the median value of the indicator, and the percentage of journals for which it exceeds 90 per cent.

Table 7.6 shows that median value of the indicator of a journal's national orientation varies from 33 per cent in chemistry to 71 per cent in humanities & arts, and 72 per cent in other social sciences, including amongst others sociology, education, political sciences, and anthropology. The percentage of journals for which the indicator exceeds 90 per cent ranges between 2 per cent in mathematics and 24 per cent in humanities & arts.

The outcomes in Table 7.6 provide evidence that in all social science disciplines and in humanities & arts, journals tend to have a much stronger national orientation than those in science disciplines. In the set of around 1,100 journals covering humanities & arts, in almost one out of four journals there is one country that contributes over 90 per cent of all papers. Such journals can hardly be qualified as international.

7.7   Discussion and conclusions

Partial indicators of coverage

Section 7.1 underlined that the analysis of the scholarly communication system presented in this chapter provides a picture 'as seen through ISI glasses'. A question that immediately follows is how reference patterns in ISI source articles compare to those in sources not covered by the ISI indexes. This question can be addressed empirically by analysing sets of cited references in non-ISI covered sources. Another approach providing at least some insight is based on the following analysis in the ISI universe.

Scholarly authors tend to publish their output not in one single journal, but rather to use a series of sources in which one can identify core sources and more peripheral ones. Within the universe of ISI source journals, there is evidence that when authors publish a paper in a particular journal, they tend to give relatively more references to other documents in that journal than they do in their papers published in other journals.

This finding is in itself not surprising. An article submitted to a journal should fit into the scope of that journal. If the work described in it depends heavily on earlier papers published in a particular journal, this may be a good reason for the authors to submit it to that journal. In addition, authors submitting a manuscript to a particular journal can be assumed to be well aware of the earlier relevant papers published in that journal. Moreover, authors may insert in their manuscripts citations to papers in the journal of their choice in order to increase the probability of its being accepted. In the referee process, a journal's editorial board members may suggest in their referee reports other relevant documents published in the same journal that submitting authors may include in their reference lists.

In view of these converging mechanisms, articles published in ISI journals can be expected to have higher shares of citations to other ISI journals than have documents in sources that were not processed for the ISI indexes. At present, however, without an additional thorough analysis it appears very difficult to give reliable estimates of the size of the effect of such mechanisms.

Importance of journals in the scholarly communication system

The analysis above revealed that in mathematics, engineering, economics, and particularly in other social sciences and humanities & arts the importance of journals in the scholarly communication system was found to be less than in other disciplines.

With respect to *mathematics* it is important to note that the database used in this study includes the *Compumath Citation Index* – covering mathematics and computer sciences – as from 1993. If sources from this database published prior to 1993 were included in the analysis, the percentage for mathematics would be somewhat higher. Interpretation of the relatively high percentage of references to non-journals in mathematics should also take into account the long publication delays of many mathematical journals. As a result, scientists often refer to *preprints*, or to accepted papers in journals of which volume and starting page number are not yet fixed.

As mentioned in Section 6.4, Garfield observed that non-journal citation is useful in distinguishing 'pure' and 'applied' research. In *engineering* and *applied sciences*, *conference proceedings* and *technical reference works* play an important role in the exchange of information. This is consistent with the outcome that among natural science disciplines, engineering shows the highest percentage of references to non-journal items, and that this percentage for applied physics and chemistry lies between that for physics and chemistry on the one hand, and that for engineering on the other. Following Garfield's criterion, outcomes suggests that biological sciences related to animals and plants (which includes agriculture) and geosciences tend to be of a rather applied nature.

One should keep in mind that engineering is an ensemble of around 35 subfields (journal categories), and that substantial differences exist among subfields within this main field. For instance, Table 7.5 revealed that, in the journal category electrical & electronic engineering, the percentage of references to *non-journals* amounts to 35, which is somewhat lower than the overall average in the main field. However, in civil engineering this percentage is 49, in various computer science categories it is between 40 and 50 per cent, whereas in transportation it is as high as 63 per cent.

In *economics*, *other social sciences* and *humanities* books play an important role. In the first field *handbooks*, and in the latter two *monographs* tend to be important sources. Several studies underlined the importance of books in the humanities. For instance, Cronin and La Barre (2004) concluded from a survey among US departments in literature and language that "granting of tenure in humanities departments still requires the production of a research monograph published by a reputable press".

It must be noted that references in a scholarly article from *humanities and arts* studying a particular text not only relate to earlier findings published by colleagues studying that text, but also to the object of study itself. In the analysis presented in this section, however, cited references to works published prior to 1980 are not included, and a large percentage of texts studied can be expected to be published before that date. For instance, citations to the works of Homer, one of the highly cited authors in the A&HCI (Garfield, 1986) are *not* included. Moreover, the analysis did not take into account references made in book reviews, dance performance reviews and other types of documents typical for the arts and humanities.

The extent to which ISI indexes cover the journal literature

With respect to the extent to which ISI indexes cover the journal literature, the following conclusions can be drawn. In the total collection of cited references in 2002 ISI source journals to journal items published during 1980–2002, it was found that about 9 out of 10 cited journal references were to ISI source journals. This is an extremely high overall percentage.

All disciplines showed a coverage percentage up to or above 80 per cent, except mathematics, engineering, other social sciences and humanities & arts. For engineering it is 77 per cent, only slightly lower than the 80 per cent level. As outlined above, for mathematics this percentage is based on incomplete data, as ISI's Specialty CD *Compumath Citation Index* is included in the analysis as from 1993. In fact, an additional analysis for this field based on the cited year period 1993–2002 reveals a percentage above 80. It can therefore be concluded that the ISI coverage of the *journal* literature is in most main fields *excellent* or *very good*, except for those parts of social sciences as sociology, education, political sciences and anthropology, and particularly for humanities & arts.

Zitt et al. (1998) described the evolution since the Second World War of scholarly communication in various disciplines as the transition from a 'nationally centred' model to an 'international' or 'trans-national' model. In the national model the 'nationally oriented' journals are dominant, publishing mainly papers of domestic authors in domestic languages. As a result, strong barriers exist to communication, competition and cooperation among scholars, publishers and language domains.

According to the international model, publishers and even languages compete for the largest international audiences, and scholars seek to publish in the most internationally visible communication media. Competition between languages has resulted in the quasi-monopoly of English as the lingua franca of primary communication, whereas other languages are mostly used for communication at a national or regional level.

The outcomes as regards the national orientation of journals covered by the ISI Citation Indexes presented in Table 7.6 suggest that in fields such as sociology, education, political sciences, anthropology and related parts of social sciences and in arts and humanities, the national model defined by Zitt et al. plays an important role. To a considerable extent the literature in these fields is dispersed among various language domains. The results are consistent with Hicks' (2004) finding that in social sciences and humanities publications in international journals, books, national journals and the non-scholarly press represent four distinct, yet partially overlapping worlds. They are also in agreement with findings by Nederhof and Zwaan (1991) for the field of language and linguistics, and with those as regards the field of law presented in Chapter 11.

But it must be emphasised that, according to Table 7.6, the classification of journals into international and national does *not* coincide with that into ISI covered and non-ISI covered journals. For instance, the ISI Citation Indexes cover a number of Law School journals in the USA. These journals publish mainly reviews of the legal literature, including a great deal of case law published by students from US Law Schools, and have a very strong national orientation. Hence, citation patterns tend to be dispersed among a variety of sources, often with a national orientation. As a result, the global journal communication system does not reveal a core-periphery structure as pronounced as it is in science. The basic principles of a citation index, outlined in Chapter 6, tend to be less appropriate in these fields than they are in science.

This conclusion is in agreement with findings of Derek de Solla Price, who observed differences in reference practices between science on the one hand and the humanities on the other (Price, 1970). These differences reflect differences in substantive contents as well as in corresponding social structures. He suggested that in the humanities, the optimal information service is a 'normal' archival library, whereas in science fields citation indexing is the most appropriate tool. The implications of the outcomes presented in this chapter for the use of the ISI Citation Indexes in the assessment of research performance in the social sciences and humanities are further discussed in Chapter 9.

Estimates of the total number of scientific and scholarly journals

Considering unique cited items instead of cited references, it was found in Table 7.2 that 80 per cent of the cited journal items were included as source items in the ISI Indexes. For cited references in source articles processed for the SCI this percentage was higher: 83 per cent. It is interesting to compare this latter percentage to an estimate made by Price (1980a). As outlined in Section 6.4, for the year 1977 setting the number of SCI journals to 2,700 and the total number of journals published worldwide to 40,000, he estimated on the basis of Bradford's law that the SCI included $\log(2,700)/\log(40,000) = 0.75$ or 75 per cent of all cited papers. This estimate is somewhat lower than the 83 per cent found in Table 7.2.

Assuming, as Price did, that the SCI includes the core of the science literature, the finding that 83 per cent of unique cited items (see Table 7.2) are in SCI source journals can be used to estimate from Bradford's Law of Dispersion the total number of scientific journals. A simple calculation yields that this number is around 20,000, which is only half of the 40,000 assumed by Price, and somewhat higher than the estimate of around 15,000 made by Mabe (2003). However, the estimate of 20,000 relates mainly to *science* journals. Applying the same approach to the data for the combined ISI Citation Indexes on CD-ROM, covering about 7,000 journals in 2002, and assuming that 81 per cent of unique cited items are in ISI source journals (Table 7.2), the total number of scholarly journals would be in the order of magnitude of 50,000. This would suggest that the number of journals in *social sciences and humanities* is in the same order of magnitude as that of *science* journals.

Chapter 8

IMPLICATIONS FOR THE USE OF THE ISI CITATION INDEXES IN RESEARCH EVALUATION

8.1   Introduction

Chapter 7 presented an analysis of coverage of the ISI Citation Indexes. Three aspects of coverage were studied. The first two were the importance of journals in the written communication system, and the extent to which the indexes cover the journal literature in a discipline. A third indicator was denoted as overall ISI coverage and is the numerical product of the first two. It measures from ISI source articles the percentage of references to journals processed for the ISI Citation Indexes. This chapter focuses on the latter indicator, and discusses implications of the analysis of overall ISI coverage from the point of view of the use of the ISI Citation Indexes in the assessment of research performance in the various domains of science and scholarship.

Table 8.1 presents a *tentative* classification of disciplines according to their overall ISI coverage into three classes, with excellent, good, and moderate coverage, respectively. Disciplines in which the percentage of references to ISI source journals is above 80 per cent constitute the class with *excellent* coverage. If a discipline's coverage is between 40 and 80 per cent it is qualified as *good*, and if it is below 40 per cent, as *moderate*. The thresholds applied in this categorisation are to some extent arbitrary. The crucial point is that there are disciplines with excellent coverage and some with moderate coverage, and there is a group in between.

Table 8.1. Adequacy of ISI coverage from the point of view of research evaluation

Excellent	Good	Moderate
Molecular biology and biochemistry	Applied physics and chemistry	Other social sciences
Biological sciences primarily related to humans	Biological sciences primarily related to animals and plants	Humanities and arts
Clinical medicine	Psychology & psychiatry	
Physics and astronomy	Other social sciences primarily related to medicine and health	
Chemistry	Geosciences	
	Mathematics	
	Engineering	
	Economics	

For a detailed description of disciplines, see Table 14.2 in Chapter 14. Biological sciences related to animals and plants includes amongst others plant sciences, ecology, biology and agriculture. Applied physics & chemistry includes amongst others the journal categories applied physics, materials science, chemical engineering, applied chemistry and instruments & instrumentation. Other social sciences related to medicine & health includes amongst others public environment and occupational health, nursing, and sport sciences. Other social sciences includes amongst others sociology, education, political sciences, and anthropology. Humanities include law.

Particularly for science fields it can be argued that uncovered sources play on average a less important role in a field's communication system than those journals do that are processed for the ISI Citation Indexes. Consequently, if the ISI coverage percentage of a field is 90 per cent, it does not follow that 10 per cent of important journals are missing (as source journals). It must also be underlined that, in order to be a valid tool for indicating intellectual influence, it is not necessary to a have a complete coverage of a field's written communication system.

On the other hand, one can argue that the fact that uncovered media are cited from ISI source journals is significant. Apparently they are important enough to be cited. They constitute a part of the knowledge base upon which the findings reported in ISI source journals were built. In addition, one should realise that ISI's assessment of candidate journals for inclusion as source journal takes place within the universe of citations in ISI source journals already included in the Index (although it may be expanded with cited references in the candidate journal itself).

If the ISI coverage percentage for a field is for instance 50 per cent, – as was obtained in Table 7.3 for ISI's coverage of the journal literature in the humanities –, one should ask whether the 50 per cent of journals covered constitute a representative sample of a larger population of important communication media in the field, and what the outcome of a citation analysis of a particular journal or research department would be if the other 50 per cent were covered rather than the part currently included.

A moderate ISI coverage percentage for a field may be caused by at least two factors. The first is that the number of journals covered is too low. Even in a field with a clear core-periphery structure in its journal communication system, such as biochemistry, one could theoretically reduce the number of journals processed to such a degree that the coverage percentage for the selected set would be 50 per cent or so. A second factor causing the ISI coverage to be moderate is the extent to which a core-periphery structure exists in the written communication system. The observed relatively high number of journals with a strong national orientation in certain parts of the social sciences and in the humanities suggests that this second factor plays an important role in these domains of scholarship.

Citation analysts in each country should be encouraged to carry out citation analyses of their uncovered journals, and establish whether or not the impact factors of their journals are as good or even better than those that are covered by ISI. This type of analysis was carried out by Stock (2004) in the field of German information science.

Section 8.2 presents four types of bibliometric research assessment studies. In three of these the ISI Citation Indexes play a crucial role, even though they may be expanded with data from other sources, whereas in a fourth type this role is absent. Overall ISI coverage is tentatively linked to one or more types of bibliometric studies. In this way it suggests which types of studies are more and which are less appropriate in an assessment of research performance in the various domains of science and scholarship.

8.2   Four types of research assessment studies

This section adopts a technical terminology described in Section 6.3. Documents subjected to a citation analysis are denoted as *target* documents, or in short as *targets*, whereas the articles from which these are cited, i.e., the articles containing references to cited documents are labelled as *source* or citing articles, or in short as *sources*. Communication media such as journals, books or proceedings volumes are labelled as *media*. Research groups, departments or institutes subjected to a citation analysis are in short denoted as *groups*. The basic characteristics of four types of citation impact assessment studies are presented in Table 8.2.

Table 8.2. Four types of research assessment studies and the role of the ISI Citation Indexes

Type of study	Cited/Target	Citing/Source	ISI coverage
1 Standard	ISI	ISI	Excellent – Good
2 Target expanded	ISI+non-ISI	ISI	Good
3 Source expanded	ISI+non-ISI	ISI+non-ISI	Good – Moderate
4. No ISI citation analysis			Moderate

1. A first type of research assessment study can be labelled as a *standard* analysis. Target articles are those that are published in journals processed for the ISI Indexes, and the universe of citing articles contains all ISI source articles. In other words, both targets and sources are from journals processed for the indexes. Documents published in sources not processed for these indexes therefore do *not* play a role.
2. A second type is denoted as *target expanded*. The citation analysis takes into account not only targets published in ISI source journals, but also those published in other media, such as books or proceedings volumes. The universe of citing articles, however, is still the total collection of papers published in ISI source journals. In short, targets are from ISI and non-ISI covered media, but sources are from ISI covered journals.
3. A third type can be labelled as a *source expanded* study. The universe of citing sources is expanded with those in media that are not covered by the ISI Indexes, by adding to the database a number of journals, books or proceedings volumes *with all references contained in them*. The target universe may be identical to the citing universe, or it may consider all types of documents, even those published in the non-ISI media added to the database.
4. A fourth type of study does *not* use data from the ISI Citation Indexes, but rather aims at measuring research performance by using different data sources and applying non-bibliometric methodologies. Typical examples are studies that create and analyse a citation index of domestic journals in a particular field, and those assessing the importance of sources on the basis of scholars' perceptions collected from interviews or questionnaires.

When research groups or departments are active in disciplines with an excellent overall ISI coverage, a *standard* citation analysis as a rule is the most appropriate type of study. Expanded studies are generally more laborious and therefore more costly, whereas it is questionable whether their outcomes provide an expression of a group's citation impact that significantly differs from that obtained in a standard analysis. A standard analysis may even be appropriate in fields with a good yet not excellent coverage. For instance, if from a preliminary analysis of a list of publications from a group results that it publishes almost exclusively in ISI covered journals, or if from their reference lists it becomes clear that they hardly cite non-ISI covered materials, it is improbable that a target expanded analysis would make much difference.

However, if the analysis of a group's publication and reference practices provide evidence that some important communication sources are not covered by the ISI Indexes, whereas the major part of important sources is covered, it is recommended to carry out a *target expanded* citation analysis rather than a standard analysis. In this case the outcomes of a standard citation analysis at the level of individual groups may be too sensitive for 'small' variations in ISI journal coverage. For instance, if a particular journal heavily used by a group and with some prominence in its field is nevertheless not covered by the ISI Indexes, a substantial part of the group's publication output, and with it, possibly a substantial part of their citation impact is discarded, whereas if the journal were ISI covered, this part could fully be taken into account.

A coverage percentage of 50 can be viewed from *two* perspectives, in the same way as a bottle containing half of its original content can be denoted either as half full or as half empty. On the one hand, it means that a number of documents or media are not covered by ISI even though scholars view these as important enough to cite them fairly frequently in ISI covered journals. But on the other hand, the number of citations to these items from ISI covered sources is so substantial that it makes sense to assess their citation impact solely within the universe of ISI citing sources. A target expanded citation analysis thus assumes that, although the collection of source (citing) documents is somewhat incomplete, their cited references may still provide reliable citation impact estimates, to the extent that the ISI source articles constitute a representative sample of a wider population of citing sources.

When the coverage percentage is between 50 and 80 per cent, a target expanded analysis tends to be appropriate, but the lower it gets, the higher is the probability that references solely in ISI sources may not be sufficiently representative for those in a wider universe of important sources. In this case, the expression of a group's citation impact in a target expanded analysis may be incomplete, and it is appropriate to *expand the citing universe* with sources not covered by ISI that play an important role in the field. For instance, in technical sciences, proceedings volumes of annual international conferences may play such an important role that it is necessary to include citation 'traffic' from one annual volume to another. Technically, this can be achieved only by adding those volumes from subsequent years and all their references to the citing universe. Data for proceedings volumes included in ISI's separate information product *ISI proceedings* could in principle be useful, to the extent that their cited references are processed as well.

It must be emphasised that selecting new sources to be included in a source expanded analysis is by no means a trivial task. *Completeness* and *adequacy of coverage* are distinct dimensions, particularly from the perspective of research evaluation. One must have a detailed knowledge of the citation universe in which counting takes place. In citation analysis one would rather not count citations from any source available, but focus on citations from sources with a certain status, satisfying at least some minimum quality standards. Any source expanded citation analysis of research groups should therefore start with analysing and identifying important sources. Citation analysis of these sources generally provides valid indications of their importance.

When the overall ISI coverage percentage in a field is substantially lower than 50 per cent, as it is in sociology, political science, education and anthropology, and in humanities & arts (including amongst others law, language and linguistics, literature, philosophy, history), it is suggested that citation analysis based on the ISI sources plays a limited role or no role at all in a research assessment study. In these fields, language barriers play a much greater role than in other domains of science and scholarship. In addition, research activities may be fragmented into distinct schools of thought, each with their own 'paradigms'. In these disciplines, source expanded analyses may be useful to the extent that important national sources are included. But even when the citing universe is expanded with national media, analyses from an international perspective, comparing groups from various countries with one another, cannot easily be made and require detailed background knowledge about communication structures and school formation in a discipline.

8.3   Examples

Typical outcomes of a standard citation impact assessment study were presented in Chapter 4. A case study on *economics* departments presented in Chapter 10 gives a good example of a target expanded citation analysis. It shows how such an analysis may in principle take into account differences in reference practices among disciplines, a distorting factor that is so well accounted for in a standard citation analysis. Although the case study relates to one of the social sciences, and to a university from one particular Western-European country, it is expected that the methodology can be fruitfully applied in the applied and technical sciences as well.

Currently, the Centre for Science and Technology Studies carries out a methodological study funded by the Netherlands Organisation for Scientific Research (NWO) aimed at exploring in the field of computer science the potentialities of a source expanded analysis, including source papers from a number of important proceedings volumes of annual international conferences not covered by the ISI Citation Indexes.

Chapter 11 describes the main assumptions and outcomes of an exploratory study developing research performance indicators in the social science field of a qualitative nature, *law*, in a particular Western-European country. In this study indicators based on citations from the ISI Citation Indexes did not play a role.

PART 2.3

ASSESSING SOCIAL SCIENCES AND
HUMANITIES

Chapter 9

DIFFERENCES BETWEEN SCIENCE, SOCIAL SCIENCES AND HUMANITIES

9.1   Introduction

Bibliometric indicators have been successfully applied in many sub-disciplines in *science*. Data from the ISI Citation Indexes play an important role in analyses of research performance in these sub-disciplines. Thus far, social sciences and humanities have not often been subjected to such analyses. At the same time, the academic authorities of many universities expressed the need to obtain an insight into the research performance in *all* departments in *all* fields of scholarship.

Those who are involved in the development of performance indicators for humanities and social sciences are confronted with the following situation. First, the need is felt in humanities and social sciences to develop methodological tools to assist evaluation agencies or policy-makers in carrying out their tasks, in the same way as the current ISI-based methodologies provide supplementary research assessment tools in basic science. Secondly, this methodology should take into account the characteristics of these domains of scholarship, their substantive contents and particularly the communication practices among scholars and the structure of the communication system.

As outlined in Chapter 7, it was Derek de Solla Price (1970) who underlined that science on the one hand and humanities on the other are two distinct domains of scholarship with essentially different substantive contents. According to Price, the different substantive contents in science and humanities ask for different "social apparatuses of information pooling and exchange". Science deals with "quantitative, highly ordered, rather certain findings". Its knowledge is "positive" and of "short term permanence". The questions addressed in its research develop rapidly. A scholar in the humanities tends to deal with fundamental questions of permanent significance, and produces "new wisdom" about them. Whereas in the latter domain of scholarship research tends to be an individual activity, in the former scientists sharing an intellectual focus are socially organised into groups, interacting at a global level at conferences and through scientific journals, and constituting the *international research front*. Close interaction with peers and knowledge about their most recent achievements are essential.

Price found the differences among the two domains of scholarship reflected in the scholarly literature. In science, authors cite recently published documents more frequently than do authors from the humanities. As discussed in Chapter 7, he defined a measure termed the Price Index, defined as the share of references in research papers to one- to five-year-old documents. This measure was found to be substantially higher in science than in humanities. He suggested that in fields with a low Price Index, the optimal information service is a 'normal' archival library, whereas in fields with a high Price Index, a citation index is the most appropriate tool.

Good examples of bibliometric studies of research performance in the social sciences and humanities using the ISI Citation Indexes are those carried out by Garfield (1986), Nederhof and Zwaan (1991), Nederhof and van Raan (1993), Glänzel (1996), and Lewison (2001). Citation based indicators of scientific status are used to empirically examine the hierarchy of the sciences, including sociology and psychology (e.g., Cole, 1983; Simonton, 2004). For a recent review of studies assessing research performance in the social sciences and humanities the reader is referred to Hicks (2004).

The social sciences constitute a broad and rather heterogeneous collection of disciplines. This is clearly reflected in the analyses of reference patterns and adequacy of ISI coverage presented in Chapter 7. Psychology, psychiatry and other social sciences related to medicine and health, and economics, are more similar to science fields, and show a good, yet not excellent ISI coverage. Other social sciences, including sociology, political science, education and anthropology tend to show more resemblance to the humanities, where ISI coverage is moderate.

In Chapter 7 it was argued that books are important communication media in social sciences and humanities. Moreover, in fields such as sociology, education, political sciences, anthropology and related parts of social sciences and in arts and humanities, the "national publication model" plays an important role. To a considerable extent the literature in these fields is dispersed among various language domains. References tend to be dispersed among a variety of cited sources, many of which have a national orientation.

As a result, the journal communication system does not reveal a core-periphery structure as pronounced as it is found to be in science. The basic principles of a citation index, outlined in Chapter 6, tend to be less appropriate in these fields than in science disciplines. Chapter 4 underlined that outcomes of citation analysis may be distorted by 'national' journals covered by the ISI Citation Indexes. National journals may even have a negative influence upon a country's citation impact in international benchmarking studies.

It can be argued, however, that genuine scholarly research, regardless of the sub-discipline and the object of research, leads to results of which the relevance and implications reach beyond a purely national viewpoint or interest. This may be less so for contributions of a more applied or practical nature. Therefore, outcomes of genuine scholarly research, even those primarily related to national aspects, deserve to be communicated – in an appropriate form – to scholars in other countries as well.

If one is willing to agree with this line of reasoning, it follows that the international orientation, or more specifically, the extent to which research findings are communicated across national or cultural boundaries, is a relevant criterion of scholarly performance in all sub-disciplines. This does not imply that *all* publications should be directed towards an international scholarly public, but rather that at least *some* publications should reach beyond a purely national or local viewpoint and be exposed to criticisms from a wide international scholarly audience.

But the findings regarding the ISI Citation Indexes summarised above suggest that it is at least questionable whether they can be used to assess this aspect properly in *all* areas of social sciences and humanities. These Indexes do cover national journals, particularly in these fields, therefore, if a scholar has published research articles in journals processed for the Indexes, it cannot be concluded without further analysis that these contributions were exposed to a wider international audience. On the other hand, the ISI coverage of the written communication in these fields is moderate. Hence, if scholars have *not* published articles in ISI covered journals, it does *not* follow that their results were exposed to a national audience only.

It must be noted that even within a single subfield, different approaches or paradigms may reveal different publication and referencing characteristics. For instance, Swygart-Hobaugh (2004) analysed differences in referencing patterns in *sociology* between journals applying quantitative methods on the one hand with those that focused on studies using qualitative approaches on the other. She found that 'quantitative' articles were more likely to cite journal articles than monographs, while 'qualitative' articles were more likely to cite monographs than journals. This finding supports Price's hypothesis that different substantive contents call for different communication structures for exchanging information. Qualitative sociology shows publication and reference patterns that are more similar to those found in the humanities.

Swygart-Hobaugh also found that journals focusing on quantitative methods almost exclusively cited other quantitative journals, whereas 'qualitative' journals referred both to qualitatively and to quantitatively oriented journals. Both her findings suggest that it is at least not unlikely that scholars in sociology applying quantitative methodologies tend to be more frequently cited than their qualitatively oriented colleagues, even if an expanded citation analysis included books as targets or sources of references. An uninformed interpretation of citation impact would value quantitative sociology more highly than qualitative sociology.

Summarising, in social science and humanities, the adequacy of ISI coverage of a country's publication output in a field varies both among countries and among fields. This variability reflects differences in substantive contents, in the degree of national orientation of research activities and publication media, and in the extent to which a country's principal journals are covered by the ISI Citation Indexes. For one country in a field the ISI coverage may be good, whereas for another it may be moderate. And ISI coverage may be good in one subfield from a particular discipline, and moderate in other subfields from the same discipline.

Therefore, methodologies for assessing research performance in social sciences and humanities, and particularly the adequacy of the ISI Citation Indexes, can be expected to be highly country- and (sub-)field-dependent. These considerations lead to the conclusion that one should be cautious in using the ISI Citation Indexes in the assessment of research performance in social sciences and humanities, particularly in subfields that have a qualitative rather than a quantitative orientation.

Much more insight is needed and many more empirical studies must be carried out in order to arrive at a more complete overview. A detailed analysis of reference practices and coverage percentages by country and discipline would constitute a useful tool. As a start of this huge project, the following chapters present the outcomes of two studies, related to the assessment of research performance of scholars active in two particular fields, in two Western-European countries. Conclusions drawn from these studies are not necessarily valid in other fields and other countries. They illustrate how one can carry out methodologies that are different from those normally applied in the assessment of research performance in basic science.

Chapter 8 distinguished four types of bibliometric studies, and proposed in fields with a good yet not excellent coverage, to carry out a 'target expanded' citation analysis based on the ISI Citation Indexes, and to give these Indexes in fields with moderate coverage a limited role or no role at all. Chapter 10 presents a case study of the research performance of Flemish academic departments in a social science field with a *quantitative* orientation: economics. Flanders is the Dutch speaking part of Belgium. It provides an illustration of a target expanded citation analysis. Chapter 11 deals with the measurement of research performance of Flemish and Dutch academic scholars in a field with a *qualitative* orientation, law. The ISI Citation Indexes do not play a role in this study. The next section presents the main elements of a general methodology one could apply in the development of appropriate research performance indicators in these fields.

9.2 Methodology for the development of research performance indicators in social sciences and humanities

A fundamental assumption is that the concepts of research performance and research quality have a meaning in all fields of scholarship, particularly in social sciences and humanities. It is also assumed that in these domains of scholarship, differences in research quality among individual scholars or groups of scholars exist.

The principal aim of the development and application of bibliometric indicators is to stimulate a debate among scholars in the field under investigation about the nature of scholarly quality, its principal dimensions and operationalisations. This aim provides a criterion of 'productivity' of the development process. A productive process enables scholars to express their views on academic quality more explicitly and clearly. In other words, a productive process establishes conditions for a more profound reflection upon what is more and what is less valuable in academic research.

The essential elements of the methodology can be summarised in the following points. First, one should collect documents containing statements of scholars in the field under study on how assessment of research performance should be conducted, and, of course, on how it should *not* be conducted. Earlier reports of peer review committees evaluating scholars in the field constitute a fruitful basis for such an inventory. The bibliometric investigator should identify the main aspects of research quality involved, issues that were raised, problems that remained unsolved, operationalisations that were applied or rejected. Secondly, scholars from the field should be involved in all stages of the study. They should be stimulated to propose or develop – even preliminary – classification systems, and to structure their own research output accordingly.

Next, bibliometrics should be used as a mirror, reflecting in a thorough analysis how scholars in the humanities and social sciences structure their activities and their research output. This structure can be examined empirically from the point of view of its consistency and the degree of consensus among scholars. Relevant issues that are worth considering in more detail can be raised in follow-up studies and conclusions from empirical materials can be derived that may illuminate such issues. It is essential to recognise the need to develop adequate *classification systems* for scholarly activities and research output prior to any comparative measurement of scholarly performance.

The interaction process between bibliometric investigators and scholars involved does not necessarily lead to a full consensus among all participants. Therefore, on the basis of their professional competence, the bibliometric investigators present to the scholarly community what they consider to be the most appropriate approach for structuring and measuring research performance. It is essential that they exercise a sufficient degree of *openness* in their presentation, both towards the scholars and to policy makers.

It is up to the scholarly community and its committees to discuss and evaluate the outcomes of the study. The process summarised above may then start again. Thus, an interactive, open process of developing performance indicators in social sciences and humanities is created.

If the extent to which research findings reach beyond a purely national or local viewpoint and are exposed to criticisms from a wide international scholarly audience is considered as a relevant criterion of research quality in social sciences and humanities, a major task would be to develop for the various subfields valid indicators of this aspect of research performance.

As argued above, it cannot be taken for granted that the ISI Citation Indexes provide valid indicators in *all* subfields of these domains of scholarship. A challenge would be to systematically explore alternative data sources and methodologies. The expertise and perceptions of scholars active in the various subfields should play an important role in such an exploration.

Chapter 10

EXPANDED CITATION ANALYSIS: A CASE STUDY IN ECONOMICS

10.1   Introduction

Chapter 8 proposed carrying out a *target expanded* citation analysis rather than a 'standard' analysis normally applied to assess basic science groups, if the analysis of a group's publication and reference practices provided evidence that some important communication sources are not covered by the ISI Indexes, while a substantial part of important sources is covered. Whereas a standard citation analysis takes into account only citations to articles that were published in journals processed for the ISI Citation Indexes, a target expanded analysis also determines the citation impact of targets published in non-ISI covered media, such as books and conference proceedings.

In *economics* the overall ISI coverage was found in Chapter 7 to be 47 per cent. Thus, about half of all the cited references in economics journals processed for the ISI Indexes are published in non-ISI covered media. This outcome justifies the carrying out of a target expanded analysis. It is assumed that, although the collection of source or citing documents is incomplete, their cited references may still provide reliable citation impact estimates, to the extent that the ISI source articles constitute a representative sample of a wider population of citing sources.

This chapter describes a methodology of a target expanded citation analysis. It is applied to research departments in the field of economics at a Flemish University. Section 10.2 technically describes in broad terms how in such an analysis a relative citation indicator can be constructed that takes into account differences in reference practices among disciplines, a distorting factor that is accounted for so well in a standard citation analysis assessing research performance in basic science. Section 10.3 analyses the extent to which the outcomes of a standard analysis differ from those obtained in a target expanded analysis, and thus provides an answer to the question whether including as targets documents in non-ISI covered media makes a difference, at least in this particular case.

Although this case study relates to a social science discipline, it is expected that its methodology can be usefully applied to other disciplines showing good yet not excellent ISI coverage, particularly in applied sciences and engineering.

10.2   Citation impact indicators for documents in non-ISI covered media

Chapter 4 described the construction in a standard citation impact assessment analysis of normalised citation impact indicators that take into account the age of the cited articles, the disciplines or subfields they cover, and the type of article (e.g., review, letter, or normal research article). In order to measure the citation impact of documents published in media not covered by the ISI Indexes – denoted briefly as non-ISI documents – in a proper way, a normalised indicator was developed that is to a large degree an analogue of that applied in a standard citation impact analysis.

A normalised citation impact indicator calculated for a group can be conceived as a ratio of the actual number of citations to a group's papers, and the expected number, given the papers' age, discipline and type. With respect to actual counts, a partly computerised and partly manual approach was applied. Generally, it is difficult to determine accurate citation counts for non-ISI sources, because the information available in the database on a cited reference is limited. It includes the first author, an abbreviated source title, the publication year, volume and starting page number only. Book or proceedings volumes titles often appear in many variants. Therefore, visual inspection of (potential) variants is necessary in order collect accurate counts.

Cited documents were assigned to one of 15 main disciplines, described in Chapter 14, according to that of the articles citing it, applying a fractional assignment whenever necessary. For instance, if a document was cited 15 times from articles assigned to physics & astronomy, and 5 times from articles in applied physics and chemistry, it was assigned a fraction of 0.75 to the former and 0.25 to the latter. Moreover, cited documents were roughly categorised into two main types: journal articles and other types of documents. In this categorisation it was assumed that the former tend to be characterised by a volume and starting page number, whereas for the latter at least one of these data fields tends to be missing.

In order to determine accurate expected citation rates – i.e., the average number of citations to non-ISI documents of a particular type in a discipline – in the ideal case one should perform a mega combined computerised and manual analysis of millions of cited documents. From a practical point of view such an analysis is not feasible. Instead, the methodology aims at determining in a computerised approach an estimate of a *lower and an upper boundary* of expected citation rates. These values correspond to two ways of defining a cited item: a strict way and a relaxed way. The former does not take into account sufficiently all variant forms of a cited document, whereas the latter may erroneously consider cited reference strings relating to distinct documents as representing the same document.

It must be noted that this indicator is based upon documents that are *cited at least once* from ISI covered journals. Therefore it is to be interpreted as a normalised citations-per-*cited*-paper ratio rather than a citations-per-paper ratio, as is the case in a standard citation analysis. Documents not cited from ISI source journals do not play a role in this type of citation analysis, although the share of documents from a group's bibliography that were never cited constitutes an informative citation impact measure in a target expanded analysis. For further details the reader is referred to Visser and Moed (2004; 2005).

10.3 Results

For researchers at 10 economics departments in a Flemish University, a list was compiled of all publications published during the period 1992–2001. These lists were verified by the researchers themselves. For each publication the number of citations received up until 2002 was determined, excluding author self-citations. Citations to articles published in journals processed for the ISI Citation Indexes were determined by means of sophisticated, computerised matching programs, taking into account the major citation errors and discrepancies outlined in Chapter 13. Citations to publications in non-ISI sources, particularly to monographs and book chapters, were collected in a partly computerised, partly manual way.

Figure 10.1 compares the normalised citation impact of a department's papers published in ISI covered journals to that of their non-ISI documents cited at least once. The former indicator is calculated from a standard citation analysis, and the latter from a target expanded analysis. For each of the two indicators a score above 1.0 indicates that a department's documents are cited on average more frequently than the world average in the discipline(s) in which it is active, also taking into account the type of document and its age. The horizontal axis relates to the citation impact of articles in ISI covered journals, and the vertical axis to that of non-ISI documents.

The figure shows that the ranking of departments according to the citation impact of their ISI covered papers significantly differs from that based on the citation impact of non-ISI covered documents. For instance, department 'B' ranks fifth in the first, but occupies the first position in the second. Hence, for several departments, the impression of their citation impact substantially changes if that of non-ISI documents is taken into account. This case study shows that a target expanded citation analysis does make a difference.

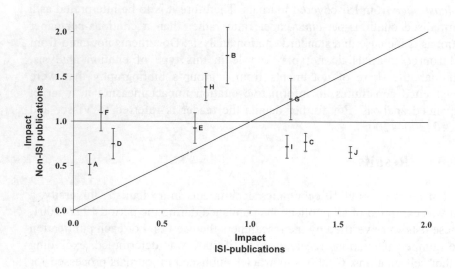

Figure 10.1. Citation impact of ISI and non-ISI covered publications for 10 economics departments

Data relate to 10 departments in the field of economics at a Flemish University. The horizontal axis relates to the average citation impact of articles in ISI covered journals, and the vertical axis to that of non-ISI documents, both compared to a proper world average. The horizontal reference line marks the world citation average for non-ISI covered publications. The diagonal line indicates points for which the citation impact of ISI publications equals that of documents published in non-ISI covered media. The plot shows that departments B and H for articles in ISI covered journals have a citation impact below world average, whereas the citation impact of their non-ISI documents is above world average. For departments I, C and J it is the opposite. A 'standard' citation analysis would take into account one dimension only, i.e., the scores displayed on the horizontal axis.

10.4   Concluding remarks

The methodology for analysing the citation impact of documents in non-ISI covered sources needs to be further developed and fine-tuned. The results presented in this chapter mark a first step. Further research in this direction is in progress (Visser and Moed, 2004). This is also true for the so-called *source expanded* citation analyses. The Leiden Centre for Science and Technology Studies recently began a large study aimed at developing appropriate methodologies for source expanded citation analysis in the field of computer science (Visser and Moed, 2005). As outlined above, assessing the importance of sources plays a crucial role in this analysis. The basic principles developed by Eugene Garfield described in Chapter 6 and applied in the construction of the *Science Citation Index* and related indexes are expected to be most useful.

Chapter 11

A CASE STUDY OF RESEARCH PERFORMANCE IN LAW

11.1 Introduction

The aim of this chapter is to further illustrate the general methodology outlined in Section 10.2, by presenting typical outcomes of a study undertaken by Luwel et al. (1999), from which results were published by Nederhof et al. (2001) and Moed et al. (2002). It was a pilot study commissioned by the Flemish Inter-University Council (VLIR) aimed at developing a methodology to assess research performance in social sciences and humanities. It related to the research activities conducted at the four larger Flemish universities.

Many scholars, particularly those in the USA, may argue that law is not a typical humanities field. It must be underlined that the results as regards the field of law presented in this chapter were drawn from a wider study in which linguistics was also analysed. The main lines of the methodology were the same in the law and linguistics analysis. For specific empirical outcomes from the latter field, the reader is referred to Luwel et al. (1999) and Nederhof et al. (2001).

In the study two questionnaires were sent out to scholars subjected to the analysis. A first collected quantitative data on many, if not all academic activities. The core was formed by publication lists, categorised by scholars themselves, according to a classification scheme including 18 types. The total number of publications listed amounted to 3,753. All publications were arranged into types. In a second questionnaire, respondents were asked to indicate 'outstanding', 'good, yet not outstanding' and 'less good' journals, and the names of Flemish scholars whose work was currently very important to their sub-discipline. The main objective was to assess to what extent the scholars' opinions corroborated the outcomes of the quantitative indicators. Response rates to both questionnaires were moderate.

11.2   Analysis of earlier assessments

A first report presented an assessment undertaken by a peer review committee of all research activities in the field of *law* at universities in the Netherlands. In its final report, this Committee expressed the need for clear guidelines and criteria for selecting and structuring the information on publication output. Such criteria should above all specify the type of publications to be included in a performance assessment.

In addition, the Committee stressed that attempts should be made to distinguish between 'genuine' scholarly contributions on the one hand, and informative publications aimed primarily at providing social services, on the other. Genuine scholarly publications conform to criteria of methodological soundness, thoroughness and significance. In the Committee's view, it is the first category of publications that distinguishes between a juridical scholar and a practitioner or a professional legal expert. Academic scholars should primarily be evaluated according to their contribution to scholarly progress, rather than to their practical activities.

In order to discriminate between substantial and small scholarly contributions, the Committee took into account the publications' length, as reflected in the number of pages. Publications with more than 5 pages were regarded as 'substantial' contributions. For each research programme to be assessed, the Committee regarded the number of single- or multi-author books (first editions only), doctoral theses and 'substantial' contributions as the most significant productivity measure. In addition, the total number of publications (of all types) was determined.

The relationship between juridical research and practice was also addressed in a second report by a committee of Deans of Flemish Law Departments. However, this Committee stated that juridical research primarily serves the 'practice', a basic characteristic that creates difficulties in distinguishing between fundamental and applied juridical research. It is worth noting that the two committees apparently did not have fully coinciding viewpoints.

According to the Committee of Deans, *the published book* ranks first in the scholarly juridical publication output. A book is viewed as the result of an often individual and personal synthesis of legislation, jurisdiction and juridical theory in a sub-discipline. A book is often the reflection of continuous, intensive scholarly research, conducted for many years. In the Committee's view, the same is true for doctoral theses. Therefore, as a rule, a doctoral thesis deserves publication as a book.

The Committee also made a distinction between *substantial* scholarly contributions and scholarly contributions *of a limited size*, published in accepted scholarly journals, anniversary volumes, seminar reports, and collective works. Typical examples of the first type are: a leading article, a review on jurisdiction or a thorough annotation, whereas a short annotation, a thorough book review or an intervention as panel member or participant in a conference are examples of scholarly contributions of a limited size. However, the Committee did not operationalise the concept of substantial contribution any further.

The Committee did not succeed in developing a classification of scholarly journals in terms of their quality or reputation. The main impediment to such a ranking was that most law journals show large variations in the quality of the papers published. In addition, some sub-disciplines are only covered by a limited number of national journals, for which no definitive ranking could be made. For a review of earlier bibliometric studies in the field of law, the reader is referred to Luwel et al. (2002).

11.3   Publication lists and classifications

Table 11.1. Classification scheme of scholarly publications in law

No.	Description	Publ. (%)
1	Book published as single author	2.9
2	Published doctoral (PhD) thesis	0.8
3	Book published as co-author	6.0
4	Unpublished doctoral (PhD) thesis	0.3
5	Substantial scholarly contribution, published in accepted scholarly journals, anniversary volumes, seminar reports,	33.1
6	Edited book or collected work	2.9
7	Published integral contribution to international conferences	1.9
8	Published abstract of lecture at international conferences	0.6
9	Published integral contribution to national conferences	3.0
10	Published abstract of lecture at national conferences	0.7
11	Scholarly contribution of a limited size, published in accepted scholarly journals, anniversary volumes, seminar	16.7
12	Teaching course notes	2.2
13	Scholarly edition of codes of Law, jurisdiction volumes, bibliographies	2.7
14	Research report circulated in the scholarly community	0.7
15	Internal research report or report on commissioned work	2.4
16	Published inaugural or valedictory lecture	0.02
17	Other publications, such as: an introduction; editorial	12.5
18	Juridical publications for a wide audience	10.8

Table 11.1 presents the classification scheme of scholarly publications in law, applied in the study. One of the key elements in the system is the distinction between *substantial contributions* (about 33 per cent of all publications listed), *small contributions* (17 per cent), *publications for a wide audience* (11 per cent) and *other publications* (13 per cent). It must be underlined that scholars in the field of law from other countries may use different classification systems.

The classification system of publication types was not always applied correctly by the respondents. Many relevant examples of erroneous classifications were collected. For instance, multi-author books were classified as single-author books. Respondents listed both the un-published and the published versions of their PhD thesis. In several cases reports of advisory committees or committees preparing legislation and teaching notes were categorised as books. It was not always clear whether published books were first or later editions. In view of the great importance of books as publications in juridical research, it was suggested specifying more precisely the criteria to be applied in determining whether or not a publication should be classified as a book.

Another important phenomenon observed in the publication lists was that the same publication may be published twice by the same author, in different sources. The two versions may be entirely identical, or show small differences. A bibliometric tool was developed to identify 'candidate' identical publications, i.e., publications published by the same author, which are probably identical. In the class of books, doctoral theses and substantial contributions, almost 8 per cent of the publications written in Dutch and listed by the same author was found to have very similar titles. A detailed analysis of printed copies revealed that most of the pairs were actually (almost) identical publications.

11.4   Analysis of classifications and quality perceptions

Publication language

The main publication language of Flemish publications in the field of law is Dutch. Of all publications 81 per cent were written in Dutch, and 10 per cent in English. Interestingly, publications published in English were rather unevenly distributed among the various sub-disciplines. In *information technology law and informatics*, *public international law*, *economics of law*, *private international law* and *European community law* the share of publications in English was greater than 25 per cent. Sub-disciplines with less than 5 per cent of publications in English were: *tax law*, *judicial law*, *contract law* and *administrative law*.

A high percentage of publications in Dutch reflects the national (or regional) character and relevance of juridical research. It is indeed plausible to assume that the international orientation of a sub-discipline is related to the object of research in that sub-discipline. From this point of view, it is perhaps not surprising that sub-disciplines such as *international law*, *international private law* and *European community law* show a relatively high percentage of publications written in English. In addition, *information technology law and legal informatics*, and *economics of law* focus on issues with a growing international interest within the framework of globalisation.

Page length of substantial contributions

Bibliometric characteristics of articles classified as substantial contributions were examined in more detail. Table 11.2 illustrates that 84 per cent of substantial contributions had a page length greater than 5. For the three other types, this percentage is near 20. Among the 16 per cent of substantial contributions containing 5 pages or less, there were several with a page length of 1 or 2. It is questionable whether such publications can be marked as substantial contributions. It is worthwhile considering whether or not it is appropriate to set a minimum page length for a publication in order to be classified as a substantial contribution. One could even take into account differences in the number of printed characters (or words) per page in the various sources.

Table 11.2. Statistics on the page length of four publication types

Publication type	Publ. with no. Pages (%)	
	<=5	>5
Substantial contributions	16	84
Small contributions	77	23
Other publications	82	18
Publications for wide audience	83	17

Publication output in journals

The role of journals was found to be less prominent in communicating research results in juridical research than it is in many fields in natural and life sciences. The proportion of journal articles among all publications listed by the respondents to the first questionnaire and published during 1992–1996, amounted to 59 per cent. In the category *substantial contributions*, it was 60 per cent. Nevertheless, this percentage was considered sufficiently high to justify a separate analysis of journals.

The data collected in the study made it possible to distinguish between scholarly journals and journals of a more applied nature, or journals directed to a wide audience. The distinction is partly based on an analysis of the classification of publications into publication types given by the respondents themselves. By arranging the classified publications by journal, one obtains an 'indirect' insight into the scholars' perceptions of the nature of the journals. A basic assumption underlying this approach is that *scholarly* journals should contain a certain minimum number of publications classified by the respondents as substantial contributions.

In addition, the number of journal publications made by respondents in the first questionnaire was compared to the number of times the respective journal was nominated in the second questionnaire. This analysis included only nominations made by Flemish scholars. There is a substantial overlap between the respondents in the first and the second questionnaire. The findings enabled one to examine the consistency of their responses. Journals in which the Flemish scholars published relatively few substantial contributions or no such contributions at all, were rarely nominated by the Flemish respondents in the second questionnaire. These journals are typical examples of applied journals or journals directed to a wide audience.

Indicators of research performance

Table 11.3. Statistical relationship between number of publications and number of nominations

No. Nominations	No. scholars	Mean			
		Total publ	Core publ	Total pages	Core pages
3–10	20	9.2	4.4	504	270
1–2	21	8.7	3.4	400	261
0	20	5.6	2.3*	321	143**

* Significantly different from mean score in class 3–10 nominations, according to Duncan's multiple range test with alpha=0.05.
** Significantly different from mean score in class with 3–10 and class with 1–2 nominations.
Mean Total Publ: The mean of total number of publications per year 1992–1996.
Mean Core publications: The mean of number of single- and multi-author books, PhD theses and substantial contributions per year.
Mean Total pages, Mean Core pages: the mean of the number of pages per scholar produced per year in all publications and in core publications, respectively.

A detailed comparison was made of the results from the second questionnaire on nominations of Flemish scholars with several bibliometric indicators based on publications, calculated for those Flemish scholars for whom publication data was available. For instance, the number of publications made by Flemish scholars receiving three or more nominations was compared with the number of publications by scholars nominated once or twice, or with that of scholars not nominated at all. Results are presented in Table 11.3.

Table 11.3 illustrates that scholars receiving three or more nominations have published a significantly higher number of *books*, *PhD theses* and *substantial contributions* than scholars who were not nominated at all, in the questionnaire on quality perceptions. Analysing the total number of pages produced, a significant difference was observed between the class of scholars with no nominations, on the one hand, and the classes of scholars with 1–2 or 3–10, on the other. With respect to the *total* number of publications or the *total* number of pages, *no* significant differences were found among the three classes of nominations. If one considers the number of nominations received as a measure of scholarly quality, as perceived by colleagues or *peers*, the statistical analysis suggests that the number of *books*, *PhD theses* and *substantial contributions* is a more appropriate indicator of research performance than the total number of publications.

11.5   Comments by Deans of law departments

Approximately 10 months after publication of the study's final report, the Committee of Deans of Flemish Law Departments gave its comments in an official letter to the Flemish Inter-University Council (VLIR). Although the Committee was unhappy with the fact that the research report was written in English, it expressed its praise for the work, and stated that many results from it would be useful for the development of performance evaluation criteria. The Committee's letter addressed three main points.

The first related to the statements in the final report concerning international orientation. Although the Committee agreed that the international orientation of Flemish juridical research needs to be stimulated, it issued a warning that this aspect should not be assessed merely on the basis of publication language. The Committee stated that contributions in English are often not of a fundamental nature, but are rather popularising works, for instance, aimed at providing an introduction to the Belgian or Flemish Law system for a larger, foreign audience. Rewarding publication in English would stimulate 'legal journalism'. Publications in English should only be given a higher weight when they are published in journals of which the quality guarantees that they go beyond the level of legal journalism.

A second point concerned rankings of journals. Although the Committee stated in its 1996 report that it is impossible to rank journals, it was now willing to reconsider this. In its view, rankings should primarily be based on expert opinion, which was based on criteria such as international orientation, severity of review procedure, a journal's circulation and its citation impact.

The third major point related to the operationalisation of the concept of substantial contribution. The Committee argued that the number of pages gives a certain indication, but that other criteria should be developed as well, such as descriptive-systematic, analytical, comparative, evaluative, innovative, critical or interdisciplinary.

Finally, the Committee stated that it would continue to work on the development of criteria for measuring research performance in the field of Law, and that it would be unfortunate if findings from the report were to be applied 'in a premature way' in university research policy.

PART 2.4

ACCURACY ASPECTS

Chapter 12

INTRODUCTORY NOTES ON ACCURACY ISSUES

12.1 Introduction

At first sight, it may seem a fairly simple task for instance to analyse an individual scholar or an institution, by searching for their names in the author and corporate address fields in the ISI Citation Indexes, or to collect citation counts for a given set of target documents. Chapters 13 and 14, however, illustrate that such a task is not as simple as it may seem. These chapters describe a number of problems of a technical nature related both to the database and to the structure of the scholarly system. They emphasise that there is *no* one-to-one correspondence between data elements stored in the database on the one hand, and 'real' entities in the scholarly system on the other. They show that most of these problems can be overcome, provided that the data collection and elementary data handling is carried out in a proper way.

It must be underlined that the chapters focus on *bibliometric* use of the ISI Citation Indexes in the assessment of research performance of individual scholars, research groups, departments, institutions and countries. An overview of the issues addressed in them is presented in Table 12.1. This chapter ends with a number of important comments on these issues by Eugene Garfield which serve as a useful background for a proper interpretation of the chapters following in this part of the book.

Table 12.1. Technical problems and their solutions presented in Chapters 13 and 14

Chapter	Problem	Solution
13	*Individual papers*	
	Citation counts may be inaccurate	Apply advanced citation matching procedures coping with major discrepancies
14.1	*Authors*	
	Homonym/synonym problem	Use verified bibliographies; let scholars check selected publications
14.2	*Institutions*	
	Variations in institutional names in address data	Use verified bibliographies; de-duplicate names but let institutions check results
	Institutions may be difficult to define	Use background information on institutions' structure
14.2	*Institutions and countries*	
	In social sciences and humanities many articles do not contain addresses at all	Be careful in those disciplines with drawing conclusions from address data
14.3	*Fields, disciplines*	
	Subfield classification system based on journal categories may be less appropriate	Use additional clustering on a paper-by-paper basis, particularly for papers in multi- or interdisciplinary journals

12.2   Notes by Eugene Garfield

"From the earliest days, it was known to ISI that there would be many variations made by citing authors in the way they cited individual articles and books. At one time more than 200 citation formats used by journals were catalogued. Clearly, such variations might affect either the retrieval of relevant papers or any bibliometric data used in citation analysis. For this reason, many caveats were published in the introductory Guides to the printed indexes.

Once the ISI data became even more visible in the CD-ROM versions of the Citation Indexes or in the on-line versions, a variety of procedures were recommended to searchers for overcoming these variations. There were also a variety of invisible procedures followed in ISI's production area that would "unify" variant data. What you see in the printed or electronic *SCI* is not necessarily what was originally reported by the author. Ignorance of these procedures led Simkin and Roychowdry to make an egregious error that led to a false theory about authors who "cite but do not read" (Simkin and Roychowdhury, 2002).

Thousands of variations in citations are corrected by these ISI procedures. Nevertheless, there is a relatively small but seemingly large number of variations in the cited reference lines reported in the *SCI*. That is because each variation occupies one line – the same space that is allocated for each correctly cited one.

As an extreme case, consider the most-cited article in the history of science – the Lowry Method. This 1951 paper has probably been cited over 250,000 times. A simple scan of the *SCI* under Lowry, J. *Biol Chem* 1951 produces hundreds of variations which occur mainly once, while the correct reference is overwhelmingly cited correctly 99 per cent of the time. In absolute terms 2,500 "errors" could be regarded as significant. However, almost none of these papers involved would be lost in a search designed to retrieve all relevant citing papers. The only search terms required to guarantee almost 100 per cent recall would be author, journal, and year. By conducting a "cited reference search" in the *ISI Web of Science*, this is easily seen.

Just as the user can decide whether or not to retrieve all of the relevant citing papers, the correct citation "metric" for this article can be tabulated in the same way. There are 724 lines of information for the 1951 Lowry paper. One has to marvel at the variety of variations and errors, but in spite of these variations, one can ferret out the data needed or desired. Very few searchers would conduct this particular search, but it might be reasonable to do so if it were part of a combination search involving Lowry OH 1951 and a key word like 'cancer'. So, to minimise information loss, one uses truncation when searching. Variations in the cited volume or page would not matter, nor would an error in the first initial. Indeed, the truncation could be carried even further by searching for Lowry by assuming that some might erroneously spell his name Lowrey (using Lowr* or Lowr# as truncated search term). Indeed, this did occur on two occasions.

Consider another well-cited example – the 1953 paper by Watson and Crick on the helical structure of DNA. This paper has been cited around 2,300 times. A few dozen citing authors managed to mangle the volume or page for that article, but those articles are nevertheless retrievable, as would be the times cited, if one were doing an article-by-article citation analysis.

If, however, one is doing a citation analysis which is "programmed", or automatic, then these discrepancies might affect the citation counts. The analyses reported later in this chapter are based on an "automatic procedure" which does not take into account the ability of the searcher or citation analyst to take into account these variations. Expert systems can be designed which do incorporate this kind of intelligence.

For research evaluation, one must always take into account variations which may seriously impact a particular study. However, one has to ask how often a discrepancy matters when dealing with the upper percentile of the cited literature. Assuming that the discrepancies are as high as 7 per cent, how often does this affect the ranking of a particular country or author?

One can always find individual cases that have egregiously failed to give a particular paper or author their due, but not when diligence is observed in checking the potential for error. Thus, in an analysis of Japanese authors, who do not use middle initials, one would have to be careful to differentiate the many homographs by using author address or other criteria.

If one accepts that there is an overall "discrepancy" in citation figures of from 1 to 10 per cent, then it is important to keep in mind that for each year the average cited article is cited only twice. In a five-year period the average article cited is cited about five times. These figures do not take into account the huge number of uncited papers, often as high as 50 per cent, in low impact journals. Over a ten-year period, the average cited article will be cited less than ten times. In this light, even a 10 per cent discrepancy is not very significant".

Chapter 13

ACCURACY OF CITATION COUNTS

13.1   Introduction and research questions

Many bibliometric indicators are based on the number of times particular articles are cited in the journals processed for the various ISI Citation Indexes, the *Science Citation Index* (SCI) being the most prominent. Thus citation links constitute crucial elements both in scientific literature retrieval and in assessment of research performance or journal impact (Garfield, 1979). The reliability of citation based indicators strongly depends on the accuracy with which citation links are identified. It is therefore essential to users of citation based indicators to have detailed insights into the types of problems that emerge and the degree of accuracy that can be achieved in establishing these links. This chapter aims at providing such insights. It builds upon the terminology described in Chapter 6.

The ISI citation indexes, including the SCI and the *Web of Science*, contain for all documents published in approximately 7,500 journals, full bibliographic data, including their title, all contributing authors and their institutional affiliations, journal title, issue, volume, starting and ending page number. The cited references from source articles are also extracted. These are the publications included in the reference lists at the bottom of a paper. From a cited reference, ISI includes five datafields: the first author, source (e.g., journal, or book) title, publication year, volume number and starting page number.

Generally, the representation of a target document subjected to citation analysis may differ from that regarded as a cited reference. For instance, an author citing a particular target article may indicate an erroneous starting page number, or may have misspelled the cited author's name in his or her reference list. The neutral term 'discrepancy' is used to indicate such differences or variations between a target article intentionally cited in a reference and the cited reference itself. A basic problem in any citation analysis holds: how does one properly match a particular set of target articles to the file of cited references, in order to establish accurate citation links between these targets and the source articles citing them, and how should one deal with discrepancies?

This chapter examines the case in which the set of target articles is a set as large as the total collection of source articles processed by ISI during a twenty-year period. In other words, it deals with citation links between ISI source articles, described in Section 6.3. The questions addressed in this chapter are: What types of discrepancies between cited references and target articles occur? How frequently do these occur? And what are the consequences of omitting discrepant references in the calculation of citation statistics?

13.2   Data and methods

The Centre for Science and Technology Studies (CWTS) at Leiden University has created a large database of all documents processed during the period 1980–2004 for the CD-ROM version of the SCI and a number of related Citation Indexes on CD-ROM. The database is bibliometric rather than bibliographic, as it is primarily designed to conduct quantitative, statistical analysis and mapping, and was used in a large series of scientific and commissioned projects conducted during the past 10 years (van Raan, 1996; van Raan, 2004a). The analyses presented below relate to as many as 22 million cited references extracted from all source articles processed in 1999, matched to about 18 million target articles, being the total collection of ISI source articles published during the period 1980–1999.

The methodology applied in this chapter builds upon work described in an earlier paper by Moed and Vriens (1989), and in a paper by Luwel (1999). It focuses on cases showing discrepancies in one datafield only. Cited references and target articles were matched in a process involving five matchkeys, each one based on four out of the five datafields available. In a first round, a matchkey was applied consisting of the first six characters of the author's family name, his or her first initial, the year of publication, volume number and starting page number. This key can be assumed to be a sufficiently unique characterisation of a journal article, and will be denoted as 'simple' matchkey. For reasons of simplicity, cited references matched in this round will be denoted as 'correct'.

In a second round, additional matchkeys were applied, including the journal title, but leaving out the author name, publication year, volume number and starting page number, respectively. Thus, discrepancies in the datafield omitted could be analysed. Cited references matched in this second round will be denoted as 'discrepant'. Discrepancies were reconstructed by finding a 'plausible' explanation for them. Therefore, a classification was designed of 32 types of discrepancies. Discrepancies for which, in the current stage of the work, no plausible explanation could be given, were assigned to a rest category.

13.3 Results

Table 13.1 presents the number of matches obtained in applying the various matchkeys. In the second round, 989,709 discrepant cited references were matched. This number equals 7.7 per cent of the total number of 'correct' references matched in the first round, applying the simple matchkey. The 32 types of discrepancies were grouped into 11 main types, presented in Table 13.2.

Many of the discrepancies showing small variations in a datafield can be attributed to inaccurate referencing by the citing authors. However, a substantial part of small variations in author names is not due to inattention or sloppiness, but rather to difficulties in identifying the family name and first names of authors from foreign countries or cultures (Borgman and Siegfried, 1992). A typical example is when Western scientists unfamiliar with Chinese names cite a Chinese author. Moreover, transliteration, i.e. the spelling of author names from one language with characters from the alphabet of another, may easily lead to mismatches. Chapter 14 further discusses problems with author names.

Table 13.1. Matches and discrepancies

Round	Datafield in which discrepancy occurred	No. refs matched	Ratio discrepant/ Correct refs (%)
1	No discrepancy ('correct' reference)	12,887,206	
2	Volume number	207,043	1.6
	Author	272,009	2.1
	Publication year	95,190	0.7
	Starting page number	415,467	3.2
	Total 2nd round	989,709	7.7

Number of ISI source/target articles (1980–1999): approximately 18,4 million. The figure for starting page number includes an estimated 20 per cent of cases in which the cited page number originally contained a character (e.g., p. L115) but was missing in the file used in this analysis.

Table 13.2. Main types of discrepancies

Main type of discrepancy	N	%
Page number in cited ref missing	165,793	16.7
Small variations in author names	159,503	16.1
Small variations in page numbers	117,683	11.9
Small variations in volume numbers	95,336	9.6
Small variations in publication years	62,837	6.3
Cited page number lies between starting and end page of target	58,853	5.9
Issue number cited rather than volume number	41,369	4.2
Citations to papers by 'consortia'	36,196	3.7
Volume number missing in cited ref (but not in target)	20,323	2.1
Secondary author cited rather than first author	19,281	1.9
Author name in target or cited reference missing	14,754	1.5
Total number of discrepancies explained	791,928	80.0
All other discrepancies in author names	42.275	4.3
All other discrepancies in page numbers	73,138	7.4
All other discrepancies in volume numbers	50,015	5.1
All other discrepancies in publication years	32,353	3.3
Total number of discrepancies not (yet) explained	197,781	20.0
Total number of discrepancies analysed	989,709	100.0

Table 13.2 shows that in the current stage of the work about 80 per cent of the discrepancies could be explained and matched with a very high probability to the intended target. For the remaining 20 per cent of discrepant references no plausible explanation of the discrepancy could yet be given. It is expected that there is a certain percentage of these that was erroneously matched to a target, particularly when they contain discrepancies in two or more datafields.

Several types of discrepancies are caused mainly by editorial characteristics of the journals cited, by referencing conventions in particular fields of scholarship, or by data capturing and formatting procedures at ISI, or by a combination of these three factors. This can be illustrated with the following examples.

–   When scholars in the field of *law* cite a paper, they often include in their reference the page number containing the statement(s) they are referring to. Thus, the cited page number is often not the starting page number, but rather a number between starting and end page. There is a striking similarity among reference lists among US law journals in this respect, all showing around 50 per cent of mismatches. Indicating a page number 'in between' also occurs, though less frequently, in references to reviews or data compilations in the natural and life sciences.

– Several journals have dual-volume numbering systems, or publish 'combined' (particularly proceedings) volumes. ISI data capturing procedures do not allow for ranges of numbers in the (source) volume number field, and therefore in a sense has to choose from several possibilities. Citing authors may make different choices, however, so that volume numbers in cited reference and target article may differ. A similar problem arises with journals of which it is apparently unclear whether the serial numbering system relates to volumes or to issues.

– Journals may publish their articles in a printed and an electronic version, and article identifiers in these versions may differ from one another. Starting and end page numbers may differ, or the electronic version may apply article serial numbers rather than page numbers. Although ISI puts an enormous effort into dealing which such differences, these may hinder proper matching of cited references and target articles, and are expected to become more onerous in the future.

– Particularly in the medical sciences, more and more papers are published presenting outcomes of a joint study conducted by a consortium, task force, survey committee or clinical trial group. Such papers normally do have authors, and ISI includes the first author on the paper in the first author field. However, scientists citing such papers indicate in their reference list mostly the name of the consortium rather than that of the first author. As a result, names in the author fields of target and cited reference do not match. The journal *Nature* is not the only journal suffering from this type of discrepancy (Anonymous, *Nature*, 2002).

It is essential to make clear that, due to their systematic nature, the discrepancies between targets and cited references are skewly distributed among target articles. Table 13.3 shows parameters of the distribution of discrepant citations among target articles. Most informative is an analysis by journal, examining the effect of including discrepancies upon its impact factor, and one by country of origin of the target articles receiving discrepant citations (Table 13.4).

The journal most affected by ignoring discrepant citations is *Clinical Orthopaedics and Related Research*. The serial numbers attached to this journal are captured by ISI as issue numbers, whereas virtually all cited references to the journal's papers include these numbers in the volume number field. Focusing on the bigger non-Western countries, (former) USSR shows the highest ratio of discrepant/correct citations (21 per cent) followed by China (13 per cent). Among the larger Western countries, Spain and Italy rank top with 7.9 and 7.0 per cent, respectively. USA and Australia show the lowest percentages, 5.7 and 5.3, respectively.

Table 13.3. Distribution of discrepant citations among cited target articles

No. Citations	Cumm Cited articles (%)	Cumm discrepant citations (%)
1	78.7	51.9
≤ 2	91.3	68.5
≤ 3	95.2	75.9
≤ 10	99.4	91.1
≤ 15	99.7	93.7
≤ 444	100.0	100.0

Table 13.3 demonstrates how the 989,709 references showing a discrepancy are distributed among target articles intentionally cited: 652,419 Targets were affected; 78.7 per cent of these received only one discrepant citation, accounting for 51.9 per cent of all cited references showing a discrepancy. About 5 per cent of the targets received at least 4 discrepant citations that account for about 24 per cent of all discrepant citations. About 4,000 targets (0.6 per cent) received more than 10 discrepant citations, accounting for 8.9 per cent of all discrepant citations. The maximum number of discrepant citations to the same target is 444. This is a 'Consortium' paper published by the Diabetes Control Complication Trial (first author Shamoon, H), in *New Engl. J. Med*, 329 (14) 977–986, (1993).

Table 13.4. Percentile values of the distribution of the ratio discrepant/correct citations among target journals and countries

Percentile	Ratio discrepant/correct citations (%)	
	Journals	Countries
P10	2.5	5.4
P25	3.4	6.3
P50	4.9	7.8
P75	7.2	9.0
P90	11.6	11.9
P95	18.3	14.2
P99	108.9	41.6

For 2,547 journals (second column) and 99 countries (third column) receiving in 1999 more than 100 'correct' citations to articles published in 1997 and 1998, the ratio was calculated of the number of discrepant and correct citations, expressed as a percentage. The distribution of ratio scores among journals and countries was characterised by their percentile values. The 50th percentile (P50, i.e. the median) is 4.9 for journals and 7.8 for countries. For 127 journals (5 per cent) the ratio discrepant/correct citations exceeds 18.3 per cent (P95), and for 5 countries this ratio exceeds 14.2. For one country it is 41.6 per cent: Vietnam.

13.4   Discussion and conclusions

The analysis presented in this chapter relates to discrepancies in a single datafield. Discrepancies in more than one datafield, containing, for instance, errors in both the author name and the volume number, were not examined. As such discrepancies cannot be assumed to be independent from one another (Lok et al., 2001), their probabilities cannot be calculated by simply multiplying those related to discrepancies in a single datafield. This issue requires a more detailed examination in future studies. The outcomes presented in this chapter provided a lower boundary estimate of the overall number of discrepancies between cited references and target articles. Another issue to be studied in more detail regards the consequences of electronic publishing, particularly the existence of different versions of publications and different numbering systems.

Simkin and Roychowdhury (2002) posted in the Eprint archive ArXiv two versions of a paper entitled 'Read before you cite', of which the first version received considerable attention from scientific journals and the non-scholarly press. From a limited number of case studies on "citation errors", applying a mathematical model in itself interesting, they concluded that citing authors copy a large percentage of references from other papers. However, apart from the fact that when an author copies a reference from another paper it does not follow that he or she did not read the cited paper, their analysis provided no empirical evidence that when two ore more citing papers contain the same discrepant reference, their citing authors actually copied it from one another. For a case study illustrating a methodology to collect this type of evidence, the reader is referred to Moed and Vriens (1989).

Focusing on the quantitative implications for bibliometric research performance assessment, it can be concluded that, due to the skewed distribution of discrepant citations among target articles, citation statistics at the level of individuals, research departments or scientific journals may be highly inaccurate when cited references are not properly matched to target articles.

The data collection procedures underlying citation based indicators must be sound and accurate. Consequently, advanced citation data handling procedures must take into account inaccurate, sloppy referencing, editorial characteristics of scientific journals, referencing conventions in scholarly subfields, language problems, author identification problems, unfamiliarity with foreign author names and data capturing procedures.

Chapter 14

PROBLEMS WITH THE NAMES OF AUTHORS AND INSTITUTIONS, AND WITH THE DELIMITATION OF SUBFIELDS

14.1   Author names

The first problem addressed in this chapter relates to the use of author names in the database's author field. Any proper use of such names must deal with the problem that one person may appear under several name variations in the author field (*synonyms*), and the phenomenon that different persons may have the same name (*homonyms*).

A personal name consists of a surname, a (given) first name, and possibly middle names. In the huge numbers of journals processed each year by ISI, personal names may appear in many different formats. As a rule, ISI parses names into their component parts and converts them into a new format, positioning the surname in the beginning of an author field, followed by the initials of the first and middle names. Hence, the author name that eventually appears in the ISI author field is determined by how a scholar names him- or herself, by technical editing and formatting conventions adopted by the publisher, and by the internal ISI reformatting process. It is important to distinguish between authors of ISI source articles, and authors of the cited references. In the latter case, the way the citing author indicates the name of the first author of the cited paper also plays a crucial role.

Borgman and Siegfried (1992) distinguished between legitimate forms of variation and typographical errors in personal names. Typical examples of sources of legitimate variations are the following.

– Transliteration of names from one alphabet or character set into another, particularly from Cyrillic, Chinese, Korean or Japanese into the Roman alphabet.

- Persons may change their surnames in the course of time, for instance, in case of marriage or divorce.
- Authors may use their full first name (Richard or Johannes) and their nickname (Dick or Hans) interchangeably, and omit middle names.
- Compound surnames, for instance Hispanic and Chinese names, may appear in many different variations, as it may be difficult for a non-expert to identify the surname.

Standard typographical errors are transposition and substitution errors, and omissions or additions of characters. In cited references, such errors are more likely to occur when citing and cited authors have different linguistic backgrounds. When bibliographical data are inserted manually into an electronic database, this manual copying of author names may lead to typographical errors, but when data are obtained by a database producer in electronic form, which is currently the case for many journals processed by ISI, errors of this type do not play a role.

Homonyms constitute a bigger problem in selecting from the author data field articles by a particular person. It is fairly difficult, however, to provide reliable estimates of how frequently homonyms occur. In a first, simple approach, author names can be identified that appear so frequently in the bylines of publications that they are likely to represent several persons rather than one.

For instance, during the four-year period 1999–2002, each of about 2,100 author names in the ISI database is linked with more than 50 articles per year. It can be safely assumed that the overwhelming number of these names relate to different persons. In this sample, about 65 per cent relate to scholars affiliated with Asian countries, particularly Japan (54 per cent), China (10 per cent) and South Korea (8 per cent). During the period considered, the Japanese names Suzuki T and Tanaka K are the most frequently appearing author names in the database, both associated with around 600 papers per year.

Some other typical examples of frequently occurring surnames in the author field are Mitchell (particularly in Australia), Olsen, Nielsen (Denmark), Martin, Martinez (France), Muller, Schmidt, Schneider, Weber (Germany), Smith, Jones, Taylor, Thomas, Wilson (UK), Kumar, Bannerjee, Singh, Sharma (India), Rossi (Italy), Wang, Zhou, Zhang (China), Lee, Kim (South Korea), Martinez, Garcia, Gonzalez (Spain), Johansson, Andersson (Sweden), Chen, Lin (Taiwan), Smith, Martin and Jones (USA). The above analysis illustrates the homonym problem well, but reveals only the tip of the iceberg.

On the one hand, a substantial number of scholars do show a one-to-one correspondence with a particular author name in the database. For those scholars, articles can be extracted easily by searching for their names in the author field. But other scholars' names may be dispersed in the database, or relate to several persons rather than one. The crucial problem is that for many given scholars it is often difficult if not impossible to know *a priori* to which class he or she belongs.

It can be concluded that, in order to properly identify articles from the database published by a particular scholar, background knowledge on the scholar's research activities is essential, particularly on the institutions in which he or she worked, the subfield or topics in which he or she is active, or the journals in which he or she has published. Under the condition that such background knowledge is available, a more sophisticated, carefully conducted search in the database may combine information from several data fields, and in this way provide much more accurate publication lists.

For a source article the ISI Citation Indexes give all publishing authors and all authors' institutional affiliations, including the names of the countries in which the institutions are located. However, at the level of individual papers, the Indexes do *not* provide a link between each author and his or her institutional affiliation. For instance, if a paper has five authors and two publishing institutions, it cannot be deduced from the database which author is affiliated to which institution, although the first address normally corresponds to the first or reprint author.

But even if a scholar's publication data are extracted in a careful way, a list may be incomplete, where background knowledge was incomplete or inaccurate. In analyses of individuals, aimed at deriving conclusions about those individuals' research activities and performance, publication lists must be fully accurate. The only way to achieve this is by enabling assessed scholars themselves to verify the compiled lists. Such a verification process enhances not only data accuracy, but also the legitimacy of the assessment procedure as a whole, as well as the acceptability of its outcomes by scholars subjected to it, and, hence, the usefulness of the bibliometric indicators in the policy domain.

14.2   Institutional affiliations

Authors normally indicate in the byline of a publication the institution to which they were affiliated when they conducted the reported research. In the ISI database this information is stored in the corporate address field, and indicates the name of the main organisation, often a sub-division or department, and, for authors designated as corresponding author, the postal address. The content of the corporate address field is first of all determined by what authors themselves indicate in the byline of their papers, and upon technical editing and formatting conventions adopted by the publisher.

Authors from the same institution, or even from the same department, may not indicate their institutional affiliations in the same way. As a result, names of main organisations may appear in many different variations in the database.

ISI developed an advanced procedure in capturing and reformatting address data. Some important elements in reformatting the institutional information are the following. When the institutional information is split into parts exhibiting some kind of hierarchical structure, ISI puts the part with the highest position in the hierarchy, often denoted as the main organisation, at the beginning of the string. Thus, the string 'Department of Astronomy, University of Cambridge' is converted into 'University of Cambridge, Department of Astronomy'. Next, institutional and cognitive words are abbreviated and standardised (e.g., Univ Cambridge, Dept Astron).

Main organisational names are to some extent de-duplicated, particularly for institutions located in the USA. In this de-duplication process errors are sometimes made. A typical example is that the names of two distinct Belgian Universities, the *Flemish Vrije Universiteit Brussel* and the *French-speaking Université Libre de Bruxelles*, are converted into a single entry, 'Free University Brussels', so that publications from these two institutions cannot be separated merely on the basis of addresses appearing in the ISI Citation Indexes. Recently, ISI has corrected this error. Although ISI applies advanced data capturing and reformatting procedures, and thus is successful to a considerable extent in standardising the huge variety in institutional affiliations from the by-lines of millions of processed source articles, the final outcomes cannot be assumed to be accurate for all main organisations.

Directors of numerous main organisations or departments have issued instructions to all affiliated scholars as to how their institutions should be named in scholarly publications. For such organisations it is expected to be a fairly straightforward task to extract from the database the major part if not all of the papers published by scholars indicating the organisations' names in the by-line of their papers. But for organisations from which their affiliates do not show such a uniform behaviour, or for those with names that are in some way distorted in the reformatting process, it may be much more difficult if not impossible to obtain accurate publication counts. It is not *a priori* clear to which class a particular main organisation belongs.

Authors do not always give full information on their affiliations. Scientists from research institutes that operate under the umbrella of a parent research council give only the name of the institute in some cases, in other cases only the name of the parent organisation and sometimes both. A similar situation occurs for authors in research institutes of a national research council located in a university, a common phenomenon, for instance, in France and Italy. Bourke and Butler (1998) discussed several problems with ISI address data related to Australian institutions.

Background knowledge about the institutions is essential. For instance, an investigator collecting publications form the University of Frankfurt (Germany) using ISI's corporate address fields must be aware that this university is also named Johann Wolfgang Goethe Universität.

Hence, in numerous cases it is extremely difficult to capture all variations under which an institution's name may appear in addresses in scientific publications. The Leiden Centre for Science and Technology Studies (CWTS) has developed methods to unify or de-duplicate institution names (de Bruin and Moed, 1990). Table 14.1 shows the number of variants found in the ISI database for the major types of institutions, and the reduction rate achieved in the de-duplication process. Although the level of accuracy is sufficiently high to analyse structural or systemic aspects of national academic systems (e.g., Matia et al., 2005), it cannot be claimed that the de-duplication is free of error.

Table 14.1. Statistics on de-duplication process of main organisational names conducted at CWTS

Type of Institution	Total Variants	Total de-duplicated Entries	Reduction Rate
Company	27,992	13,231	53%
Hospital	24,256	8,981	63%
Research Inst	28,363	8,535	70%
University	54,242	10,562	81%

Apart from technical problems in measuring an institution's publication output using corporate address data, there are conceptional problems as well. It is not always clear how an organisation must be properly institutionally defined. The role of 'affiliated' institutes or umbrella/parent organisations is particularly problematic. For instance, in some countries 'academic' hospitals are a part of the parent university, whereas in other countries they are separate entities.

From numerous experiences made in research performance assessments of scientific institutions conducted during the past two decades, it must be concluded that bibliometric evaluations and assessments of individual research organisations tend to produce fiercely-debated, and sometimes controversial, outcomes that are politically highly sensitive, as the institutions' prestige is at stake and institutions – especially universities – become more and more competitive, particularly within the European context.

These experiences lead to the conclusion that an appropriate identification scheme of an organisation's publication output must involve detailed background knowledge provided, or at least thoroughly checked by, the organisations themselves. Verification by representatives of the organisations is indispensable for obtaining outcomes that are sufficiently accurate and hence can be properly used in policy analysis and the public domain.

The corporate *country* field in the ISI database is accurately de-duplicated. Therefore, one may be inclined to assume that it is a relatively simple task to extract a country's publication output from the database and analyse longitudinal patterns in publication counts, or conduct cross-comparisons among countries. But this section highlights an important technical issue that should be taken into account, and that has implications for analyses at lower aggregation levels as well, particularly at the level of institutions, or even individual scholars.

Not all source articles included in the ISI database contain data on the institutional affiliations of their authors. An analysis of normal articles, letters, notes and reviews published during the period 1993–2002 revealed that the percentage of articles included in the *Science Citation Index* (SCI) without address amounted to only 2.4 per cent. For articles included in the *Social Science Citation Index* (SSCI) but not in the SCI, this percentage was 14, whereas for articles included in the *Arts and Humanities Citation Index* (A&HCI) but not in the SCI or SSCI, is was found to be 49 per cent. If one analyses all types of source items including, for instance, editorials, meeting abstracts and book reviews as well, the percentage of items without address are even higher: 4 per cent in the SCI, 19 per cent in the SSCI and 56 per cent in the A&HCI. There are in principle two reasons why items do not have authors' institutional affiliations in the ISI database. The most important one is that the indexed documents simply do not contain any author addresses at all. A second, less important factor is that in some papers addresses are not included in the byline of the item, but at some other position in the text.

The conclusion is that, if one determines publication counts per country using merely the corporate country field in the ISI database, about half of the articles in the A&HCI and about 15 per cent of articles in SSCI will not be counted at all. A more detailed analysis per journal could reveal how these articles without address are distributed among the countries of origin of the publishing authors.

A conceptual problem is that paper counts from a country in the corporate address field do not always properly reflect the state of a national scholarly or science system. The institution from which the findings were presented in a paper can be assumed to be located in the country indicated in its geographical affiliation, but the link between it and the national scholarly system may be so weak, that its papers do not reflect the country's performance. This is particularly true for internationally funded institutions or facilities, for instance, in high energy physics and astronomy, such as CERN in Switzerland and astronomical technical facilities in South America.

14.3 Discipline and subfield delimitations

There is a huge literature on bibliometric methodologies that aim at identifying cognitive or social structures in scholarly research activities. Important methodologies are based on an analysis of cited references – bibliographic coupling or co-citation techniques – or on cognitive terms in titles, abstracts, or key word lists – co-word techniques – of individual articles. These methodologies deserve much more attention than can be given within the framework of this book. They provide tailor-made delimitations of scholarly and technological fields, often on a paper-by-paper basis, based upon co-citation analysis (e.g., Small, 1974; 1977; Small and Sweeney, 1985; Small et al., 1985; Schwechheimer and Winterhager, 2001); co-word analysis (e.g., Callon et al., 1983; Bhattacharya and Basu, 1998; Noyons et al., 1999; Lewison, 1999; Widhalm et al., 2001); combined co-citation and co-word analysis (e.g., Braam et al., 1991); and author co-citation analysis (White and Griffith, 1981; McCain, 1990; White and McCain, 1998). The reader is referred to Noyons (2004) for an overview.

A classification often applied in bibliometric analysis is that of *journal categories*, based on a grouping of journals into scholarly subfields. The number of journal categories is in the order of magnitude of 150. This classification is based partly on an analysis of citation patterns among journals, and partly upon the journal titles. ISI, CHI Research and other institutions such as CWTS have their own classification systems.

One of the major problems is the positioning of so-called multidisciplinary journals that cover a broad variety of subfields. Typical examples are the journals *Nature* and *Science*. Such journals basically do not fit into such a system, and are assigned to the category 'multidisciplinary'. Other journals cover an entire discipline rather than a subfield, such as *Physical Review Letters* or the *Journal of the American Chemical Society*. Such journals are assigned to a broad category termed 'physics general' or 'chemistry'. As a result, the journal category system contains categories representing distinct levels of aggregation.

In this book, a classification of journals into 15 disciplines is used, by aggregating ISI journal categories. It is presented in Table 14.2. *Clinical medicine* is the largest field in terms of number of source items published in 2002, with a share of 18.7 per cent, and *economics* the smallest, with 1.3 per cent of all papers. Although journal categories were primarily categorised according to their cognitive contents, an analysis of reference patterns in the papers covering them also played an important role. Journal categories that had similar cited reference characteristics were grouped, particularly those with similar percentages of references to papers published in ISI covered journals, denoted in Chapter 7 as overall ISI coverage.

An attempt was made to separate the *more clinically oriented biomedical specialties* from the more *basic biological sciences*, and to roughly discriminate in the latter between *biological sciences* primarily related to *humans* and those predominantly dealing with *animals and plants*. A group of journals dealing with *applied research in physics and chemistry* was taken as a separate field apart from the more basic oriented fields *physics & astronomy* and *chemistry*.

In *social sciences*, *psychology and psychiatry* constitute a separate field. Other social science journals primarily dealing which medical or health-related research were grouped into a field '*Other social sciences primarily related to medicine and health*', including public environment and occupational health, nursing, sport sciences, rehabilitation, substance abuse, family studies, geriatrics, health policy and several other journal categories. Economics constitutes a separate field as well. The field '*Other social sciences*' includes sociology, education, political sciences, anthropology, geography, internal relations and several smaller journal categories. The group 'Other' comprises the journal category 'multi-disciplinary'. *Humanities and arts* includes the field of law. Other major journal categories in this main field are literature, history, art, classics, language and linguistics, philosophy, archeology, poetry, dance, and music.

It should be noted that it is impossible to establish a strict separation of these domains of scholarly research, as many journals cover several domains rather than just one. However, a rough categorisation is feasible. When journal categories showed a substantial overlap in journals, they were combined. This is the case for instance with the journal categories in the main field labelled as *molecular biology & biochemistry* that covers both human, animal and plant-related molecular biology and biochemistry.

The overlap in papers among the main fields is much smaller than that among journal categories. Roughly speaking, about 20 per cent of the 2002 source items were assigned to more than one discipline. The largest overlaps exist between *engineering* and *applied physics & chemistry*, and between *clinical medicine* and *biological sciences primarily related to humans*.

Table 14.2. Classification of journal categories into 15 disciplines

Discipline/ Main field	Source items (%)	Important journal categories included (Non-exhaustive list)
Applied physics & chemistry	10.3	15 categories, incl. applied physics, materials science, optics, chemical engineering, mechanics, applied chemistry, acoustics, instruments & instrumentation
Biological sciences primarily related to animals and plants	6.6	16 categories incl. plant sciences, ecology, zoology, marine & freshwater biology, veterinary sciences, agriculture, food science, biology
Biological sciences primarily related to humans	10.3	12 more basic oriented categories primarily related to humans, incl. neurosciences, pharmacology, immunology, endocrinology, microbiology, virology, medicine, research
Chemistry	9.6	General, physical, organic, inorganic & nuclear, analytical and electro-chemistry, polymer science
Clinical medicine	18.7	34 predominantly clinical categories, including oncology, medicine general, surgery, cardiology & cardiovascular system, gastroenterology
Economics	1.4	Economics, management, business
Engineering	7.6	34 Engineering categories, incl. electrical eng, nuclear science and technol., mechanical eng, computer science
Geosciences	3.5	12 categories, incl. environmental sciences, geosciences, meteorology & atmospheric sciences, oceanography, geology, mineralogy
Humanities & arts	4.2	Law, literature, history, art, classics, language and linguistics, philosophy, archeology, poetry, dance, music
Mathematics	3.0	Mathematics, applied mathematics, statistics & probability, miscellaneous mathematics
Molecular biology & biochemistry	7.0	Biochemistry & molecular biology, cell biology, biophysics, biotechnology, developmental biology, biochemical research methods
Other social sciences primarily related to medicine & health	2.3	Public environment and occupational health, nursing, sport science, rehabilitation, substance abuse, family studies, geriatrics, health policy
Other social sciences	3.1	Sociology, education, political sciences, anthropology, geography, internal relations
Physics & astronomy	8.2	Atomic, molecular & chemical, condensed matter, nuclear, and mathematical physics, physics of particles and fields, and fluids.
Psychology & psychiatry	2.8	All categories related to psychology, psychiatry and behavioural sciences
Other	1.8	Category multidisciplinary

PART 2.5

THEORETICAL ASPECTS

Chapter 15

WHAT DO REFERENCES AND CITATIONS MEASURE?

15.1 Introduction

What do citations measure? Citations are manifestations of underlying processes that may be studied from various disciplinary perspectives. In order to understand what citations indicate, and to relate citation counts to concepts commonly used in evaluative bibliometrics such as 'research performance', 'scholarly quality', 'influence' or 'impact', insight is needed into the nature of such processes. Their theoretical understanding contributes to what is often denoted as a '*theory of citation*'.

This chapter presents a concise overview of the literature addressing this issue. It briefly discusses theoretical positions of a number of scholars who have contributed to a more profound understanding of citation-based indicators by quoting and briefly discussing some key passages from their works. An overview of these scholars and some of their key notions are presented in Table 15.1. One of the scholars included in this overview is Paul Wouters. Following his suggestion, what *references* and *citations* measure are treated as two distinct issues (Wouters, 2000).

In order to cognitively locate the various scholars, Section 15.2 briefly sketches five main disciplinary viewpoints from which citation based indicators are constructed, used, interpreted or theoretically founded: a *physical*, *sociological*, *psychological*, *historical* and an *information-* or *communication-scientific* viewpoint. Each disciplinary viewpoint embraces several distinct approaches or 'paradigms'. It should be noted that one scholar or study may adopt more than one viewpoint.

Table 15.1. Views on what is measured by references and citations

Author	*References conceived as*	*Citations measure*
Garfield, Salton	Descriptors of document content	
Garfield	Manifestations of scholarly information flows	Utility (quantity of formal information use)
Small	Elements in a symbol-making process	Highly cited items as concept symbols
Merton, Zuckerman	Registrations of intellectual property and peer recognition	Intellectual influence
Cole and Cole		Socially defined quality
Gilbert	Tools of persuasion	Authoritativeness
Cronin	The character and composition of reference lists reflect authors' personalities and professional milieux	It is unclear what citations measure; the interplay between institutional norms and personal considerations must be studied first
Martin and Irvine	References reflect both influence, social and political pressures, and awareness	Differences in citation rates among carefully selected matched groups (partially) indicate differences in actual influence
Zuckerman	Referencing motives and their consequences are analytically distinct	Citations are proxies of more direct measurements of intellectual influence
Cozzens	References are at the intersect of the reward, rhetorical and communication system but rhetorics comes first	Recognition, persuasiveness and awareness each generate a certain portion of variation in citation counts
White	Inter-textual relationships mainly reflect straightforward acknowledgement of related documents	Co-citation maps provide an aerial view and measure a historical consensus as to important authors and works
van Raan	References are partly particularistic but in large ensembles biases cancel out	The upper part of the distribution of a 'thermodynamic' ensemble of many citers measures 'top' research
Wouters	The reference is the product of the scientist	The citation is the product of the indexer. Validity of citations cannot be grounded merely in reference behaviour

15.2   Disciplinary approaches

Physical approaches

Derek de Solla Price, one of the founders of the 'science of science', is an outstanding representative of the physical approach to the quantitative study of scholarly activity and construction of indicators. He argued that the various available science indicators should be interrelated by simple laws, in order to gain a feeling for their phenomenological interpretation.

> Somewhat cautiously it may be suggested that we need a social scientific equivalent of the Newtonian masterstroke that took such vaguely used terms as force, work and energy, redefined them with simple equations [...] and brought order into previous meanderings (Price, 1980b, p. 1).

Recent studies adopting Price's approach are inspired by modern developments in the physics of non-linear phenomena rather than by Newton's classical, deterministic laws of terrestrial mechanics (e.g., Katz, 1999; van Raan, 2000; Amaral et al., 2001).

Gerald Holton, who had the same disciplinary background as Price, formulated a somewhat different perspective. In his contribution to the important book, *Towards a Metric of Science*, he argued:

> I propose that the term indicator is properly reserved for a measure that explicitly tests some assumption, hypothesis or theory; for mere data, these underlying assumptions, hypotheses or theories usually remain implicit. (Holton, 1978, p. 53). The indicators cannot be thought of given from 'above', or detached from the theoretical framework, or as unable to undergo changes in actual use. They should preferably be developed in response to and as aids in the solution of interesting questions and problems (ibid., p. 55).

Holton advocated plurality in theoretical development, allowing for a diversity of models and corresponding indicators.

> The absence of any explicit theory to guide the making and use of indicators may not be good; but the adoption of a single one is likely to be worse (ibid., p. 57).

But at the same time Holton suggests developing "theory invariant" concepts. One could argue that Price's notions show more affinity to experimental physics, and those of Holton to theoretical physics. Among the scholars discussed below, Anthony van Raan can be denoted as an exemplar of the physical approach in bibliometric research.

Sociological approaches

A sociological approach to scholarly performance investigates how a research community socially appraises the significance of some piece of work under study, by drawing inferences from how scholars act, what they state, what and how they cite in their publications. This approach therefore deals with scholars' perceptions and conceives both scholars' statements and their publication and referencing practices as *social acts*.

In sociological research, bibliometric analysis of the scholarly literature is considered as one of several possible research techniques. But research techniques are not theoretically neutral: in social sciences they can themselves be conceived as social acts (e.g., Mulkay, 1974). Their interpretation is based on an implied theory of publishing and citing. Moreover, the use of bibliometric techniques may also influence a study's outcomes in several ways.

Within the sociology of science, distinct perspectives were developed upon science as a social activity. As an illustration, one may compare the theoretical work of Robert K. Merton (e.g., Merton, 1968) with that of Michel Callon (Callon et al., 1986). Whereas Merton conceived of a scientist primarily as a disinterested seeker of scientific truth, Callon focused on the scientist as an entrepreneur, and conceived of the leader of a research department primarily as a director of a small or medium-sized knowledge production firm. Whereas Merton studied the 'internal' normative system within science and how it ensures the advancement of valid knowledge despite 'external' pressures, Callon's theoretical work aimed at analysing how science is embedded in and influenced by the society in which it is employed.

A micro-sociological perspective on scholarly activity focuses on the work-a-day life and its special circumstances, the personal motivations and strivings of individual scientists, and their interactions with colleagues and with policy makers. This micro-sociological perspective is reflected in the following passage:

> Another area of interest is the production of scientific papers. They are written in situations that are peopled by such significant others as administrators, professors, anticipated audiences, recalcitrant research assistants, typists, colleagues, husbands and wives. These situations refer to laboratories, promotions, salaries, research grants, equipment, computer time and mortgages. Thus, for example, any study which uses scientific papers as data should take cognisance of the situations in which they are written (Law and French, 1974).

Another sociological perspective upon references and citations was put forward by Leydesdorff, based upon Luhmann's system-analytical conception of social processes (e.g., Leydesdorff, 1998).

Among the authors discussed below, Stephen and Jonathan Cole and Harriet Zuckerman built upon the theoretical framework developed by Merton, whereas Nigel Gilbert further developed some of the notions found in the work of Callon. Blaise Cronin underlined the relevance of the micro-sociological approach.

Psychological approaches

These approaches focus on the psychology of referencing. Among the authors discussed below, it is Blaise Cronin who emphasised the potentialities of a psychological approach to the study of the citation or reference, particularly the relationship between cognitive style and individual's personality.

Typical examples of studies following this approach are those analysing citer motivations. These are often based on questionnaires sent out to scholars to obtain their scores on a predefined list of possible motives, and show a large variety of such motives. Good examples are studies on citer motivations undertaken by Brooks (e.g. Brooks, 1986).

Historical approaches

One type of historical studies focuses on the cognitive dimension of scholarly activity, and sketches the historical developments of scholarly ideas and their principal contributors. Typical examples of such studies using bibliometric techniques are those conducted by Cees le Pair and co-workers on nuclear magnetic resonance and the electron microscope and the contribution of Dutch scientists to the development in those fields (e.g., Chang, 1975; Bakker, 1977).

The work on historiography carried out by Eugene Garfield has generated a powerful tool to trace the development of scientific ideas using citation analysis (e.g., Garfield et al., 2003). Longitudinal analysis of the structure and development of research specialties can also be categorised under this type of historical studies, such as the work by Small (1977) and co-workers using co-citation analysis.

A second group of studies focuses on the social, economic and institutional conditions under which research activities were carried out, either at the level of individual scholars or research departments, or at that of the global science system as a whole. The studies by Derek de Solla Price

(Price, 1961; Price, 1963) are excellent examples of this second group of historical studies.

Information- and communication-scientific approaches

Borgman defined scholarly communication as follows:

By scholarly communication we mean the study of how scholars in any field (e.g., physical, biological, social, and behavioral sciences, humanities, technology use and disseminate information through formal and informal channels. The study of scholarly communication includes the growth of scholarly information, the relationships among research areas and disciplines, the information needs and uses of individual user groups, and the relationships among formal and informal methods of communication (Borgman, 1990).

Paul Wouters (1999) distinguished between two theoretical concepts of information. The first, attributed to Shannon, conceives information as a formal entity from which all meaning is purged. The second, defined by Bateson, focuses on meaning and defines information as "any difference which makes a difference". Wouters denotes this concept as "paradigmatic". In the study of scholarly communication, both theoretical information concepts are further developed. It must be noted that the information scientific approach borrows elements from physical or sociological approaches. For instance, the concept of information may be modelled analogously to the physical concept of entropy, and citation or author relationships may be used to reveal social structures.

Of the authors discussed below. Eugene Garfield's work on the analysis of the journal communication system using citation relations was based upon the formalised concept, whereas Henry Small's ideas about citations as "concept symbols" focused more upon the paradigmatic concept of information. Howard White takes an intermediary position, to the extent that he underlined both the utility of formal clusters, but at the same time the relevance of "narratives" that tell a cluster's story. Finally, Ben Martin and John Irvine, Blaise Cronin, Susan Cozzens, and Paul Wouters employed a more general perspective exceeding that of a single disciplinary approach or paradigm.

15.3   Views of scholars

Eugene Garfield

Garfield's notion is that references cited in a document can be viewed as subject terms of that document. The cited work is symbolic of specific content, such as a method, a particular concept, or a hypothesis. The citing document has a substantive form of subject relevance to the ideas symbolised by the cited item (Garfield, 1964).

In his view, reference lists are regulated by the standards of good science exposition and the practice viewing a good bibliography as a sign of scholarship. This makes them more appropriate for indexing purposes than, for instance, document titles. Salton (1963), too conceived references as indicators of document content that can be used as document descriptors. Citation indexing, and particularly the ISI Citation Indexes as bibliographical search tools are founded in these notions.

The notion of references as subject terms or descriptors primarily points towards properties of the citing document. But as bibliographies are regulated by standards of good exposition and scholarship, they express ways of thinking about the cited documents – the descriptors themselves – as well. Thus, while from the point of view of the citing document a cited reference is an indicator of document content, it is from the point of view of the cited document an expression of its importance or utility.

> Since authors refer to previous material to support, illustrate, or elaborate on a particular point, the act of citing is an expression of the importance of the material. The total number of such expressions is about the most objective measure there is of the material's importance to current research. The number of times all the material in a given journal has been cited is an equally objective and enlightening measure of the quality of the journal as a medium for communicating research results (Garfield, 1979, p. 24).

The latter statements refer explicitly to the use of Citation Indexes in the identification of important documents, and in the study of the structure of the scholarly communication system, analysing relationships among journals and identifying the most important or 'core' journals in it. This type of use relates to the assessment of 'utility', 'impact' or 'influence' of documents, authors or communication sources, based on the ways in which – and particularly the frequency at which – they are subsequently cited.

Henry Small

Henry Small further developed Garfield's notion of references as subject symbols und thus contributed to the theoretical basis of the use of citation indexing in information retrieval. He focused on the question of what kinds of "subjects" are indicated, especially by references to very highly cited documents.

> In the tradition of scholarship, the references are the 'sources' which the author draws upon to give further meaning to his text. Reversing this view, as I am

suggesting here, the author is imparting meaning to his 'sources' by citing them. [...] Referencing viewed in this way is a labeling process. The language pointed to by the footnote number labels or characterises the document cited - or, in other words, constitutes the author's interpretation of the cited work. In citing a document an author is creating its meaning, and this, I will argue, is a process of symbol making (Small, 1978, p. 328).

A cited document stands for – is a symbol of – a concept. Concepts include experimental findings, methodologies, types of data, metaphysical notions, theoretical statements or equations. Small argued that most references given by an author are his or her "own private symbols". But other cited documents have a significant content that is shared by a community of scientists. Such documents tend to be frequently cited and are termed as "concept symbols".

Small's hypothesis is that "a scientist carries with him a repertoire of such collective concepts and their corresponding document symbols". His empirical work on testing such a hypothesis analysed the passages in research articles' full texts citing a particular 'highly cited' document, and examined the extent to which its symbolic content was actually shared among citing authors (Small, 1978).

Robert K. Merton

Robert K. Merton viewed publication and reference behaviour of scholarly authors within a wider framework of a set of general norms in scholarly activity, that in their turn are related to the scientific or scholarly method and its ultimate goal, the advancement of valid scholarly knowledge. Scholars do strive for personal fame and recognition. But the scholarly system, particularly the system of open publication, is organised in such a way that its institutional goal – augmenting scholarly knowledge – and the personal rewards are tied together.

> Like other institutions also, science has its system of allocating rewards for performance of roles. These rewards are largely honorific, since even today, the pursuit of knowledge is culturally defined as being primarily a disinterested search for truth, and only secondary a means of earning a livelihood (Merton, 1957, p. 659).

The principal way for a scholar to be rewarded for his contribution to the advancement of knowledge is through recognition by peers. In order to receive such an award, scholars publish their findings openly, so that these can be used and acknowledged by their colleagues. At the same time, they have the obligation of acknowledging the sources containing the knowledge claims they have built upon in their own works. The latter obligation is often summarised as 'to give credit were credit is due'. Scholars have no choice: one's private property is established by giving it away, and in order to receive peer recognition, they must provide it to others.

> The reference serves both instrumental and symbolic functions in the transmission and enlargement of knowledge. Instrumentally, it tells us of work we may not have known before, some of which may hold further interest for us; symbolically, it registers in the enduring archives the intellectual property of the acknowledged source by providing a pellet of peer recognition of the knowledge claim, accepted or expressly rejected, that was made in that source (Merton, 1996, pp. 334–335).

The notion of citations as indicators of influence and as tools to assess the value of scholarly contributions emerges explicitly from the following statement:

> For if one's work is not being noticed and used by others in the system of science, doubts of its value are apt to rise (Merton, 1977, pp. 54–55).

It was not Merton, however, who further developed this type of use of references or citations, but rather several of his students, including Stephen and Jonathon Cole and Harriet Zuckerman, the work of whom is briefly discussed below.

Jonathan Cole and Stephen Cole

Jonathan and Stephen Cole further developed citation analysis as a research tool in sociological research. They assumed that citations can be used as an indicator of influence, or of what they termed "socially defined quality". In methodological terms, citation measures are conceived as indicators or operationalisations of an abstract, theoretical concept, 'research quality', and their validity can be empirically tested by correlating them to other, more direct measures of the concept, including quality judgements expressed by peers (Cole and Cole, 1967; 1971).

They build upon the theoretical work of Merton, particularly on the notion of intellectual property and the symbolic function of references sketched above. This work provided a theoretical foundation for exploring the use of citation analysis as a research tool.

Their main objective was to develop a research tool that could be used in sociological research to test hypotheses related to social stratification and related issues. They observed in several research fields positive correlations between citation rates of individual papers or authors and peer judgements, and concluded that citation analysis was in principle useful for the type of research they had in mind.

The use of citations as a sociological research tool should be distinguished from their application in an evaluative context for the assessment of research performance of individuals or groups. The former type of use eventually aims at testing some kind of hypothesis or revealing a structure. The latter may lead to statements on the performance of particular, designated individual scientists in the research system.

> Citations are a very good measure of the quality of scientific work for use in sociological studies of science; but because the measure is far from perfect it would be an error to reify it and use it to make individual decisions. [...] In sociological studies our goal is not to examine individuals but to examine the relationships among variables (Cole, 1989, p. 11).

The sociological perspective developed by Merton and followers is often denoted as the 'normative' view or paradigm (e.g., Cronin, 1984). Reference behaviour is essentially norm-regulated. It does not follow that all scholars at all times strictly conform to those norms, rather it states that that there is a general notion among practitioners that these norms are consequential upon the advancement of science and scholarship itself. References give credit where credit is due. They acknowledge the community's intellectual debts to the discoverer.

Nigel Gilbert

A second sociological perspective can be denoted as the social construction of references. This constructive view takes the position that scientists cite to advance their interests, defend their claims against attack, convince others, and thus gain a dominant position in their scientific community. For instance, Nigel Gilbert introduced the idea that referencing is an aid to persuasion. In order to support their research findings, authors will tend to cite documents which they assume their audience will regard as "authoritative".

> The participants in a mature field will share a belief that some published work is important and correct, some other work is trivial, perhaps some is erroneous, and much is irrelevant to their current interests. Hence, authors preparing papers will tend to cite the 'important and correct' papers, may cite 'erroneous' papers in order to challenge them and will avoid citing the 'trivial' and 'irrelevant' ones (Gilbert, 1977, p. 116).

In an explicit confrontation with the normative view, Gilbert stated:

> One can therefore argue that the scientific 'norm' that one should cite the research on which one's work depends, may not be a product of a pervasive concern to acknowledge 'property rights' but rather may arise from scientists' interest in persuading their colleagues by using all the resources available to

them, including those respected papers which can be cited to bolster their own arguments (ibid.).

From this perspective, citations measure authoritativeness of a paper, or, more generally, its rhetorical strength, defined as the extent to which a cited paper fits into the rhetoric of the citing author.

Blaise Cronin

In his monograph '*The Citation Process*' (1984), Blaise Cronin argued that, in order to obtain a deeper insight into the citation process, one must move into the *psychology* of science, and analyse the interplay between "institutional norms and personal considerations".

> Citation needs to be thought of as a process. The outcomes of this process (on a recurring basis) are citations attached to scholarly papers. The character and composition of the lists reflect authors' personalities and professional milieux. The elements in the chemistry of citation are almost infinite, and it is this fact which necessitates particularistic accounts of citation (Cronin, 1984, p. 83).

He rejected the 'Mertonian' notion that citation is governed by "adherence to a specific and universally recognised set of norms", but at the same time, the citation process is in his view "not characterised by randomness and inconsistency". He distinguished between an "internalistic" and an "externalistic" approach to citation analysis. The former focuses on quantities and frequency distributions, whereas the latter concentrates on the contexts within which, and the processes along which, authors compile their reference lists. In order to obtain a deeper understanding of what citations measure, these two approaches need to be combined.

Referring to a micro-sociological viewpoint as expressed by Law and French quoted in the previous section, he advocated an "externalistic" approach as follows:

> Citation is not something which happens in a void, and citations are not separable from the contexts and conditions of their generation. [...] Future studies should therefore concentrate on the content of citations, and the conditions of their creation and application (ibid., p. 86).

If references are rhetorical devices to persuade, and should be interpreted in the social context in which they were made, with all its particularities and special instances, how could one possibly relate citations to research performance? How should an attempt to theoretically ground the notion of citations as indicators of impact, significance or influence of a cited work incorporate – or at least account for – the insights obtained from the micro-sociological studies socially or psychologically constructing the reference?

Below the notions are discussed of seven authors who reflected upon this question: Martin and Irvine (1983), Cozzens (1989), Zuckerman (1987), White (1990), van Raan (1998) and Wouters (1999).

Ben Martin and John Irvine

Ben Martin and John Irvine made a distinction between research quality, importance and impact of a scientific publication. Quality is conceived as a property of the publication and the research described in it. Importance refers to the potential influence of a piece of research upon surrounding research activities, if there were "perfect communication" in science. Impact is defined as actual influence.

Citation rates constitute an indicator of impact of a piece of work, rather than of its importance or quality. Thus, they essentially adopted the notions explored by Cole and Cole of citations as "imperfect" measures of influence. But they are aware of the possible effects of other, "disturbing" factors upon citation rates, that partly relate to what Cronin terms "personal considerations" or "particularistic" use of references.

> The citation rate is a partial indicator of the impact of a scientific publication: that is, a variable determined partly by (a) the impact on the advance of scientific knowledge, but also influenced by (b) other factors, including various social and political pressures such as the communication practices [...], the emphasis on the numbers of citations for obtaining promotion, tenure or grants, and the existing visibility of authors, their previous work, and their employing institution (Martin and Irvine, 1983, p. 70).

They underlined that it cannot *a priori* be assumed that the effect of the "other", mainly political and social, factors upon citation rates is small compared to that of the quality or importance of an evaluated piece of work, nor that the former comprise a set of random influences that cancel out when data samples are sufficiently large.

In their view, systematic biases may play a significant role. A proper way of using and interpreting citation rates is by carefully selecting matched groups, thus comparing "like with like", and by calculating several performance indicators rather than a single one, and analysing the extent to which the outcomes converge.

Susan Cozzens

Susan Cozzens distinguished between a reward system and a rhetorical system in science. The first is captured by the work of Merton and embodies a citation etiquette, which stipulates that when a new published idea is used, its progenitor should be explicitly cited. Following Gilbert and others, the latter is ruled by the strategic use of references as weapons to defend knowledge claims and persuade colleagues of their validity.

She claimed that "a citation is first and foremost a portion of a power seeking text" (Cozzens, 1989). In other words, the rhetorical system is the dominant one. The reward system and its citation etiquette constitute only a set of secondary criteria in selecting references. Other important elements from this system are direct praise from colleagues, being promoted, and receiving grants and awards.

> [...] it is clear that the primary function of a document is to argue a knowledge claim persuasively and that the art of writing scientific papers consists in marshalling the available rhetorical resources – conceptual and honorific – to achieve that goal (Cozzens, 1989, p. 445).

Cozzens hypothesised that the variation in citation counts can be divided into a portion generated by the reward system and a portion generated by the rhetorical system. In her view, bibliometric indicators aimed at measuring the reward system should be constructed in such a way that "all measurable effects of rhetoric and communication have been taken into account".

Harriet Zuckerman

In a reply to Gilbert's notion of references as aids to persuade, Harriet Zuckerman defended the position of citations as measures of intellectual influence in the following manner. She argued that, even if the well-known work of a famous scientist is cited in order to persuade, such a citation might reflect cognitive influence. She emphasised that motives – of citing authors – and their consequences – revealing influence – are analytically distinct.

If one assumes, as Gilbert did, that authors tend to cite important or authoritative papers in order to be persuasive, what is it that makes such cited works important or authoritative?

> Presumably, these authoritative sources have been assessed by the pertinent collectivity of peers having made sound and consequential contributions. As Gilbert himself observes, it is the papers seen as "important and correct" which are "selected because the author hopes that the referenced papers will be regarded as authoritative by the intended audience". In short, it is peer recognition of the cognitive worth of the sources grown influential, initially reflected in high rates of citation, that makes them authoritative (Zuckerman, 1987, p. 334)

Following Cole and Cole, she claimed that citations can be used as *proxies* for other, direct assessments of intellectual influence, such as peer judgements and honorific awards.

Howard White

Howard White made a distinction between two groups of analysts following distinct approaches to the study of references and citations. The first approach he denoted as "bibliographical", and it focuses on particular instances and individual peculiarities or "vagaries". The second looks for patterns in highly aggregated data, which exist at a high degree of abstraction.

> Because such groups work at such different levels of reality, the rift between them cannot really be closed. It is as if each were studying a town but could do so in only one way: either by living among its people or by flying over it. The "ground level" and the "aerial level" views lead to descriptions of reality that at some point become incommensurable (White, 1990, p. 91).

White emphasised the potentialities of analysing large data files.

> When one sees that scores, hundreds, and even thousands of citations have accrued to a work, an author, a set of authors, it is […] difficult not to believe that individual vagaries of citing behavior cancel each other out, corrected by the sheer numbers of persons citing. […] Why not believe that there is a norm in citing – straightforward acknowledgement of related documents – and that the great majority of citations conform to it? (ibid.).

He argued that co-citation maps or citation analyses in general constitute a tool for doing intellectual history. In his view, they represent "the history of the consensus as to important authors or work". Such a consensus is not explicit, in the sense that practitioners in a field have knowingly given their assent, but rather an implicit one, which he qualified as a "social construct like 'a climate of opinion' or a 'market', and perhaps all the more powerful than that" (ibid., p. 106).

According to White, the co-citation maps are "objective" in the sense that they are based on algorithms working on large data files, that they are replicable, and that their perspective is "broader than can be achieved by any individual scientist". But he emphasised that "they do not claim that their methods render human judgement unnecessary or vitiate the traditional "subjective" methods of interviewing people and reading primary documents" (ibid., p. 98).

Anthony van Raan

Anthony van Raan argued that an analysis of the referencing behaviour of authors is not the most appropriate way to investigate the validity of citation analysis.

It is as if a physicist would strive for creating a framework of thermodynamics by making a 'theory' on the behaviour of individual molecules (van Raan, 1998, p. 136).

Van Raan argued that the major number of cited papers in a reference list are typically "modal" papers, receiving few citations, whereas a small fraction is highly cited. The analysis of citing behaviour thus mostly deals with large numbers of citations to modal papers, whereas in citation analysis of research performance the relatively few highly cited papers are the most significant ones.

He proposed a "thermodynamic" theory of citing, which does not focus on individual citers, but rather on "ensembles" of many citers, applying a statistical approach in terms of distribution functions of "behavioural characteristics" of citing authors.

> Pressure, volume and temperature are the main parameters of the thermodynamic ensemble of very many molecules. Likewise, citation analysis is at the 'thermodynamic side': it concerns an ensemble of many citers. Certainly, the individual characteristics of the citers are interesting, but the distribution functions of these characteristics are the make-up of that part of the world which is relevant to bibliometric analysis (ibid.).

Reference behaviour may to a certain extent be particularistic and therefore lead to "citation biases". However, according to van Raan "there is no sound evidence that citation biases are the predominant character of reference lists in scientific papers, and that less predominant citation-biases do not cancel each other out" (ibid., p. 135).

Paul Wouters

Wouters distinguished between two types of science representations built upon two distinct theoretical concepts of information. The first representation, attributed to Shannon, is denoted as "formalised", and is based on the concept of information as a formal entity from which all meaning is purged. The second is a paradigmatic representation, focusing on meaning and embracing a concept of information defined by Bateson as "any difference which makes a difference".

In his view, science indicators can be conceived as a result of statistical operations upon "meaningless" symbols (e.g., citations), and thus constitute a formalised science representation that initially neglects meaning. In order to be useful, allocation of meaning to the indicators is necessary, but this can be "postponed". Allocation of meaning occurs in "indicator theories" developed in various, often competing, "paradigmatic science representations".

A theoretical foundation of science indicators – or scientometrics in general – is provided by what Wouters terms a "reflexive indicator theory". It is reflexive to the extent that it is not merely a theory about indicators, but also a theory about indicator theories.

> Because of the emergence of the formalized representations, stimulated by the creation of the SCI, multiple relations have been created between the formalized and the paradigmatic representations of science (and technology). Every existing science or technology indicator theory is the embodiment of one possible type of relation within the domain of all possible relationships. Encompassing all this is not a sociological theory, but simply this proposal: to recognize the two different domains, to position each indicator theory accordingly, and to establish their interrelations (Wouters, 1999, pp. 212–213).

Wouters further contributed to the development of the reflexive indicator theory by underlining the relevance in the debate on citation theories of the distinction between references and citations and their corresponding viewpoints: reference behaviour from the perspective of the citing documents and their authors on the one hand, and citation counts from that of cited documents on the other.

> The citation as used in scientometric analysis and science and technology indicators is not identical to the reference produced at the scientist's desk. [...] The citation is the product of the citation indexer, not of the scientist (ibid., p. 4).

In Wouters' view, the reference belongs to the citing text. But in a Citation Index, cited references are no longer organised according to the documents in which they are contained, but rather according to the documents they point to. In Wouters' words, "they become attributes of the cited in stead of the original, citing text". This has important consequences for the development of a more profound insight into what citations measure.

> Because of the difference between the reference and the citation, the legitimation of citation analysis should be analytically distinguished from the study of citing behavior in science (ibid., p. 212). The results of research into citing behaviour of scientists may still be relevant but cannot, contrary to received wisdom in scientometrics and science studies, be regarded as sufficient to explain the role and function of the citation (ibid., p. 12).

Wouters claimed that, in the quest for an encompassing citation theory, the sociological studies of reference behaviour are a "dead end". These studies contribute to a reference theory rather than a citation theory.

Chapter 16

TOWARDS A THEORY OF CITATION: SOME BUILDING BLOCKS

16.1   Introduction

It is essential that methodologies and indicators applied in policy studies of scholarly activity and performance are properly tested and theoretically founded. Obviously, analysts of scholarly performance should not employ methodological practices that they would condemn as inadequate in the work of those scholars under evaluation (e.g., Hull, 1998).

In Section 15.2 it was argued that quantitative science and technology studies is a multi-disciplinary field, and that even within a discipline fundamentally distinct paradigms were developed. If quantitative science studies is a multi-disciplinary research field, the quest for a comprehensive theory of citation can be conceived as the fairly difficult task to transform a multi-disciplinary activity into an interdisciplinary one. Participants in the 'theory of citation' debate do not always properly recognise this fundamental problem. The existence of distinct paradigms within a single discipline makes this even more difficult.

The development of science indicators in a scholarly, multi-disciplinary context does not necessarily result in a broad consensus among its practitioners upon what such indicators reflect and how they are properly used in a policy context. Generally, the social sciences often embrace schools of thought, each with its own fundamental assumptions and principles. This is particularly true in the sociology of science.

This condition has important consequences for the debate on 'citation theories' aimed at providing a framework for interpretation of citation-based indicators. Not infrequently, the quest for a citation theory seems to assume that it would be feasible to develop one 'single' – comprehensive or 'grand' – theoretical framework shared by all practitioners, thus at the same time settling all disputes among the various schools. But it is invalid to assume that a theoretical foundation is sound only when there is a strict consensus among practitioners involved, and that, whenever various, competing theoretical positions exist, it follows that there is no theoretical foundation at all.

Wouters' proposal of a reflexive indicator theory is fruitful, as it does *not* assume the primacy of any existing citation theory, but rather creates a theoretical openness by proposing to further develop a framework in which each approach eventually finds its proper place. Below a number of observations and comments follow that can be conceived as contributions to Wouters' project of a reflexive indicator theory. Although they aim at contributing to a deeper understanding of referencing practices and what citations measure, they do not claim to develop a full, encompassing theory. They focus upon the validity citation analysis in research evaluation, i.e. the extent to which citation counts indicate aspects such as 'importance' or 'influence' of scientific achievements.

As a background, *Section 16.2* presents basic quantitative characteristics of reference lists in research articles. It is argued that reference lists have a limited length and that authors have to be selective in including cited documents. It is shown that reference lists are unique in the sense that very few papers have identical lists, but that at the same time they contain more commonly used cited references. Hence, there is a large variability in citation counts among individual papers, and the distribution of citations amongst papers in any field is skewed. The crucial issue at stake is which factors account for this skewness, and how these are related to research performance.

Section 16.3 introduces a distinction between a 'citation analytical' and a citation*ist*', and between a constructive and a constructiv*ist* viewpoint of what citations measure. It is argued that both a citation analytical and a constructive viewpoint are valuable approaches. However, a citation*ist* and constructiv*ist* viewpoint represent extreme positions that tend to have a negative influence upon the quest for a scholarly foundation of the use of citation analysis in research evaluation.

Section 16.4 presents a critical discussion of the views of the various scholars outlined in Chapter 15. It is concluded that citation analysis applied in an evaluative context does not aim at capturing motives of individuals, but rather their consequences at an aggregate level. It embodies a fundamental shift in perspective from that of the psychology of individual citers towards what scientists jointly express sociologically in their referencing behaviour about the structures and performances of scholarly activity. On the other hand, it is emphasised that using large data samples does not necessarily rule out all sorts of biases.

Section 16.5 broadens the viewpoint often adopted in library and information science of research articles as separate 'entities', by incorporating relevant notions from a sociological perspective. It conceives papers as elements from coherent publication ensembles of research groups carrying out a research programme. It is hypothesised that citing authors acknowledging a research group's work do not distribute their citations evenly among all papers emerging from its programme, but rather cite particular papers that have become symbols or 'flags' of such a programme. This tendency accounts for a part of the skewness observed in citation distributions of individual papers. But on the whole, some groups or programmes are more frequently cited than others.

In order to further develop a theoretical perspective upon reference behaviour – and also the hypothesis of the existence of 'flag' papers mentioned above – a crucial challenge is to account for the increasing importance of reference lists as content descriptors in the scholarly information system, and for the increasing role of citations in research evaluation practices. *Section 16.6* proposes conceiving a reference list as a *distinct* part of a research paper with proper functions related to the use of references bibliographically in citation indexing, and bibliometrically in research evaluation in the broadest sense.

It is hypothesised that citing authors tend to ensure that important research groups and their programmes are represented in the reference lists of their papers. Including works in a reference list can still be interpreted in terms of cognitive influence, but its expression in the citing text may be vague or implicit.

Chapter 9 underlined differences in referencing practices of authors from science fields (including the natural and life sciences) on the one hand, and those from the social sciences, and particularly the humanities, on the other. The reflections presented in this chapter primarily relate to science, or, more generally, to subfields with a fairly quantitative substantive content and strongly developed international social and communication networks. The extent to which the various observations made below are also valid for other domains of scholarship is an issue that needs further study.

16.2   Reference lists are selective and contain both unique and more commonly used cited references

Reference lists have a *limited length*. The average length of references varies among disciplines and type of source paper, but it is plausible to assume that authors must be selective when they compile their reference lists. A reference list should not be viewed as a complete list of influences exercised upon the work described in the citing paper. This notion can also be found in the work of Small (1987), Zuckerman (1987) and van Raan (1998).

Several journals actually specify an indicative or a maximum number of references. A cited work may generate influence through other papers citing that work. Authors may therefore refer to some of the papers citing that particular work rather than explicitly referring to the work itself. Thus, intermediary publications may serve as "cognitive conduits" (Zuckerman, 1987). Other works may be generally conceived as so crucial and firmly incorporated into the current state of a field that authors do not feel the need to cite them explicitly This phenomenon is termed by Zuckerman "obliteration by incorporation".

A reference list is generally *unique*, in the sense that hardly any papers with references have identical lists. From an analysis of source papers included in the 2001 SCI, it emerges that almost 91 per cent contain at least one reference that is cited in the particular source paper *only*. Evidently, this percentage increases with increasing length of reference lists. In fact, for source papers with 20 references, being the mode of the distribution of number of references among source papers, 94 per cent of source papers contain at least one unique reference, and for papers with 40 references this rises to 96 per cent.

The 'particularistic' aspect of referencing highlighted by Cronin is thus clearly reflected in citing authors' reference lists. The unique references relate to sources that, in the year that they are cited, do not have a citation impact upon other papers, but that may nevertheless constitute an important basis of the work described in the citing paper.

A reference list thus contains a certain fraction of unique references, but at the same time there is also a considerable amount of *similarity among reference lists*. A reference list normally contains a portion of references to documents that are cited in other reference lists as well. This is precisely the profile that one would expect to find in papers making original contributions to a common cause, the advancement of scientific knowledge.

In the total collection of 2001 SCI source papers, the 10 per cent most frequently cited papers account for 33 per cent of all citations. The latter percentage varies across research discipline, and is 26 per cent in engineering and 39 per cent in physics & astronomy (Moed and Garfield, 2004). It was found that 93 per cent of all source papers in a year contain at least one reference to a document included among the ten per cent most frequently cited items in that year. For source papers with 20 and 40 references, this percentage is 98.4 and 99.7 per cent, respectively. Hence, there is a large variability in citation counts among individual papers, and the distribution of citations amongst papers in any field is skewed. Which factors account for this skewness, and how are these related to research performance?

16.3 Extreme positions are not useful in the debate on citation theories

It is useful to make a distinction between a social constructive and a constructiv*ist* view on referencing behaviour, and between a citation analytical versus a citation*ist* viewpoint. These distinctions are crucial in any attempt to relate the various existing indicator theories with one another. A social constructive view of referencing behaviour analyses the social conditions and interactions involved in the publication process. It does not negate that a cited paper has a reality of its own, or an identity that also exists outside the world of the citing author, but its primary interest lies in analysing how it may be influenced by the social environment in which it is produced.

A constructiv*ist* view denies such a proper identity, and claims that a cited paper is *merely* what the citing author makes of it. In other words, it assumes that a constructive approach is the only one valid. Inasmuch as many authors cite the same paper, the citations are merely an aggregate of a wide variety of individual motives and special circumstances. There is essentially *no* aspect that the citations have in common, because motives and circumstances producing them were different, and therefore there is no rationale for counting them, and attempting to understand what properties of the cited paper are reflected in the counts.

A second relevant distinction is that of a citation-analytical and a citation*ist* approach. The first assumes that – under certain conditions – citation analysis may provide valid indications of the significance of a document. Such indications may be denoted as objective in the sense that they reflect properties of the cited document itself, and that they are replicable, and based on the practices and perceptions of large numbers of (citing) scientists rather than on those of a single individual scientist.

A citation*ist* view holds that citations are the only valid measures of research quality, and that it is merely their quantitative character and the magnitude of the data files from which they are drawn that makes them objective, even to the extent that no further theoretical foundation is needed to justify their application. According to this view, it would be extremely difficult if not impossible to provide such a foundation, as any potential empirical evidence would tend to be 'subjective' and can therefore hardly have implications for the status of the objective tool. Perhaps the most extreme position is expressed in the circular argument that 'citations measure quality because quality is what citations measure'.

The author of this book does acknowledge the potential usefulness of citation based indicators and of the social constructive approach, but he rejects both a constructiv*ist* and a citation*ist* viewpoint. Although none of the authors discussed in Chapter 15 adopts such an extreme, constructiv*ist* or citation*ist* viewpoint in the debate on what citations measure, positions of scholars sometimes tend to be criticised *as if* they are extreme in the sense outlined above, and this tendency may hamper theoretical progress.

The extreme theoretical positions have their correlates in the ways citation analysis can be applied in research evaluation and policy. A citation*ist* view would justify if not stimulate a rigid, formulaic use of bibliometric indicators as if these are the only valid measures of research performance, whereas a constructiv*ist* view would reject them by qualifying them as totally irrelevant constructs.

16.4   Comments on the views of scholars discussed in Chapter 15

The micro-sociological school analyses, from the point of view of an individual author, how particular motives or circumstances influence or regulate the selection of cited references. However, it often seems to disregard what the citing authors' selection of references expresses as regards the way they conceive the outside world, particularly the research front at which they operate. Scientists do not *merely* cite papers because the cited contents fit into the logical structure of an argument, but *also* because the cited paper or its authors have, in their perception, earned a certain status during the past and can substantiate or add credibility to statements or claims made in a paper. A cited paper can be a strong weapon in persuading colleagues only if it has a certain significance.

The relevance of taking into account what citing authors express as regards the 'outside world', can be further underlined by confronting Wouters' claim that "the citation is the product of the indexer" with the notion of concept symbols developed by Small. The latter focused on what is *common* in reference practices. He combined reference and citation analysis rather than separating them. Although a highly cited reference is embedded in a number of different citing texts, these texts have some element in common. They use the reference in a similar way. The reference has an 'identity' of its own, and is not *merely* a construct of the citing authors, even if it appears to be a split identity, in the sense that different networks of researchers may establish distinct symbolic applications of a particular cited work (Cozzens, 1982). In this sense, the citation is not *merely* a product of the citation indexer as Wouters seems to suggest, but *also* of the scientist. Conformity in reference patterns provides a basis for aggregating articles containing the same reference, and hence for counting – or more generally, analysing – citations to a particular document.

The distinction made by Zuckerman between *motives* and *consequences* of referencing behaviour is particularly useful in this context. The author of this book agrees with Zuckerman's reply to Gilbert that, even if a citing author intends to persuade, the reference may express intellectual influence. Authoritative papers tend to be authoritative because of their influence upon practitioners in a field, reflected in their high citation rates.

Cozzens suggested that the reward, rhetoric and communication system each attribute a certain portion to the variance in citation counts, and that, in order to use citations as measures of reward, these portions should be separated from one another. But although some rhetoric or communication factors can thus be accounted for – for instance in so-called 'normalised' citation indicators discussed in Chapters 4 and 5 of this book – it is questionable whether the reward and the rhetoric system can be fully separated, since citations reflect both aspects at the same time. It is a matter of distinct theoretical perspectives, each with its own validity, rather than a matter of separate factors in a variance analysis. Leydesdorff and Amsterdamska (1990) made a similar argument, by underlining the "inherently multidimensional character of citation".

Cronin argued that one should concentrate on the 'personal', 'motivational' content of citations, and on micro-sociological conditions of their creation and application. Leydesdorff and Amsterdamska (1990) rightly argued that analysing scientists' motives for citing through interviews and questionnaires on the one hand, and studying the role of the cited reference in the argumentation structure in the citing text on the other, represent two analytically distinct levels of analysis. Their empirical research revealed that motives or perceptions of citing authors do not directly correspond to the rhetorical function of cited documents in the citing text. This outcome underlines once more the relevance of the distinction between citing authors' motives and their consequences referred to above.

White's idea of co-citation maps as aerial views measuring a historical consensus as to important authors and works is based on the notion of references as "acknowledgements", and thus adopts the 'normative' view on referencing behaviour. He assumed that in the analysis of large data files, individual "vagaries" in referencing behaviour cancel out.

However, enlargement of data samples tends to neutralise random errors, but not necessarily systematic errors or biases. Following White's metaphor on the aerial view, one may ask whether the methodology generating a proper *aerial* view of a town also provides sufficiently detailed and valid information to describe and 'evaluate' an *individual* living in the town. This issue is particularly relevant in the use of citation indicators in research evaluation of individual entities such as authors, research groups or institutions.

Regarding van Raan's "thermodynamic" model describing large ensembles of citers analogously to ensembles of molecules, it must be noted that according to the thermodynamic model, molecules obey the laws of mechanics. One may therefore ask what the 'general laws' are that underlie reference behaviour of authors. Van Raan apparently assumes that references essentially reflect influences of the cited works upon the citing paper, regardless of whether the referenced works are "modal" or not.

The author of this book agrees with Zuckerman that, on the one hand, the presence of error does not preclude the possibility of precise measurement and that the net effect of certain sorts of error can be measured, but that on the other hand the crucial issue is whether errors are randomly distributed among all subgroups of scientists, or whether they systematically affect certain subgroups (Zuckerman, 1987, p. 331).

Thus, it cannot *a priori* be assumed that any deviations of the norm cancel out when data samples are sufficiently large. Martin and Irvine clearly expressed this insight in their methodological work. Their method of multiple converging partial indicators involves a quest for biases in any of the indicators used, but they also noted that convergence itself does not guarantee that the outcome is free of bias (Martin and Irvine, 1983, p. 87).

To the extent that the micro-sociological approach adopts a constructiv*ist* viewpoint, the author of this book agrees with Wouters' claim that in the quest for an encompassing citation theory, the micro-sociological studies of reference behaviour are a "dead end". However, he would not agree with the claim that studies constructing the reference merely contribute to a reference theory and not to a citation theory. Reference and citation theories, although analytically distinct, should not be separated from one another. A satisfactory theory of citation should be grounded in a notion of what scientists tend to express in their referencing practices. In the next two sections, two notions are described that could be conceived as building blocks in such a theory.

16.5   Research articles are elements of publication ensembles of research groups carrying out a research programme

One source of variation or skewness in the distribution of citations among cited papers emerges from the notion that research articles should be conceived as elements of a publication ensemble of a collection of scientists who are working in a particular institutional environment – a research group

– and who carry out a scientific or technological goal or mission – a research programme.

An academic research group normally consists of research students working on their PhD thesis, supervised by senior scientists or by post-doctoral students. Normally there is one group leader. Research groups may have a more *permanent* character and consist of scientists working together for a period of years. But they may also be formed on a *temporary* basis to carry out a specific task or project, and be dissolved when their mission is accomplished. An individual scientist may even participate in more than one research group at the same time.

The term 'research programme' has a heavy burden philosophically, but is used here as a term from daily scientific practice. In operational terms its core is comprised in the few slides a group leader would show in a presentation introducing the work of his or her group. It includes a mission statement, the principal lines of research, the main achievements, the names of the principal investigators, and the main funding sources. To the outside world of colleagues in the field, the programme and the group are closely connected. A programme may be symbolised by the names of the principal investigators, and vice versa. Both the programme and the group thus have a cognitive and a social interpretation.

A research group produces results, published in scientific papers. It is hypothesised that a group's papers can be subdivided roughly into two types, denoted as 'bricks' and 'flags'. Bricks contain elementary, or more-or-less 'normal' contributions, and can be distinguished from flag papers, presenting either overviews of the research programme carried out by the group – mostly in review papers – or the few research articles describing the very significant progress made by members of the group.

Both types of papers are essential elements of the output of the group's programme. There are no flags without bricks, and in principle no bricks without flags either. Review articles may be born, so to say, as flag papers. Other articles, however, may present outcomes that appear to be so significant that they become flags of the programme from which they emerged. Flag articles are symbols for a range of studies conducted in the framework of a research programme. In other words, authors who need to refer to a research programme, its general principles and main outcomes, tend to cite that programme's flag papers. By citing a flag paper, they implicitly cite many, if not all, related brick papers.

Considering highly cited articles as flags or symbols of research programmes of research groups rather than as 'concept symbols' as suggested by Small, may account for the phenomenon of 'split citation identity' observed by Cozzens (1982). A research programme may embody several concepts, and authors referring to it do not necessarily use one and the same concept. In addition, papers may start as significant brick papers, initially cited because of particular results, and transform in a later phase, when their high significance is generally acknowledged, into flag papers. During its lifetime a paper may therefore represent different concept symbols.

From the point of view of citation impact, the relationship between flag articles and brick papers is complex. On the one hand, flag papers in a sense lure citations away from brick articles. The principle of cumulative advantage is at stake here: the more a paper is cited, the more colleagues tend to see it as a flag paper, and the more citations it subsequently attracts. On the other hand, however, flag papers increase the visibility of the programme as a whole, and hence of the brick papers without which they would never have become flags at all.

The citation distribution of a research group's articles is thus essentially skewed. Disregarding the effect of age, a typical distribution of citations among a group's articles reveals a limited number of highly cited papers, and a much larger share of uncited or moderately cited papers. This pattern can be found both for leading groups making key contributions to their field and for less prominent groups. The existence of flag papers, however, is *not* the only factor accounting for the observed skewness in citation distributions. Leading groups tend to have higher citation rates to their flag papers and relatively lower shares of uncited brick papers than less prominent ones.

16.6   A reference list constitutes a distinct part of a paper with proper functions

Reference lists in a sense have a 'life of their own': they can be viewed, evaluated, and analysed to some extent separately from the text in which they were made. This does not mean that references have no function in the rhetorical structure of a scientific paper. References are attached to specific points in the text. Thus, a rhetorical viewpoint on references is appropriate and fruitful.

But references are also elements of a reference list, which can be conceived as a distinct part of a text with proper functions. One may distinguish between two functions. The first relates to the use of references as document content descriptors. For instance, in order to obtain an impression of its contents, potential readers of a full paper tend to browse not only through its title and abstract, but also through its list of references.

A second function relates to the increasing awareness of citing authors that references, when converted into citations, may play a role in the broad domain of research evaluation. This domain not only comprises the process of peer review of submitted manuscripts, but also the use of citation based indicators in research performance assessment.

In practice it is difficult, if not impossible, to distinguish this function from that related to the role of references as content descriptors. Both functions influence a paper's reference list and both are enforced by the increasing use of citation indexes, particularly those produced by the Institute for Scientific Information, for bibliographic and bibliometric purposes.

From this perspective a reference list marks a paper's 'socio-cognitive location', reflected in the special mix between unique and common references. In this way citing authors tend to ensure that important works, scientists or groups are represented in their reference lists. Including works in a reference list can still be interpreted in terms of cognitive influence, but its expression in the citing text may be vague or implicit.

This hypothesis explains why in citation context analyses relatively large proportions of references were qualified as 'perfunctory' (Moravcsik and Murguesan, 1975; Hooten, 1991), 'providing a background' (e.g., Oppenheim and Renn, 1978), or 'setting the stage' (Peritz, 1983; Cano, 1989). From the perspective of rhetorical analysis of citing texts one may conclude that such references have little information utility to the authors of citing papers. But from the perspective of the use of citation analysis in research evaluation, it is not the information utility within the citing text that is of primary relevance, but rather the extent to which works or groups are cited in references 'setting the stage'.

In any field there are leading groups active at the forefront of scientific development. Their leading position is both cognitively and socially anchored. Cognitively, their important contributions tend to be highlighted in a state-of-the-art of a field. But to the extent that the science system functions well in stimulating and warranting scientific quality, leading groups, and particularly their senior researchers, tend at the same time to acquire powerful social positions, as institute directors, journal editors, conference organisers, peer committee members or government advisers.

Since leading groups tend to be represented more frequently in scientific articles' reference lists than less prominent groups, their publication ensembles, and particularly their flag papers, tend to be more frequently cited. Thus, citations can be interpreted as manifestations of intellectual influence, even though such influence may not directly be traced from the citing texts. They can be viewed as instances of citing authors' socio-cognitive location that reflect their awareness of what are the important groups or programmes that must be included in their reference lists.

Chapter 17

IMPLICATIONS FOR THE USE OF CITATION ANALYSIS IN RESEARCH EVALUATION

17.1 What do citations measure?

What are the consequences of the notions outlined in Chapters 15 and 16 for the validity of citation analysis as a tool in research evaluation? Chapter 15 illustrated that referencing behaviour and citations can be studied and interpreted from various disciplinary viewpoints, and within a discipline from various perspectives or 'paradigms'. In principle, all these perspectives are valid: they all illuminate referencing practices.

It is therefore extremely difficult if not impossible to express what citations measure in a single theoretical concept that covers all the interpretations covered by the various approaches. Citations measure many aspects of scholarly activity at the same time. The term *impact*, coined by Garfield and later used as a key concept by Martin and Irvine, is often used, but it is suggested to use the term *citation impact*, as it expresses the methodology along which impact is measured.

Citation impact is basically a quantitative concept that can be operationalised in elementary, or in more sophisticated ways – for instance, through crude citation counts or an advanced, normalised measure. Absolute citation counts, as such, have a limited significance. Measurements of citation impact should always be viewed in function of the universe of citing publications, i.e., the database in which they took place, and have a comparative nature, in the sense that the outcomes for a particular entity should be related to that of other, similar entities.

Concepts as 'intellectual influence' and 'contribution to scholarly progress' are essentially theoretical concepts of a qualitative nature, and can be assessed only by taking into account the cognitive contents of the work under evaluation. The issue at stake in this book is whether citation analysis can be used in research evaluation. Therefore, the relationships between citation impact on the one hand, and intellectual influence or contribution to scholarly progress on the other, need to be clarified.

Chapter 16 argued that in principle it is valid to interpret citations as indicators of intellectual influence. It was hypothesised that citing authors tend to ensure that certain important groups and their programmes are represented in the *reference list* of their papers. Including works in a reference list can be interpreted in terms of intellectual influence, but its expression *in the citing text* may be vague or implicit. An author may cite works of colleagues because they have a powerful position in their fields, but these references may reflect intellectual influence, to the extent that such colleagues acquired that powerful position because their work is influential, and that this position enables them to enforce their influence. But the concepts of citation impact and intellectual influence do *not* coincide. Whether or not citation impact properly reflects intellectual influence also depends upon how the latter concept is defined. In addition, it is crucial how it is related to the concept of contribution to scholarly progress.

In Chapter 4 of this book, a case study illustrated the huge short-term citation impact of a paper on 'cold fusion', which claimed that the process of nuclear fusion had been done at room temperature in an electrolytic cell. Attempts to repeat the work by major, reputable laboratories, were unsuccessful. The paper was highly cited, particularly during the first years after publication. The 'cold fusion' case may be an extreme one, and the author of this book definitely does not want to suggest that all highly cited publications report findings are as controversial as in this particular case. On the contrary, most significant discoveries are reported in papers that are cited with high frequency, for instance, the paper by Watson and Crick on DNA structure mentioned below, and that by Lowry on protein measurement mentioned in Chapter 12. This is well illustrated by the thousands of Citations Classics reported at *http://garfield.library.upenn.edu/classics.html*. However, it can be used to further illustrate the point that citation impact on the one hand, and intellectual influence or contribution to scholarly progress on the other, do not coincide, and that the first may not properly reflect the latter two.

The citation impact of this work can be interpreted in terms of intellectual influence. If one disregards the permanence of the intellectual influence, its cognitive direction and its longer term implications, this concept becomes more similar to that of citation impact. On the other hand, if an evaluator considers these aspects of intellectual influence as important attributes in a qualitative assessment, discrepancies between a work's citation impact and the assessment of its intellectual influence are apt to rise.

Even if one adopts Merton's notion of the symbolic function of the reference, it must be underlined that registering the intellectual property of a knowledge claim on the one hand, and evaluating the merits of such a claim in terms of acceptance or rejection on the other, are distinct aspects. A reference does not necessarily reflect acceptance of a claim, but rather by whom and in which work the claim was made. Citations to the 'cold fusion' paper may be registrations of intellectual property of a knowledge claim, but one may at least ask whether their sheer number ('citation impact') is proportional to the claim's contribution to scientific progress in the field.

Even if one assumes that citations measure intellectual influence, it must still be underlined that intellectual influence needs to be valued in a wider cognitive framework, and does not necessarily properly reflect a work's contribution to scholarly progress or its 'intrinsic quality'. This notion is clearly expressed by Garfield in the following passage, referring to one of the most highly cited papers in the SCI:

> It is arguable whether the Watson-Crick elucidation of the structure of DNA was more or less "significant" than numerous other discoveries before and since. Perhaps the fact that it is only one in a thousand papers that have been cited as much tells us something important about the way scientific knowledge cumulates. It is precisely because it is difficult to assign numeric values to this or that discovery or breakthrough that we should not confuse intrinsic value with the "intellectual influence" reflected in citation counts (Garfield, 1985, p. 408).

Another way to further illustrate that citation impact and intellectual influence, or any other qualitative concept, do not coincide, is to take into account the concept of bias. The latter relates to the problem that citation impact may be affected by factors that have no apparent relationship to the intellectual influence or any other evaluative concepts intended to be measured, and therefore throw obstacles in properly interpreting the former in terms of the latter.

As argued in Chapter 16, it is true that random errors can be expected to cancel out when analysed data samples are sufficiently large; but systematic biases may still remain. They do not necessarily cancel out in large data samples. Hence, individual vagaries in referencing behaviour cancel out, but the results of citation analysis must still be analysed for systematic biases. It must be emphasised, however, that biases do not merely relate to referencing practices of citing authors (the 'citing side'). As authors cite works or groups that have a reality of their own, particularities and special circumstances of the cited objects ('the cited side') may cause biases in citation impact as well. Any attempt to interpret citation impact in terms of intellectual influence must be aware of this. But the concept of bias is not theoretically neutral. Whether or not a particular factor distorts the outcomes of citation analysis is not merely a matter of quantitative-statistical considerations, but also depends upon how the concept to be measured is defined. Distorting factors negatively define such a concept, in terms of 'what it is not'.

The considerations made above may explain why empirical studies statistically comparing the outcomes of citation analysis with peer judgements of scholarly quality found weak or moderate, but no perfect, positive correlations between these two. On the one hand, the fact that the correlations were found to be positive provides an empirical justification for relating the concept of citation impact to that of intellectual influence and similar qualitative concepts, and to examine, within an evaluative framework, whether in a particular case the former properly reflects an evaluator's notion of the latter. On the other hand, the effect of distorting factors and the fact that citation impact does not necessarily reflect a peer's qualitative judgement are responsible for this lack of total correlation.

17.2   Implications

The author of this book recognises that distinct notions of the concept of intellectual influence may exist, and that evaluators assessing scholarly work may have different views upon what are the most crucial aspects to be taken into account. It follows that, in order to be useful and properly used in research evaluation, citation impact must be further interpreted, by assessing what it expresses regarding the aspects to be assessed in the evaluation. In other words, outcomes of citation analysis must be *valued* in terms of a qualitative, evaluative framework that takes into account the substantive contents of the works under evaluation.

An important implication is that *evaluators* should make the evaluation criteria they applied sufficiently clear in advance. In addition, *bibliometric investigators* should inform users of citation analysis of the theoretical assumptions that underlie it, and of possible bias. In this way they establish necessary conditions for properly interpreting outcomes of citation analysis and valuing citation impact within a wider evaluative framework.

The interpretation of citation impact can be conceived as a quest for possible biases, distortions, or measurement 'errors'. From this perspective, it is crucial at which level of aggregation citation analysis is carried out. It is proposed to distinguish two types of use of citation analysis in research evaluation. A first aims at making statements about an individual 'entity' subjected to evaluation, such as an individual scholar or a research department. In this case, the particular, individual characteristics and circumstances of the evaluated entity may affect the outcomes of a citation analysis and should therefore be taken into account.

A second type of use analyses aggregates of entities rather than an individual unit. The entities have some aspect in common, and it is this aspect that provided the basis of their aggregation. Analysis of the aggregate can be carried out in such a way that 'extreme' cases such as that of 'cold fusion' tend to affect the outcomes less strongly, and that the effects of special characteristics and circumstances of individual entities to some extent cancel out. It must be underlined that systematic biases as regards the aggregate as a whole, may still occur and should be taken into account. Therefore, analysing aggregates does not necessarily rule out all sorts of bias, but may, when properly conducted, reduce bias to a considerable extent.

PART 2.6

CITATION ANALYSIS AND PEER REVIEW

Chapter 18

PEER REVIEW AND THE USE AND VALIDITY OF CITATION ANALYSIS

18.1   Introduction

Citation analysis and peer review can be related to one another in the following ways.

- Bibliometric indicators are applied as supplementary tools in peer review processes.
- The outcomes of peer reviews are used as a validation instrument of bibliometric indicators.
- Bibliometric indicators are applied as tools for monitoring and studying peer review processes.

Part 2.6 of this book dedicates attention to each of these three factors. Section 18.2 presents a brief overview of a number of important studies analysing peer review processes of submitted journal manuscripts, grant proposals, and the past performance of research departments. Section 18.3 deals with the use of citation analysis within a peer review process, and Section 18.4 with validation of citation impact indicators using peer judgements. The next two chapters in this part present two case studies using citation analysis to analyse peer review processes. These studies focus on the *outcomes* of such processes, particularly peer ratings of the past performance of research departments (Chapter 19) and grant proposals (Chapter 20).

18.2   About peer review

The scholarly community has developed many institutionalised forms of internal evaluation in which peers assess manifestations of scholarly work. The aim of a peer review process is not to settle scholarly debate, but rather to contribute to the fulfilment of conditions under which it meets professional standards. According to Robert K. Merton, the 'ethos of science' demands that scholarly work should be judged on the basis of purely scholarly merits (Merton, 1972). Judgements should not depend upon the personal or social attributes of the authors of the work to be reviewed. Therefore peer reviewers should manifest disinterestedness and maintain a professional distance not only with respect to their own activities, but also regarding the work being evaluated.

Peer review of *submitted manuscripts* takes place within the context of a journal's editorial policy. But evaluating the significance or methodological soundness of the reported materials on the one hand, and the decision whether or not a manuscript's content fits into the scope of the journal on the other, are distinct issues in which different types of criteria need to be applied. An excellent manuscript may be rejected when the editors feel it does not fit into the journal's scope. Whereas for some journals the assessment of these two aspects is separated, in the sense that peer reviewers deal with the former and editors with the latter, for other journals peer reviewers may be asked explicitly by editors to judge both aspects.

Peer review plays an important role in procedures to evaluate *grant proposals*. In most countries, national research councils grant submitted research proposals on the basis of their scholarly merits. Peers assess the expected contribution to scholarly progress made by the work described in a proposal; the extent to which the research team is sufficiently qualified to carry out the research, focusing both on the team's viability, the adequacy of its institutional setting and its past research performance; and the appropriateness of the budget requested relative to the objectives outlined in the proposal. The quality of a research proposal and the question whether or not it should be granted are two distinct aspects. In some procedures, assessment of these aspects may be fairly strictly separated, leaving the granting decision to a Council's management. In other procedures, such separation may be less strict.

Other forms of peer review can be found in the allocation of *scholarly prizes and awards*. For instance, the Nobel Prize has been awarded annually since 1901. Peer review plays a crucial role in identifying the key scientists who made outstanding contributions to the advancement of scholarly knowledge in a particular domain of scholarship.

A more recent phenomenon is the installation by policy agencies of peer review committees with the task evaluating past or expected future performance of *research departments* in scholarly institutions or disciplines. Good examples are the research assessment exercises carried out in the UK, and periodical evaluations per scholarly discipline of academic research in the Netherlands. Such exercises may have several distinct objectives. They may primarily aim at making manifest research quality, particularly scientific excellence, for the 'outside' world, i.e., for scholars from other disciplines, for potential external users of research results, and for the general public. A second aim is to provide departments subjected to evaluation with information that may enable them to improve their research performance. A third objective is to provide tools in making decisions about the allocation of research funds.

In 1977 Stephen Cole, Leonard Rubin and Jonathan Cole presented a statistical analysis of the evaluation procedures on which the US National Science Foundation (NSF) based its decisions whether or not to fund submitted grant proposals (Cole et al., 1977). Their analysis addressed several important criticisms of the peer review system in general, expressed both by members of the scientific community and by politicians. They focused on the validity of what they termed the "old boy hypothesis", stating that "the proposals of eminent scientists are apt to be rated more favourably by eminent researchers than by other reviewers". They analysed internal NSF data regarding several thousands of peer ratings of more than 1,000 applications from a number of basic science disciplines in the year 1975, and calculated several measures of eminence of applicants and their departments, including indicators based on publication and citation counts, as well as the applicants' recent NSF funding record.

They found no empirical evidence in favour of the 'old boy hypothesis'. Applicants from high ranking departments were found to be rated lower by reviewers from high ranking departments than they were by reviewers from lower ranked departments. Somewhat to their own surprise, they also found that an applicant's past performance – although one of the most important criteria in the NSF procedure – had only a marginal influence upon the probability of his or her proposal being granted.

Stephen Cole, Jonathan Cole and Gary Simon (Cole et al., 1981) examined the degree of chance and consensus in peer review by comparing peer ratings of grant proposals from solid state physics, chemical dynamics and economics submitted to the NSF to ratings given in a second review by independently selected panels of reviewers. From an analysis of variance they concluded that "… the fate of a particular grant application is roughly half determined by the characteristics of the proposal and the principal investigator, and about half by apparently random elements which might be characterised as the 'luck of the reviewer draw'" (ibid., p. 885).

Ben Martin and John Irvine (1983) described peer evaluation as a method "based on individual scientists' perceptions of contributions by others to scientific progress, perceptions arrived at through a complicated series of intellectual and social processes, mediated by factors other than the quality, importance or impact of the research under evaluation" (p. 72–73). They identified three major problems in using the outcomes of peer evaluation in a policy context. First, evaluators may be influenced by political and social pressures within the scientific community, such as the possible implications of their judgements for their own work and that of their colleagues. Secondly, peer reviewers tend to evaluate in terms of their own research interests, and may not possess all the knowledge that is needed to form a balanced judgement. Finally, peers tend to conform to conventionally accepted patterns of belief, and may, for instance, be influenced by a scientist's reputation rather than his or her actual contribution to scientific progress.

Cicchetti (1991) presented a thorough review of studies addressing the reliability of peer review of journal manuscripts and grant proposals. The concept of reliability relates to the extent to which peer reviewers agree in their judgements on the quality of manuscripts or proposals. Regarding the evaluation of journal manuscripts, Cicchetti distinguished between two main types of scholarly disciplines: general and diffuse, and specific and focused. The author concluded from a number of earlier studies that reviewers and journal editors in the former type of disciplines tend to agree more on rejection than on acceptance of submitted manuscripts, whereas in the latter more agreement was found on acceptance than on rejection.

Cicchetti further analysed the data samples studied by Cole et al. (1981), and found that the degree of agreement among reviewers for proposals with *low* ratings was significantly higher than that for proposals with *high* peer ratings. The author concluded that "referees of grant proposals agree much more about what is unworthy of support than about what does have scientific value" (Cicchetti, 1991, p. 119). He noted that several systems of grant review exist that differ according to who selects the reviewers, how grants are evaluated, and whether or not peer review panels carry out site visits at applicants' institutions. He underlined the relevance of further research into how such differences influence the reliability and validity of peer reviews of grant applications.

Langfeldt (2001) reviewed numerous studies of peer review processes. She identified one group of studies focusing on the degree of agreement among reviewers ('reliability') and the effects of possible biases, and a second group primarily analysing evaluation criteria applied by review panels. Studies from the first group tended to report low degrees of agreement among reviewers, and identified various kinds of bias, including the applicant's academic status and gender, institutional and cognitive bias. The second group of studies revealed that reviewers tend to use a common set of evaluation criteria. She concluded that the combination of these findings indicate that "while there is a certain set of criteria that reviewers pay attention to – more or less explicitly –, these criteria are interpreted or operationalised differently by various reviewers" (Langfeldt, 2001, p. 821).

In her own empirical work she analysed the effect of guidelines, budgets and particularly rating scales and ranking methods upon the assessment of grant proposals submitted to the Research Council of Norway, an organisation that applied several models of grant review. She found that the guidelines given to the review panels had little effect upon the criteria they emphasised, but that the outcome was affected by rating scales, ranking methods and budgets (Langfeldt, 2001).

18.3 Use of bibliometric indicators within peer review

Peer review processes are normally carried out without documentation of the bases for conclusions. It is therefore difficult to assess the extent to which citation and publication data are used in peer review. When citation analysis does not constitute an official source of information in a peer review process, it does *not* follow that citation or publication data do not play a role at all. Peers may directly consult ISI's *Web of Science* or other bibliographic versions of ISI's Citation Indexes, or they may have obtained information from earlier bibliometric studies or rankings, published in journals or made available through the internet. This type of use can be denoted as '*informal*'.

A good example of an evaluation system in which bibliometric indicators play a *formal* role is the system installed in the early 1990s by the Association of Universities in the Netherlands (VSNU), aimed at assessing periodically and by discipline all research departments located at Dutch academic institutions. The system was essentially based upon peer review, but in several disciplines – particularly physics, chemistry and biology – systematic bibliometric analyses of all departments involved constituted one of its inputs. Although this assessment procedure was recently transformed into a system of self-evaluation, in the disciplines mentioned above citation analysis still plays an important role (van Leeuwen, 2004b). Publication data used in the citation analysis were verified by the departments themselves, and the evaluation protocol gave their leaders the opportunity to comment on the bibliometric outcomes.

Norris and Oppenheim (2003) proposed using citation analysis as one of the assessment tools in the UK research assessment exercises: "whilst citation analysis is not a perfect tool, it is recommended that it should be adopted as the primary procedure for the initial ranking of university departments". It must be noted that in the research assessments in the Netherlands mentioned above, the outcomes of the citation analysis in most cases did not constitute the "primary procedure" for initial rankings in the peer review process as suggested by Norris and Oppenheim. Instead, the peer committees formulated initial judgements without knowledge of the bibliometric outcomes, and in a later phase used the indicators, combined with information obtained at site visits, to further substantiate and finalise their judgements.

18.4   Validation of bibliometric indicators regarding individual scholars and research departments

During the past 50 years, numerous studies examined from the point of view of validation of bibliometric indicators, statistical correlations between peer judgements about the research performance of individual scholars or research departments on the hand, and the outcomes of citation analysis on the other. This section mentions only a few typical, interesting examples. Clark (1957) asked a panel of experts in the field of psychology to name the psychologists who contributed most to the advances in this field. He correlated the number of times a person was nominated with several other performance indicators and found that citation counts revealed the highest correlation.

Jonathan and Stephen Cole carried out important validation studies in the late 1960s and early 1970s, especially in the area of physics (Cole and Cole, 1971). Small (1977) conducted a co-citation analysis of a research specialty working on collagen research. He identified and clustered a number of highly cited documents in this specialty. A questionnaire survey demonstrated that the highly cited documents were significant documents in the perception of specialists in the field, and that the authors of these papers were viewed as leading researchers.

Nederhof and van Raan (1987) analysed the citation impact of the work of candidates for a doctoral degree in physics and chemistry, and found that citation rates of recipients of the honours degree *cum laude* were on average significantly higher than those of candidates who did not receive this qualification. For an overview of other earlier studies using citation analysis the reader is referred to Spiegel-Rösing et al. (1975) and Nederhof (1988).

Eugene Garfield and co-workers have conducted a series of studies in which publication and citation counts for individual authors were correlated with Nobel Prizes. They summarised their main findings in two papers published in 1992 (Garfield and Welljams-Dorof, 1992a; 1992b). They determined the frequency at which Nobel laureates appeared in the top of rankings of authors based on total or average citation counts to their published papers. For instance, among the 50 most cited primary authors in the *Science Citation Index* of 1967, six authors had already won the Nobel Prize prior to 1967 (denoted as 'post-Nobelists'), and eight others became laureates after that year ('pre-Nobelists'). The latter outcome revealed the power of citation analysis to *forecast* Nobel Prize winners. Among the 50 most highly cited authors in economics during the period 1966–1986, fifteen scientists had won the prize prior to 1986, and two others received it between 1987 and 1991.

Garfield qualified the scientists among the top one per cent most cited authors as being "of Nobel class", and emphasised that only a small number of these can eventually win a Nobel Prize. In two studies analysing the top 300 and 1,000 authors, he found that papers of all Nobel authors – including both post- and pre-Nobelists – were cited on average 25 per cent more than an average non-Nobel paper in the top lists. For papers of pre-Nobelists, this percentage was found to be only 15 per cent. Papers of post-Nobelists had 38 per cent higher citation impact than those of pre-Nobelists.

Garfield's analysis is one-sided in the sense that it focused on the extent to which highly cited authors receive Nobel awards, but did not give statistics about how many Nobel Prize winners were highly or poorly cited. He underlined that some studies are based on 'first author counts' only, disregarding work of which a scientist is a co-author; that the counts are 'lifetime' counts, which may bias his selections in favour of older scientists; and that the analysis does not take into account differences in publication and citation practices among scholarly disciplines, which may bias selections in favour of fields in which authors publish and cite frequently. He argued that annual forecasts of Nobel Prize winners based on citation analysis are useful as "they lower the probability that scientists who are less visible despite the high impact of their work will be overlooked", but that "a purely algorithmic identification of candidates on the basis of either productivity or citation admittedly would be absurd" (Garfield, 1990).

In 1995, The US National Research Council (NRC), the working arm of the National Academy of Science and the National Academy of Engineering, published a report presenting a quality rating of PhD programs at 274 US institutions in 41 fields, based on surveys sent to faculty (Goldberger et al., 1995). This was a follow-up report to a study carried out in the early 1980s. The survey was designed to gather the views of a sample of about 8,000 faculty at U.S. universities on the scholarly quality of the program faculty in their field and the effectiveness of those programs in educating research scholars.

The NRC report also presented bibliometric indicators based on publication and citation data extracted from the ISI Citation Indexes, but these indicators were *not* used by the NRC for ranking purposes. Using the terminology outlined in Chapter 8 of this book, the citation analysis carried out in the NRC report was a standard analysis, in which citation target publications were those published in journals processed for the ISI Citation Indexes. It analysed publications and citations during a fixed period of five years, and calculated for each PhD program citation densities, defined as the number of collected citations to the papers emerging from a program divided by the number of faculty in that program.

Diamond and Graham (2000) further analysed the NRC data and concluded that "reputational ratings showed a strong positive correlation with citation densities", in the sense that the institutions appearing in the top of the former tended to be highly ranking on the latter as well. However, younger and smaller "challenging" institutions tended to have higher positions in the citation impact rankings than in the reputational rankings. The authors concluded that such institutions "break into the upper ranks when measured by their research achievements rather than by a perceived level of prestige".

Other analysts have pointed towards the limitations of the citation analysis in the NRC study, and their implications, particularly for the ratings of PhD programs in social science fields. For instance, Holcombe (2004), who focused on the field of economics, underlined that the NRC analysis counts only a subset of publications and citations, which in his view "would favor top departments in the citation count process".

In a series of research papers, Charles Oppenheim and co-workers statistically analysed the UK Research Assessment Exercises (RAE) of the past performance of research departments, conducted periodically by the UK Higher Education Funding Councils. Peer reviews of publications made by the departments subjected to evaluation play a crucial role in these exercises. The authors found in several research disciplines statistically significant correlations between the RAE ratings on the one hand and bibliometric indicators based upon citation analysis on the other (e.g., Norris and Oppenheim, 2003).

Smith and Eysenck (2002) correlated citations received by staff members in each of 38 university psychology departments in the United Kingdom with the Research Assessment Exercise (RAE) grades awarded to them in 1996 and 2001. The correlations they obtained were around 0.8, and qualified by the authors as "extremely high". They concluded that "the two approaches measure broadly the same thing".

Rinia et al. (1998; 1999) examined statistical correlations between bibliometric indicators and peer ratings for research programmes in the field of physics, carried out at academic institutions in the Netherlands. They found significantly positive rank correlation coefficients of around 0.5 between several bibliometric indicators on the one hand, and the overall peer ratings on the other (Rinia et al., 1998). The normalised citation impact indicator presented in Chapter 4 showed the strongest correlation. For programmes in applied physics, however, these correlations were somewhat lower than they were for basic physics programmes. The authors found evidence that the quality of the research team was an important criterion in the peer review, but that other criteria played a role as well.

In a second study (Rinia et al., 1999) the authors analysed a sub-set of programmes and included indicators of research interdisciplinarity. They found no bias in peer ratings or bibliometric indicators against interdisciplinary research. In the next chapter of this book, the data analysed by Rinia et al. also play a role, but, jointly with outcomes of research assessment exercises in other science disciplines, they are analysed from a different perspective, namely the extent to which bibliometric indicators and peer ratings converge in discriminating between 'excellent' and 'good yet not excellent' research performance.

Chapter 19

ANALYSIS OF PEER ASSESSMENTS OF RESEARCH DEPARTMENTS

19.1 Introduction

This chapter compares the outcomes of peer reviews of the past research performance of research departments with bibliometric indicators of their publication output. As outlined in Chapter 18, such a comparison can be made from two distinct points of view. The first is that of validation of bibliometric indicators. These indicators are tested using peer judgements as a benchmark. Thus, it is assumed that peer review provides a more direct measure of research quality, and to the extent the bibliometric indicators correlate with peer judgements, they are validated.

A second point of view critically examines peer ratings of particular evaluation panels. In this analysis bibliometric indicators are applied as a benchmark. The basic assumption holds that bibliometric indicators are valid indicators of research performance, and thus can be used to assess peer judgements, and raise questions about how peers evaluated, which criteria they applied, and whether their judgements were biased. It is on this second perspective that this chapter focuses. It aims to show how citation analysis can be a useful tool in analysing peer review processes, by presenting a number of significant observations, and raising critical questions regarding the ways peers evaluated the past performance of research departments.

Statistical relationships between peer ratings and bibliometric indicators of evaluated entities are often expressed as rank correlation coefficients for the study population as a whole. Although these statistics are also calculated below, it must be noted that they only reveal an overall tendency in the data. It is more informative to examine agreement between the two types of outcomes in function of the hypothesised quality of the entities under evaluation. Similarly to the analysis by Cicchetti (1991) of agreement among peers regarding highly versus lowly rated submitted manuscripts or grant proposals, this chapter compares bibliometric and peer ratings of research departments in function of their classification into 'excellent', 'good', and 'less good' departments. The principal research question addressed in this chapter is: To what extent did the peer review committees succeed in identifying 'less good' and 'top' research?

19.2   Data and methods

Data analysed in this chapter relates to a number of peer reviews of the performance of research departments in the natural and life sciences. All applied the same peer rating system and the same set of evaluation criteria. Three reviews were conducted during the 1990s on behalf of the Organisation of Universities in the Netherlands (VSNU), and assessed Dutch academic research in biology, physics and chemistry. A fourth review was carried out in 2001 on behalf of the central management of one of the larger Western-European universities.

In the three VSNU reviews the outcomes of a detailed bibliometric study were provided to the peers during the review process. Hence, peer ratings and bibliometric indicators are not constructed independently from one another, and their correlation can hardly be interpreted in terms of validation of citation impact indicators. In a fourth review, peers had no information about the outcomes of the bibliometric study.

In the VSNU reviews only the final peer ratings of the committees were available in the analysis. A committee consisted of around 8 members, jointly evaluating all departments. There was no further information on judgements of individual peers and the extent to which they agreed with one another. In the university review, 40 peers rated independently from one another on average 8 departments in a (sub-)discipline. Each department was rated by three or four peers. The analysis below relates to a department's mean peer rating.

Table 19.1. Peer rating system applied in the four assessments

Rating	Qualification	Short description
5	Excellent	Among the world's best in the field
4	Good	Above world average; some elements may be excellent
3	Satisfactory	At world's average; some aspects are important nationally
2	Unsatisfactory	Below world's average in the field
1	Poor	Far below world's average

Peers rated the departments' quality using five qualifications described in Table 19.1. The qualifications were ranked by descending quality, and their rank orders (from 5 to 1) were conceived as ratings and subjected to further data analysis. The qualification 'poor' was given to only one department, in the university review. Hence, in the VSNU studies peer ratings ranged between 2 and 5.

For each department a series of bibliometric indicators was calculated. This chapter focuses on the normalised citation impact indicator described in Chapter 4. A ratio above 1 for this measure indicates that the average citation impact of a department's papers is above the world average in the subfields in which it is active. Departments were categorised on the basis of their citation impact into four citation impact classes, ranked from very high (rating 5) to very low (rating 2), in such a way that the distribution of citation impact ratings among departments was equal to that for peer ratings. For instance, there were as many departments with impact rating 5 as there were with peer rating 5.

19.3   Results

Table 19.2 shows the distribution of peer ratings among departments for all four studies. In addition, for departments receiving a particular peer rating it shows the mean value of their citation impact. In all four studies departments with a high peer rating had on average a higher citation impact than departments with lower ratings. In the total sample of 404 departments evaluated in the four studies, the mean citation impact of departments rated as poor, unsatisfactory, satisfactory, good, and excellent was 0.0, 0.6, 0.9, 1.3 and 1.7, respectively. Each study showed such an increase in mean impact as peer ratings increase.

In the VSNU biology, chemistry and physics reviews, the Spearman rank correlation coefficients between peer judgements and citation impact were 0.73, 0.58 and 0.50, respectively. In the university review, in which peers did not use bibliometric indicators, a rank correlation coefficient of 0.46 was obtained, only slightly lower that those obtained in the VSNU studies.

Table 19.2 shows that the mean citation impact of the departments included in the various reviews varied substantially from one study to another. In the VSNU studies on biology, chemistry and physics it amounted to 1.2, 1.3 and 1.5, respectively, whereas in the university study it was 0.9. On the other hand, all four peer reviews generated approximately the same peer rating distribution, with about 20, 45, 30, 5, and 0 per cent of departments rated excellent, good, satisfactory, unsatisfactory and poor, respectively.

Table 19.2. Percentage of departments and their average citation impact per peer rating

Peer rating	Total (n=404)		Biology (n=68)		Chemistry (n=158)		Physics (n=80)		University (n=98)	
	%	IMP	%	IMP	%	IMP	%	IMP	%	IMP
1	0	0.0	0		0		0		1	0.0
2	4	0.6	4	0.7	4	0.6	1	0.5	7	0.5
3	29	0.9	28	0.8	31	0.9	29	1.0	28	0.5
4	46	1.3	47	1.4	43	1.3	46	1.4	49	1.0
5	21	1.7	21	1.7	22	1.6	24	2.1	16	1.3
Total	100	1.2	100	1.2	100	1.3	100	1.5	100	0.9

%: The percentage share of departments with a particular peer rating.
IMP: The mean value of the citation impact compared to world citation average of departments with a particular peer rating. For an insight into the variability of citation impact scores among departments with a particular peer rating, see Table 19.3.
Peer ratings: 1: Poor; 2: Unsatisfactory; 3: Satisfactory; 4: Good; 5: Excellent.

The next analyses related to the three VSNU field assessments only. As noted above, in these assessments a detailed bibliometric study constituted one of the sources of information in the review process. The matrix of peer ratings versus citation impact ratings is presented in Table 19.3.

A first analysis examined the top of the quality distribution, and analysed the extent to which the two methodologies converge in discriminating between 'excellent' or 'top' research on the one hand, and 'good yet not excellent' departments on the other. Table 19.3 shows that among the 68 departments rated excellent by peers, the number with a low or very low citation impact was 6 (9 per cent). But the number of departments with a very high citation impact did not substantially exceed those with a high citation impact: 36 versus 26 (53 versus 38 per cent). In other words, the peer qualification 'excellent' discriminated very well between departments with a citation impact below world average and those that were above that average, but it discriminated less well between very high and high impact departments.

Conversely, in the set of 68 departments with a very high citation impact, the number of departments rated 'less good' (satisfactory or unsatisfactory) was only 3 (4 per cent). However, the number of departments rated excellent was similar to that qualified by peers as good (29 versus 36). Thus, a very high citation impact discriminated very well between departments rated excellent or good and those receiving lower peer ratings, but it did not discriminate so well between good and excellent departments in the perception of the peers[1].

Table 19.3. Peer ratings versus citation impact in VSNU field assessments: full matrix

Peer rating	Citation impact Class				Total
	Very low (0.0–0.5)	Low (0.5–1.0)	High (1.0–1.7)	Very high (1.7–5.0)	
Unsatisfactory	3	7	0	0	10
Satisfactory	6	51	31	3	91
Good	1	27	80	29	137
Excellent	0	6	26	36	68
Total	10	91	137	68	306

Numbers in the cells indicate the number of departments with a particular peer rating and citation impact class. Numbers between parentheses in the column headings indicate the range of values for the citation impact indicators of the departments in each impact class. It is noteworthy that the procedure for categorising citation impact scores described in Section 19.2 resulted in the (unintended) outcome that the cut-off point between the second (low) and third (high) citation impact class lies exactly at the value 1.0, which corresponds to a citation impact equal to the world average.

Table 19.4. Peer ratings versus citation impact in VSNU field assessments: bottom approach

Peer rating	Citation Impact Class					
	Very low or low		High or very high		Total	
	N	%	N	%	N	%
Unsatisfactory or satisfactory	67	22	34	11	101	33
Good or excellent	34	11	171	56	205	67
Total	101	33	205	67	306	100

The next analysis focused on the lower part of the quality distribution. Combining the two lowest and the two highest peer rating and citation impact classes, respectively, resulted in a two-by-two matrix presented in Table 19.4. It shows that 56 per cent of all departments had both a high or very high citation impact and a good or excellent peer rating, and 22 per cent had a low or very low rating for both aspects. Another 22 per cent showed a discrepancy between peer rating and citation impact. Thus, to the extent that the evaluation procedure aims at discriminating between good or excellent departments on the one hand and less good departments (rated either satisfactory or unsatisfactory) on the other, the citation impact indicator agreed with the peer rating in almost 80 per cent of the cases.

19.4   Discussion and conclusions

The analyses presented above represent case studies, and as always one should be cautious in drawing more general conclusions from them. Notwithstanding these inherent limitations of citation analysis outlined in Chapters 4 and 17, the outcomes obtained in the previous section give rise to the following observations and questions.

It was found that the distributions of peer ratings among departments in the four studies were statistically similar, whereas the departments' average citation impact differed substantially from one study to another. This finding suggests that a peer rating system tends to generate a peer quality distribution that depends upon the rating system itself, and that is to some extent independent of the overall level of quality of evaluated departments.

Analysis of the three field reviews demonstrates that if those responsible for the evaluation had *not* conducted a peer review at all, but had commissioned *solely* a bibliometric study, the outcomes of the latter – in terms of whether departments had a citation impact above or below world average – would correctly predict a peer rating – in terms of good or excellent versus less good (satisfactory or unsatisfactory) – in about 8 out of 10 cases. In about one out of 10 cases, the bibliometric study alone would rate a department higher than peers would have done, and in another one out of 10 cases, it would rate a department lower.

But it was also found that among the departments with a very high citation impact, the number of departments rated excellent was similar to that evaluated as good by the peers[2]. If one assumes that the applied citation impact indicators reflect excellence adequately, it follows that the peer review committees were able to identify 'good' or 'valuable' research meeting minimum quality standards, but that they were not very successful in identifying genuinely excellent or top research.

It should be noted that the number of peers in the VSNU field review committees is limited to about eight. It must be an extremely difficult task for such a small committee to jointly collect detailed insights into a field as broad as an entire discipline. Possibly, peers are more able to identify what is qualitatively 'less good' than what is excellent or 'genuine top' research, particularly when they are cognitively rather distant from most of the research activities they have to evaluate. This hypothesis is consistent with conclusions drawn in earlier studies on the evaluation of grant proposals and journal manuscripts in 'general' or 'diffuse' subfields stating that referees tend to agree much more upon what is unworthy of support than about what does have scientific value (Cicchetti, 1991, see Section 18.2).

This conclusion underlines the need for policy makers who organise research assessment exercises at a national level to thoroughly reflect upon the objectives of such exercises. If these exercises aim primarily at identifying the bottom or the *lower* part of the quality distribution of departments in a discipline, the citation analysis provides evidence that they have been effective. But if the principal objective is to indicate *excellence* in the *top* of the quality distribution, one may ask whether the organisation of the review process provided proper conditions to meet that objective.

It must be emphasised that it does not follow that research assessment exercises aimed at identifying excellence should be based merely upon citation analysis, and that the latter should thus replace peer review. Nor does the author of this book wish to question the competence and integrity of the peers involved in the reviews studied in this chapter[3]. In addition, the observed discrepancies between peer ratings and citation analysis can also be discussed in terms of validity of the latter, and may lead to the invention of new, more valid indicators, a perspective further developed in Chapter 25. But the outcomes underline the need to further reflect upon organisational settings and tools that are needed to enable peer reviewers to carry out their task. The cost effectiveness of the evaluation procedure should be taken into account as well.

Notes

1   A secondary analysis showed that when the threshold for having a very high citation impact was increased, the ratio of excellent and good departments in the perception of the peer reviewers remained more or less constant. The department with the highest citation impact was rated excellent.

2. Their absolute numbers are 36 against 29, accounting for 53 and 43 per cent of all departments with a very high citation impact, respectively. On the one hand, one could argue that the percentage share of departments in the entire population rated excellent by the peers was much lower than that share for good groups: 22 against 45 per cent. Hence, compared to the distribution within the entire population, excellent departments are over-represented in the class of those with a very high citation impact: from the point of view of validation of bibliometric indicators, this observation would be significant, were it not that the peers did actually use the outcomes of the bibliometric study. However, in an analysis of the validity of peer review, using citation analysis as a benchmark, it is inappropriate to relate the share of good and excellent departments in the class of high citation impact departments to that of the total population, as the latter is merely based upon peer ratings.

3. It should be noted that the peers evaluated not only the departments' research quality, but also several other aspects, including their viability. Possibly peers' judgements on these other aspects influenced their quality rating to some extent.

Chapter 20

ANALYSIS OF A NATIONAL RESEARCH COUNCIL

20.1   Introduction

This chapter presents a quantitative analysis of the evaluation and funding procedures carried out by a National Research Council from a smaller Western-European country, in which peer review of grant proposals plays a crucial role. It illustrates how quantitative, bibliometric methods can fruitfully contribute to an internal debate within funding agencies on funding procedures and evaluation criteria, and to a public debate between a funding agency and the national science policy sphere.

The Research Council provides funds for research projects and scholarships on the basis of an inter-university competition. Its total annual budget in 2001 was approximately 80 million Euros. The Council has installed some 25 expert committees, jointly covering all domains of science and scholarship and being responsible for the evaluation of submitted proposals. An expert committee covers a sub-discipline. Applicants indicated the sub-disciplines covered by a proposal, and in this way nominated the committees that in their view should evaluate the proposal. They could nominate more than one committee whenever appropriate.

About 40 per cent of experts was appointed to a professorship in an institution located in the country itself. Committees ranked applications on the basis of their merits ('*priority ranking*'), particularly the significance of the research described in the proposal, and the past performance of its applicants. Such priority rankings were partly based on comments by external experts reviewing a proposal. Granting decisions are made by the Council's Board of Directors, a body that includes the Rectors of the universities within the country. In 2001, for the first time, an independent, quantitative, partly bibliometric study, commissioned by the minister responsible for research, played an important role in the negotiations on the renewal of the agreement between this Council and the national government.

This chapter focuses on *project* applications in the natural and life sciences and addresses the following research questions.

– What is the distribution of submitted and granted applications among expert committees? How did rejection rates vary among committees?
– What is the statistical relationship between the priority ranking made by a committee and the final granting decision?
– What is the statistical relationship between an application's probability of being granted on the one hand, and the citation impact of the applicants, the trans-disciplinary nature of their research, and their proximity relationship with the evaluating committee, on the other?

The latter three factors were analysed because government representatives wished to assess whether the Council's procedures rewarded researchers of high international quality, whether trans-disciplinary research was hampered, and whether proximity relationships between applicants and evaluating committees made the outcomes of the procedure inequitable.

20.2   Data and methods

The Research Council provided the names of all committee members, and detailed information about 10,000 applications made during the period 1991–2000, including the names and affiliations of the applicants, the sum requested, the judgement (priority ranking) made by the evaluating committee, the final granting decision and the sum granted.

The expert committees rated the applications priority using five categories: excellent, very good, good, promising and 'not classed'. The latter qualification was given to applications that in the committees' view should not be granted.

For 3,300 applicants and committee members active in science fields, bibliometric output and citation impact indicators were calculated with respect to the period 1980–2000, derived from the Citation Indexes produced by the Institute for Scientific Information.

The key citation impact indicator applied in the study is the normalised citation impact indicator, defined as the average citation rate of a scientist's papers relative to the world citation average in the subfields in which he or she is active. Indicators of trans-disciplinary citation impact were based on the degree to which a scientist's papers were cited from journals outside the sub-discipline in which he or she is active. Two indicators were calculated: absolute and relative. Details are given in Table 20.1. The index of proximity between applicants and the Council's expert committees is defined in Table 20.2.

Table 20.1. Indicators of trans-disciplinarity

Indicator	Definition
Trans-disciplinary citation impact of a journal J	% Citations to J's articles given in papers outside the subfield(s) covered by J
Trans-disciplinary citation impact of the articles of group G published in journal J	% Citations to G's articles published in J, given in papers outside the subfield(s) covered by J
Relative trans-disciplinary citation impact of group G's articles published in Journal J	Trans-disciplinary citation impact of G's articles in J ÷ Trans-disciplinary citation impact of J
Trans-disciplinary citation impact of the total collection of articles published by group G	% Citations to all G's articles, given in papers outside the subfield(s) covered by the journals in which G published, evaluated on a journal-by-journal basis
Relative trans-disciplinary citation impact of the total collection of articles published by group G	Trans-disciplinary citation impact of G's articles ÷ Trans-disciplinary citation impact of the journals in which G has published

Table 20.2. Index of proximity between applicants and expert committees

Index	Proximity
0	Applicants are/were not a member of any Council's expert committee
1	Co-applicant is/was a member of a committee, but not of those evaluating the proposal
2	First applicant is/was a member of a committee, but not of those evaluating the proposal
3	Co-applicant is a member of the committee(s) evaluating the proposal
4	First applicant is a member of the committee(s) evaluating the proposal

A core analysis was a logistic regression analysis of submitted applications with the final granting decision or priority ranking of the evaluating committee as the dependent variable, and the citation impact of the applicants, their trans-disciplinary citation impact, and the proximity between the applicants of a proposal and the committee evaluating the proposal as independent variables. As control variables the analysis took into account the total sum requested in the project application, and the university to which the first applicant was affiliated. Projects applying for a total sum exceeding 250,000 Euro were categorised as 'big', and all others as 'small'.

20.3   Results

Table 20.3 presents statistics on submitted and granted applications and budgets. It shows that 46 per cent of submitted applications and 28 per cent of the total amount of funds requested in all submitted applications was granted. However, focusing on *granted* applications, only 50 per cent of the total requested budget was granted.

Table 20.3. Statistics on submitted and granted applications and budgets

Number of applications submitted (1991–2000)	4,008
% Applications granted	46
Total budget requested (MEuro) in submitted applications	1,200
% budget granted for all submitted applications	28
% budget granted for granted applications only	50

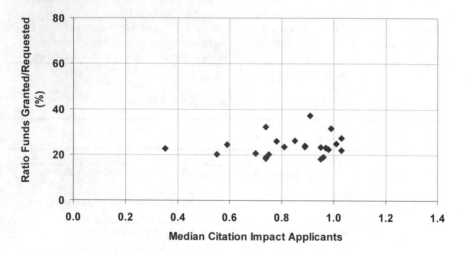

Figure 20.1. Ratio of funds granted/requested versus citation impact of national applicants per discipline

Data relate to the period 1997–2000. Figure 20.1 shows that the ratio of granted to requested funds tends to be constant over committees. It follows that the distribution of granted funds for projects among committees was largely determined by the number of applications submitted. In other words, the rejection rate regarding the total budget requested in submitted applications was about the same for all committees. The citation impact of national researchers in the discipline(s) covered by a committee did not play a significant role.

The next analysis focused on the distribution of funds for granted applications among expert committees. Figure 20.1 relates the ratio of granted to requested funds in a discipline to the median citation impact of the papers published by scientists active in that discipline and submitting applications to the Council. The figure shows that during the period 1997–2000 the ratio of granted/requested funds tended to be the same for all committees. In other words, all committees showed more or less the same rejection rate with respect to the total budget requested in submitted applications. Citation impact of national researchers in a sub-discipline did not influence this ratio in a statistically significant way.

Figure 20.2 gives the distribution of expert ratings among submitted applications. It shows that this distribution varied among the years. In the years 1998 and 1999 the Council's total budget available for granting new applications dropped significantly. In 1999 particularly the percentage share of applications rated as excellent or very good declined, whereas that of not classed applications increased considerably.

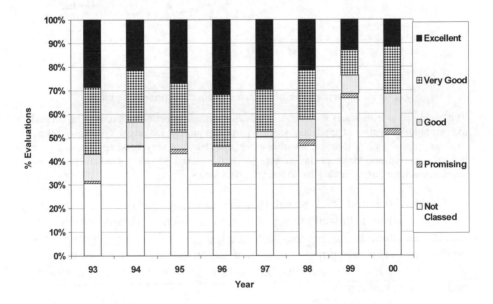

Figure 20.2. Expert committees' classification of submitted applications

The horizontal axis indicates the year in which applications were submitted, and the vertical axis the percentage share of applications with a particular priority ranking made by the expert committee evaluating it. These shares varied significantly over the years, in the years 1998–1999 due to the Council's budgetary restrictions.

Figure 20.3 presents the percentage share granted by the Council for applications receiving a particular committee rating. As from 1997, the overwhelming majority of applications rated as excellent or very good by the committees were granted. The drop in the Council's total budget in 1998 and

1999 is also visible in this figure. The applications rated as good or promising were rarely granted in those years.

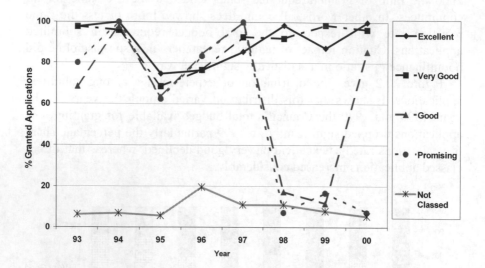

Figure 20.3. Granting decisions versus committees' priority rankings

The horizontal axis indicates the year in which applications were submitted, and the vertical axis gives for each class of applications with a particular priority ranking the percentage share that was granted by the Council. As from 1997, excellent and very good applications were normally granted, and those not classed were not. In the years 1998–1999 good and promising applications were rarely granted due to budget restrictions.

Figures 20.2 and 20.3 reveal that the granting decision made by the Council as a rule followed the priority ranking given by expert committees, within the boundaries of the total budget available for funding new applications. This outcome suggests that expert committees not only made priority rankings of applications, but de facto also made granting decisions and allocated budgets.

Figures 20.5 to 20.9 present key findings as regards statistical relationships between an application's priority ranking or its probability to be granted on the one hand, and the proximity between its applicants and the expert committees evaluating it (Figures 20.4 and 20.5), applicants' citation impact (Figures 20.6 and 20.7), and his or her trans-disciplinary impact (Figure 20.8).

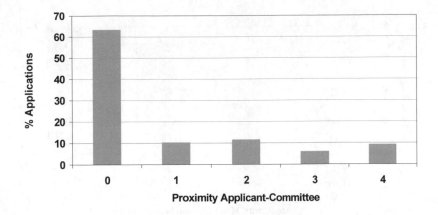

Figure 20.4. Distribution of applications for projects according to proximity between applicant and evaluating expert committee

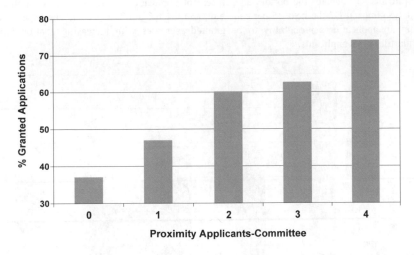

Figure 20.5. Percentage of applications granted versus the proximity between applicant and evaluating expert committee

Figure 20.4 shows that for 15 per cent of applications, an applicant (either the first (proximity index=4) or a co-applicant (proximity index=3)) was a member of the committee evaluating the application. Figure 20.5 reveals that an application's probability to be granted increased with increasing proximity between applicants and evaluating committee. For a definition of the proximity index see Table 20.2 in Section 20.2.

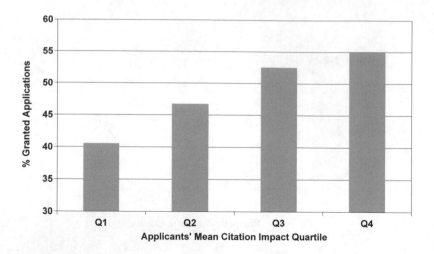

Figure 20.6. Percentage of applications granted versus applicants' citation impact

Applications were grouped into quartiles on the basis of the citation impact of their applicants. Q1 denotes the bottom 25 per cent of applications in terms of their applicants' citation impact, Q2 the next 25 per cent, etc., and Q4 the top 25 per cent. The figure shows that an application's probability to be granted increases with increasing citation impact (quartile) of its applicants.

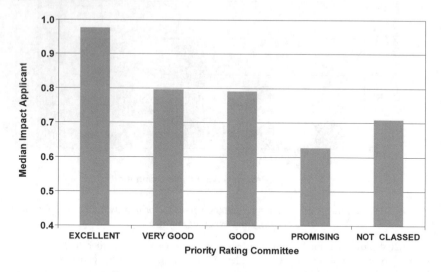

Figure 20.7. Applicants' citation impact versus committees' priority rankings

Figure 20.7 shows that the median citation impact of applicants of proposals rated excellent is 0.98. This score is higher than that for all other applications. There are no differences in applicants' citation impact between 'very good' and 'good' applications in the perception of the Council's expert committees.

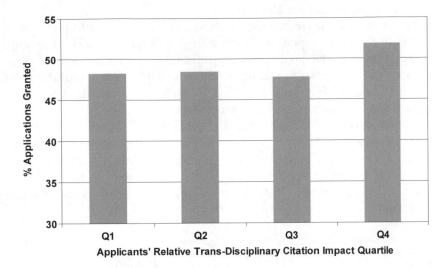

Figure 20.8. Percentage of applications granted versus applicants' trans-disciplinary citation
impact

Applications were grouped into quartiles (Q1–Q4) on the basis of their applicants' trans-disciplinary citation impact. For the definition of trans-disciplinary citation impact see Section 20.2. Figure 20.8 displays relative trans-disciplinary citation impact. Outcomes based on an absolute measure are similar. It shows that an application's probability of being granted hardly varies with the trans-disciplinary citation impact of the work of its applicants.

Table 20.4 presents the outcomes of a logistic regression analysis of applications with the probability to be granted as the dependent variable, and proximity to the expert committees, citation impact and trans-disciplinary citation impact of their applicants as independent variables. The size of the project in terms of total budget requested, and the first applicant's institution are control variables. From this table and Figures 20.5 to 20.8 above the following conclusions can be drawn.

– Applications submitted by applicants who were members of the evaluating expert committee showed a much higher probability of being granted than those submitted by scientists who have never been a member of any committee.

– No differences were found in applicants' citation impact between applications rated by the expert committees as very good and those qualified as good, even though Figure 20.3 showed that in some years the former had a much higher probability of being granted than the latter.

– Applications submitted by researchers who were among the top 25 per cent of applicants in terms of their citation impact, had a higher probability of being granted than those submitted by researchers who were among the bottom 25 per cent.

– According to the regression analysis, all variables but one had a significant effect upon the probability of being granted. The only exception was the applicants' trans-disciplinary citation impact. This factor did not significantly influence their applications' probability of being granted. There are therefore no indications that the procedures were biased against trans-disciplinary research.

– Measured by the Chi-Square statistic, the largest influence was generated by the proximity between applicants of a submitted application and the expert committee evaluating it. Although committee members were found to have a somewhat higher citation impact than other researchers active in the country, the logistic regression analysis takes this into account.

Table 20.4. Maximum likelihood analysis of variance table

Source	DF	Chi-Square	Prob
Intercept	1	18.47	0.000
Citation impact applicants	3	26.97	0.000
Relative trans-disciplinary citation impact applicants	1	0.29	0.593
Proximity applicant–committee	2	112.50	0.000
Sum requested	1	45.47	0.000
Institution applicant	4	25.94	0.000
Likelihood ratio	199	230.23	0.064

Results are outcomes of a logistic regression analysis using the procedure CADMOD available in the SAS System. The number of applications involved in the analysis was approximately 2,500. They were submitted during the period 1991–2000 and covered the natural and life sciences only. Similarly to the analysis presented in Figure 20.6, applications were grouped into quartiles on the basis of the citation impact of their applicants. With respect to the relative trans-disciplinary citation impact, applications were grouped into an upper and a lower half. Proximity between applicant and committee was measured on a three-point scale rather than the five-point scale presented in Table 20.2, and did not discriminate between first and co-applicant. The Likelihood ratio of 0.064 indicates that the model adequately describes the data and that no interaction terms need to be included. An analysis based on applications from the four most recent years (1997–2000) provided similar outcomes. The only difference is that the institution of the applicant has no significant effect. This factor was politically rather sensitive but is not further discussed in this chapter. Applications involving 'big' projects (requesting more than 250,000 Euros) have a higher probability of being granted than those submitting smaller projects.

20.4   Discussion and conclusions

A public report was published, presenting all outcomes of the study. It included numerous notes and comments made by representatives of the Research Council, stating the views of the Board of Directors on particular issues and providing relevant background knowledge. The report concluded that the evaluation and granting procedures adopted by the Council did take into account and to some extent did reward the citation impact of applicants of submitted proposals, and that there were no apparent impediments to trans-disciplinary research activities. The report raised a number of issues that can be summarised as follows.

- To what extent is the budget allocated to a granted application sufficient to carry out the research activities described in the proposal?
- To what extent should the distribution of funds among disciplines be influenced by the citation impact of national researchers active in those disciplines, or more generally, by the level of national performance in a discipline?
- Is it necessary to adjust the procedures for handling applications submitted by members of expert committees in order to make the procedures more equitable?
- Is there a need for expert committees to discriminate more rigorously between very good and good applications?
- Is there a need to develop ways to stimulate more strongly trans-disciplinary research?
- Is it appropriate that expert committees evaluate applications, decide on granting and fix budgets at the same time?

The study provided evidence that funding procedures based on peer review may be negatively affected by factors that do not relate to the intrinsic quality of proposals or to the past performance of their applicants. Peer review processes of grant applications may be biased in favour of applicants who have a close proximity to the peer committees evaluating applications. The outcomes of the study stimulated a policy debate, both within the Research Council itself, and between its Board of Directors and the national government. It focused on the need to develop instruments for distributing funds among disciplines, to sharpen the quality criteria applied by the committees, to stimulate trans-disciplinary research, and to adjust the procedures related to applications submitted by members of evaluating committees.

PART 2.7

MACRO STUDIES

Chapter 21

DID GLOBAL SCIENTIFIC PUBLICATION PRODUCTIVITY INCREASE DURING THE 1980s AND 1990s?

21.1   Introduction

During the past decades, public funding of research has become more and more dependent upon performance criteria based on the value-for-money principle. The science system and its institutions were stimulated to enhance their productivity. Collaboration, globalisation and economic relevance became main incentives. Research evaluation and performance assessments, in which bibliometric indicators played an increasingly important role, were conducted on a regular basis. Their application may have influenced scientists' publication strategics.

A thorough analysis of the effects of these trends upon the global science system and their interrelationships has a high policy relevance, as its outcomes are expected to provide a sound basis for future informed research policy and effective policy measures. This chapter assesses the *net* effect of these trends upon scientists' publication productivity, expressed by the number of published research papers per scientist. In view of the vital importance of basic research and all the efforts to improve its productivity, one would perhaps expect it to increase during the past decades. But did it increase? And if not, why not? Or did it even decrease, as several bibliometric investigators suggested?

A meta analysis of all articles in journals processed during 1980–2002 by the Institute for Scientific Information (ISI) for the *Science Citation Index* and related Citation Indexes on CD-ROM showed that the annual number of papers increased, with a mean annual growth rate (MAGR) of 2.5 per cent, from 480,000 to 810,000. An estimated 80 per cent of papers is published by academic institutions and publicly funded research institutions. The number of unique authors publishing in a year almost doubled from 540,000 to 1,100,000. The total number of times scientists authored a paper in a year increased with an MAGR of 4.5 per cent, to over 3 million in 2002.

Table 21.1. Indicators and their interpretation

Indicator	Interpretation	1980	2002	MAGR 1980–2002
Papers	Global publication output	478,000	814,000	+ 2.5 %
Unique publishing authors	Total number of authors publishing in a year	545,000	1,095,000	+ 3.3 %
Authorships	Number of times scientists authored a paper	1,187,000	3,081,000	+ 4.5 %
Authorships per paper	Scientific collaboration, average team size	2.48	3.79	+ 1.9 %
Authorships per publishing author	Papers in an 'average' author's annual publication list	2.17	2.81	+ 1.2 %
Papers per unique publishing author	Publication productivity	0.88	0.74	- 0.7 %

MAGR: Mean annual growth rate during 1980–2002.

Three ratios were calculated. The first was the number of *authorships per paper*, reflecting collaboration, particularly the average size of the team producing the papers. It increased by almost 2 per cent per year, from 2.5 to 3.8 authorships per paper. The second was the number of *authorships per publishing author*, reflecting the number of papers an 'average' author adds in a year to his or her publication list. In everyday language one would use the term '*papers* per publishing author' rather than '*authorships* per publishing author', but in this chapter the latter term is used in order to clearly distinguish this ratio from a third ratio defined below. It increased by 1.2 per cent per year, from 2.2 to 2.8 authorships per publishing author. Thus, in 1980, a team of 2.5 authors published 2.2 ISI papers, whereas in 2002, a team of 3.8 authors produced on average 2.8 ISI papers.

A third ratio is defined as the total number of papers published jointly by all authors, divided by the number of unique publishing authors, and can be termed as annual *publication productivity*. It declined, with a mean annual decline rate of 0.7 per cent, from 0.88 to 0.74 papers per unique publishing author per year. A decline was also observed in earlier studies covering the same time period (Persson et al., 2004) or for an even longer time period (Mabe and Amin, 2002). These studies were rightly cautious in drawing conclusions in terms of trends in scientific productivity. The next section argues that this outcome cannot be interpreted as a genuine decline in global publication productivity.

21.2   Further analysis at an aggregate level

An in-depth analysis inspired by Derek de Solla Price (1980a) categorised authors publishing in a year into *continuants*, *movers*, *newcomers*, and *transients*. It took into account a fixed publication 'window' of four years, being the typical duration of a PhD period. Their definitions are illustrated in Figure 21.1, and defined in its legend. It was found that the percentage share of continuants slightly increased during 1984–1998 by 0.25 per cent per year, whereas those for movers, newcomers and transients declined by -0.45, -0.05 and -0.70 per cent, respectively. In 1998 their percentage shares were 65.9, 9.3, 12.0 and 12.8, respectively.

	T-4	T-3	T-2	T-1	T	T+1	T+2	T+3	T+4
Continuant			X		X			X	
Newcomer					X		X		
Mover		X			X				
Transient					X				
Active but not publishing			X			X			

Figure 21.1. Categorisation of authors in a given year

The grey cells indicate the publication window that is taken into account in the definition of the various author categories for a particular year T. As an example, cells marked with 'X' indicate particular years in which authors may have published at least one paper. Authors publishing in year T who had at least one paper during a period of four years preceding T and at least one paper in the four years following T, were defined as *continuants* in year T. *Newcomers* in year T were defined as authors with no papers in the preceding 4 years and at least one paper in the 4 subsequent years, and *movers* as authors with a paper in the 4 preceding years but no publications during the 4 subsequent years. *Transients* in year T have only published papers in T and no papers in the four preceding or subsequent years. In this way authors could be categorised for the years 1984–1998. *Active though not publishing scientists* in year T were defined as authors who did not publish in year T, but who did publish at least one paper during a time period of P1 years preceding T and in the P2 years following T, with the constraint that P1+P2 does not exceed 4.

It can be assumed that continuants are on average more productive than those who are at the start or end of their careers, or those who publish only occasionally. Apparently, the observed decline in publishing authors' publication productivity cannot be explained by a relative decline of continuants in a particular year.

Price (1980a) defined *active* scientists in a year as scientists who *published* in that year. But active scientists do not necessarily publish papers in each year of their career. Therefore, a new measure of the number of scientists active in a year assumes that active scientists publish at least one paper every *four years*, and includes not only scientists who published in the particular year, but also those who did not publish in that year, but who did publish papers shortly before and after. Details are given in Figure 21.1 and its legend.

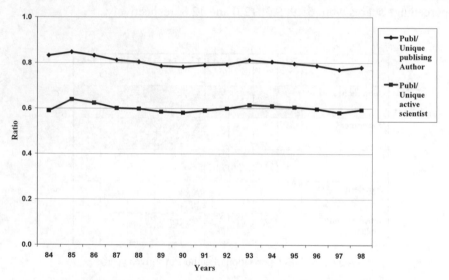

Figure 21.2. Global publication productivity measured in two ways

The upper graph in Figure 21.2 gives the annual publication productivity as defined by Price, assuming that the number of scientists active in a year equals the number of authors publishing in that year. It shows a slightly declining trend. The lower graph is based on the assumption that a scientist active in a particular year publishes at least one paper every four years, but not necessarily in that year itself. It fluctuates around a level of about 0.6 papers per active scientist per year. The deviations from this level reflect rapid expansions of the coverage of the ISI Citation Indexes on CD-ROM in the years 1985 and 1992-1993.

In the total population of scientists active in a year, the proportion of scientists *not* publishing in that year declined by 1.3 per cent per year, from 29 per cent in 1984 to 24 per cent in 1998. The annual productivity measure defined in Section 21.1 *over*estimates the productivity per active scientist, as it takes into account only authors who published in a year. An annual productivity ratio calculated as the number of papers per unique active (publishing or non-publishing) scientist in a year revealed a more-or-less constant level of about 0.6 papers per unique active scientist per year. This is shown in Figure 21.2.

21.3 Analysis by discipline

Table 21.2 presents indicators per discipline. The second column in this table gives the mean annual growth rate in the *percentage share of active scientists in a discipline*, relative to the total number of active scientists across all disciplines. This calculation relates to the period 1993–1998, as changes in the coverage of the ISI Citation Indexes on CD-ROM in earlier years would too strongly distort the figures. It shows that in physics and chemistry disciplines this share declined over the years, whereas in medical and biological sciences it increased. The third column gives this percentage share of active scientists in 1998, the most recent year for which it could be calculated.

The mean annual growth rate (MAGR) in *the number of authorships per paper* – reflecting collaboration or team size – was in most disciplines around the overall score of 2.5[1]. The *number of authorships per active scientist* – reflecting the number of papers an average scientist adds in a year to his or her publication list – increased in all fields, although in physics and chemistry it increased more rapidly than in medical-biological disciplines.

Moreover, in the former group of disciplines the *number of papers per unique active scientist* – measuring publication productivity – showed an increase, with mean annual growth rates between 1.3 and 2.5 per cent, whereas in the latter it declined, with MAGR between -1.1 and -0.2 per cent. In the group of other science fields, engineering and particularly mathematics revealed an increase, and geosciences a decline in this indicator. All disciplines from social sciences also showed a decline, but humanities & arts showed an increase.

Table 21.2. Indicators per discipline

Discipline	% Active scientists		Authorships/ Active scientist		Papers/unique Active scientist	
	MAGR 1993– 1998	Score in 1998	MAGR 1984– 1998	Score in 1998	MAGR 1984– 1998	Score in 1998
* Total ISI *			2.4	2.1	0.1	0.59
Physics & chemistry						
Appl phys & chem	-0.2	9.2	4.8	2.4	2.5	0.68
Chemistry	-0.8	9.3	3.0	2.5	1.6	0.71
Physics & astron	-0.7	6.8	4.6	3.3	1.3	0.76
Medical & biol sci						
Biol Sci - anim & plants	0.5	7.9	1.1	1.4	-1.1	0.47
Biol Sci - humans	0.6	13.1	1.4	2.0	-0.7	0.48
Clin medicine	0.0	27.3	2.1	2.4	-0.2	0.53
Mol biol & biochem	0.8	6.9	1.7	2.0	-0.4	0.50
Other science						
Engineering	0.3	5.5	2.6	1.4	0.7	0.53
Geosciences	0.9	3.4	1.7	1.4	-0.6	0.46
Mathematics	1.5	1.6	2.8	1.4	1.6	0.76
Social sci & humanties						
Psychol, psychiat	0.5	2.7	1.1	1.5	-1.0	0.55
Economics	-0.2	1.0	0.7	1.2	-0.5	0.69
Social sci~medicine	3.2	1.4	1.5	1.3	-0.9	0.44
Other social sci	-2.0	1.9	0.4	1.0	-1.0	0.62
Humanities & arts	-3.9	2.2	1.1	1.1	0.4	0.90

MAGR: Mean annual growth rate expressed as a percentage.

All ISI papers were categorised into 15 main disciplines, and authors were assigned to the discipline in which they had the highest percentage share of their papers. For the definition of disciplines, see Table 14.2 in Chapter 14.

% Active scientists in a discipline are relative to the total number of active scientists across all disciplines.

Authorships/Active scientist gives the number of papers an 'average' scientist adds in a year to his or her publication list.

Papers/Unique active scientist gives the total number of papers published by active scientists in a discipline (counting only a fraction if a paper is published by authors from more than one discipline) divided by all scientists active in the discipline. In a fractional scheme a paper published by n1 authors from discipline D1 and n2 from D2 contributes a fraction n1/(n1+n2) to the counts of D1 and a portion n2/(n1+n2) to those of D2.

21.4 Discussion and conclusions

As outlined in Section 21.1, many factors influence global publication productivity, and the analysis presented above assessed their *net* effect. Therefore, it marks only a first step of a more detailed study aimed at measuring effects of individual factors. A first, exploratory discussion is presented from two distinct points of view:

– Possible effects of the use of various types of bibliometric indicators in research evaluation upon scholars' *publication practices*: salami-style of publishing; authorship inflation; and a shift from a 'quantity' to a 'quality of publication' strategy.

– Possible effects upon the scholarly system of recent policies, aiming to enhance its efficiency and productivity, economic relevance, scientific collaboration, and globalisation.

Changes in publication practices

It has been claimed that the 'publish or perish' incentive forced scientists more and more to a *salami-style of publishing*, cutting slices from an integral piece of work that in the past would have been published in a single paper, and publishing each slice in a separate paper, thus increasing their publication output. This would positively influence scientists' publication productivity. Unless it is neutralised by other factors, the observed constant number of papers per active scientist in science and scholarship as a whole does not provide evidence for such a trend during the 1980s and 1990s. This conclusion is similar to that drawn by Mabe and Amin (2002). The analysis by discipline, however, revealed that global publication productivity tended to increase in physics and chemistry fields, and to decline in medical and biological sciences. Following the salami-style of publishing hypothesis, this outcome may indicate a growing tendency towards such a style of publishing in the former group of fields.

However, if the trend towards higher shares of medical-biological active scientists observed in the ISI Citation Indexes reflects a relative shift in the targets of global research funding in favour of the medical-biological sciences, the increase in publication productivity of researchers in physics and chemistry fields could also be interpreted as a *compensation effect*. Scientists in these fields compensated the *relative* decline in funding by jointly producing more papers per scientist. Such a compensation effect was suggested by Braun et al. (1989) as regards the British science system in their discussion on the decline of British science.

In addition, one may distinguish several publication strategies that influence the size of publication output in opposite directions and are correlated with distinct types of bibliometric indicators in the evaluation sphere. The first may be denoted as the *quantity of publication* strategy, of which salami-style of publishing is an extreme manifestation. Its bibliometric correlate in the evaluation sphere is the sheer number of papers published. Other strategies take into account the *'quality' of the publications*. An extreme form is a strategy aiming to publish as many papers as possible in 'top' journals (Moed, 2000; Lawrence, 2003). It is rewarded in assessments on the basis of the number of papers in journals with a high journal impact factor. Other strategies may seek a balance between these two extremes, and may conceive publications as proper means to account for research funding, but are reluctant to overemphasise quantity, as it is expected to produce a 'dilution effect' with a negative influence upon a group's citation per publication ratio (see Chapter 25).

If a shift towards the 'quality of publication' strategy played any role at all, findings suggest that during the past two decades it was more often adopted in medical and biological disciplines than in physics and chemistry fields. It would follow that the number of papers in 'high impact' journals was more frequently applied in performance assessments in the former fields than it was in the latter. However, there is evidence that physics and chemistry disciplines are catching up in this respect. The number of submissions to 'top' journals in chemistry has increased so strongly that the editors of these journals recently decided to limit the number of manuscripts entering the formal peer review process by rejecting in advance a substantial fraction of them (e.g., Stang, 2005).

In order to become an author of a paper, the size of the contribution of a scientist to the work described in it must exceed a certain minimum, and it is claimed that this threshold declined over the years. This process could be termed as *authorship inflation*, and is stimulated by the increasing use of multi-partnership and the length of participants' publication lists as criteria in research assessment exercises and funding decisions.

It would lead to an increase in the average number of authorships per paper, but not necessarily to an increase in the number of papers per active scientist. The same pool of scientists may publish a constant numbers of papers over the years, but by increasing co-authorship each individual author may augment the annual number of papers listed in his or her curriculum vitae. The observed overall pattern in the data is consistent with such a process. But as outlined below, it does not follow that authorship inflation is the only factor augmenting the number of authors in the byline of a paper.

Although electronic publishing, particularly in *e-print archives* is becoming increasingly important, the extent to which it actually replaces traditional publishing in the serial literature is unclear and needs to be analysed in more detail. This factor could at best negatively influence author publication productivity in ISI covered journals in recent years, but would not explain the patterns found during the entire period 1980–2002.

Productivity, economic relevance, and globalisation

It is true that the role of publicly funded scientists as inventors in *patents* is important in science intensive fields (Noyons et al., 2003; Schmoch, 2004), and that their involvement in technical-innovative activities has grown over the years. Generally, growing emphasis on *economic relevance* may negatively affect author publication productivity in international journals processed for the ISI Citation Indexes. But it is questionable whether this factor had a very strong negative influence upon academic publishing. In order to attract funds from external agencies, including those from the private sector, university groups contributing as inventors to patents need to remain visible at the international research front by publishing papers.

Rising numbers of authorships per paper do not merely reflect authorship inflation. Increasing *scientific collaboration* within institutions or among groups from various countries also positively affects this parameter. If this factor is dominant and not neutralised by other factors, however, it apparently has had *no positive* effect upon scientists' publication productivity. This finding suggests that the amount of energy and resources absorbed by collaborative work and globalisation is so substantial, that it held overall publication productivity back from an increase. Following this line of reasoning, increasing research productivity or efficiency on the one hand, and collaboration and globalisation on the other, are to some extent conflicting policy objectives.

Notes

[1] In all science fields it ranged between 2.2 and 2.7, in social sciences between 1.3 and 2.0, whereas in humanities and arts it was 3.2. The number of authorships per paper in most disciplines is higher than that for the total database (1.9 per cent according to Table 21.1), as a discipline's counts include co-authorships of collaborating scientists from other disciplines.

Chapter 22

MEASURING TRENDS IN NATIONAL PUBLICATION OUTPUT

22.1 Introduction

Measuring national research performance with the use of bibliometric indicators is an activity with a long tradition. Price (1978), Price (1980b), Narin (1976), Braun, Glänzel and Schubert (Braun et al., 1988), and many others made important contributions to this topic. Very recently, Godin (2005) published a book presenting an historical overview of the development of statistics on science and technology. Nowadays many countries publish National Science Indicators Reports and analyse what bibliometric indicators express about the state of a nation's research system, and about the level of its research performance. Data from the Citation Indexes produced by the Institute for Scientific Information plays a crucial role in the construction of such indicators.

For instance, *Science and Engineering Indicators 2002* is a report of the US National Science Board, the governing body of the National Science Foundation (NSF, 2002). The bibliometric indicators presented are derived from the Science Indicators Database produced by CHI Research for the US National Science Foundation, based on raw data material from ISI's *Science Citation Index* and *Social Science Citation Index*. The French Observatoire des Sciences et des Techniques (OST, 2004), the Netherlands Observatory of Science and Technology (NOWT, 2004) and the Flemish Steunpunt voor O&O Statistieken (SOOS, 2003) publish national science indicator reports, and present bibliometric indicators derived from special databases they constructed themselves from raw data obtained from the ISI Citation Indexes. The European Commission publishes S&T indicators reports (EC, 2003). Thomson Scientific publishes ISI Essential Science Indicators of the research performance of countries on a regular basis. These indicators are used for secondary analysis by several national agencies (e.g. King, 2004).

Interpreting bibliometric indicators at the macro level is by no means an easy task. Some indicators are based on absolute numbers, and others on simple percentages or more sophisticated 'relative' measures. Some reflect pure 'output' or production, whereas others either implicitly or explicitly relate 'output' to 'input'. Studies assessing a particular aspect of national research performance normally do not present a single indicator for that aspect, but rather a series of indicators. This is in itself appropriate, as knowledgeable users of statistical data are aware that one should not rely too strongly upon a single indicator. But what if the various indicators seem to lead to different conclusions? Next, the various producers of macro indicators do not apply the same methodology. They found different solutions to a number of major methodological problems. Different methodologies may lead to different outcomes, and hence, potentially, to different conclusions. Finally, even when producers use the same methodology and find the same quantitative pattern, their interpretations of that pattern may differ from one another.

Grupp and Mogee discussed the current status of S&T indicators, and focused on newer developments towards composite indicators, benchmarking, and scoreboarding. They illustrated what they denoted as "the vulnerability of S&T indicators to manipulation", by showing in particular cases how rank positions of countries depend upon which indicators were selected and how they were transformed into a composite index. They concluded: "It seems not to be too difficult to argue for a 'country friendly' selection and corresponding weighting of indicators. Thus the use of scoreboards opens space for manipulation in the policymaking system" (Grupp and Mogee, 2004, p. 75).

Selective use may occur not only in the construction and interpretation of complex composite indicators, but also with respect to more simple, elementary ones based on publication counts. Conclusions regarding a decline or increase in national publication output or productivity may strongly depend upon the type of indicators calculated, and the time period taken into account. In many cases a country may show an increase in one indicator and a decline in another.

The principal remedy bibliometricians have against misinterpretation or selective use of their indicators is to explain as accurately as possible how these indicators were constructed; what assumptions underlie them; what methodological problems are involved in their construction and how these problems were solved; which factors should be taken into account in interpreting them; and how, from an integral perspective, outcomes depend on the type of indicators used. The aim of this chapter is to provide such information related to the use of publication-based macro indicators. Thus, this chapter provides information of a more technical nature that may assist a user in properly interpreting such indicators.

Persson and Danell (2004) have demonstrated the relevance of "decomposing national trends" in bibliometric macro indicators, by disaggregating a national system into its principal components (e.g, particular fields or institutions), and statistically examining the influence of particular entities upon the macro trend. This chapter focuses on general tendencies in the data collected for 20 major countries. Its aim is not to assess particular countries' research performance. This latter task could be carried out properly only within the framework of specific policy questions that one seeks to answer, and by using information from other sources, as is normally carried out in national science indicators reports.

It must also be noted that national publication counts represent a rather elementary type of macro indicators. More sophisticated indicators take into account for instance the citation impact of a country's papers, or relate bibliometric indicators to input statistics of a country's R&D activities, such as those compiled by the OECD (e.g., Luwel, 2004). Braun (2004) developed macro indicators based upon an analysis of patterns in editorial gate keeping, focusing for instance on the country of origin of editors of major scientific journals.

22.2   Difficulties in constructing and interpreting publication based macro indicators

At first sight it may seem a simple task from a technical point of view to determine in a scientific literature database the number of papers 'published from a country', or more precisely, by scientists who are affiliated to institutions located in a particular country. One counts the number of papers per country of origin using the institutional affiliations in the byline of papers and included in ISI's corporate address field. Next, one analyses trends in some comparative perspective.

However, any attempt to carry out analyses at the level of individual countries is confronted with a number of methodological problems. One of the most crucial is how to handle papers reporting on collaborative work, published by authors affiliated with institutions from different countries. Three technical ways to handle internationally co-authored papers are denoted as 'fractional', 'integer' or 'whole', and 'first author' counting, respectively. The following example may clarify these schemes. If a paper is published by authors from three institutions located in country A, and from two institutions in country B, a fractional scheme attributes to that paper a fraction 3/5 to country A and 2/5 to country B, whereas an integer scheme assigns the paper integrally (or wholly) both to A and to B.

A country's integer count gives the number of papers in which at least one of its authors participated. In short, it measures participation. A fractional count gives the number of papers 'creditable' to a country, assuming that all authors or institutions made equal contributions to an internationally co-authored paper, and that all contributions add up to one.

A third scheme assigns an internationally co-authored paper integrally to the country of its first or reprint author. It assumes that the first or reprint author made the largest contribution to such a paper. This indicator was applied in earlier work by Braun et al. (1988). In this book it is further explored in Chapter 23. This chapter focuses on the fractional and integer scheme, since these are applied in more recent studies discussed in this chapter.

In a series of research articles published in the late 1980s and early 1990s, Ben Martin and colleagues analysed patterns in annual counts of publications from the UK. In their 1987 paper entitled "The continuing decline of British science" they analysed indicators from the Science Indicators Database produced by CHI Research (Martin et al., 1987). These indicators were based on a fractional counting scheme of internationally co-authored papers. They concluded that "publication and citation data for the period up to 1984 indicate that the relative decline in British science is continuing, albeit at a slower rate than in the 1970s".

Science and Engineering Indicators 2002 presented indicators for the USA produced by CHI Research, applying basically the same methodology as that used in the studies by Martin et al. It was found that the during the period 1992–1999 the US publication output declined by 10 per cent (NSF, 2002, Table 5.16, pp. 5–39 to 5–41).

Comparing the two studies, one notices a difference in the way the publication based macro indicators are interpreted. Whereas Martin et al. interpreted the observed decline in the UK's proportion of (fractionally counted) papers in the SCI database as evidence of a decline of British science, the US Indicators Report concluded that "the number of U.S.-authored papers appear to have fallen from the level in the early 1990s", but that "the reasons for this development remain unknown". It stated that the fractional counting scheme is biased against growth, and highlighted the possible effect of displacement of papers from 'established' countries, particularly the USA, by those from developing ones. In addition, it observed that the absolute – wholly counted – number of US papers did show growth, and seemed at least to suggest that this pattern may reflect more properly the trend in the US science system's performance than the fractional counting method.

A study by David A. King (2004) analysed essential science indicators for countries provided by Thomson Scientific/ISI. The solution it found to the problem of internationally co-authored papers and changes in database coverage is rather different from that suggested by CHI Research. It applied an integer counting scheme and calculated for each country the percentage of papers from the total database to which it contributed. Due to the fact that an internationally co-authored paper was fully attributed to each participating country, the sum of this percentage over all countries exceeded 100 per cent, a statistical property strongly criticised by Martin et al. Analysing data for the period 1993–2001, the UK was identified as the "top of the premier league" on the basis of its author productivity (number of publications per author) and several other indicators relating research outputs to inputs.

22.3   Eleven indicators and their interpretation

A basic unit in the analysis presented in this chapter is the author. For each author the most probable country of origin was determined, on the basis of a number of plausible assumptions and decision rules. Papers were assigned to countries on the basis of the country of origin of their authors. The outcome of this procedure provided a unique basis for a rough, statistical analysis of patterns in authorship by country and in international scientific collaboration. 'Country of origin' should be interpreted as the country where the institution is located to which the author is affiliated, and not in terms of nationality. Authors of a paper assigned to a country who are from that country are denoted below as *domestic* authors, and those who are from abroad as *foreign* authors.

Table 22.1 presents mean annual growth rates (MAGR) in 11 indicators for 20 countries. The analysis relates to the five-year period 1998–2002. These growth rates were expressed as a percentage and were rounded to the nearest integer percentage value. For instance, mean annual growth rates between -0.5 and +0.5 per cent are indicated as 0 per cent. It presents outcomes for the top 20 countries in terms of the raw number of papers published during the period 1998–2002, given in the second column of Table 22.1. These countries account for 89 per cent of all papers in the ISI Citation Indexes used in this study. The time period is rather short and could easily be extended, but is often applied in national science indicators reports. Countries are ranked by descending MAGR in the raw number of papers presented in column 3. They are arranged into four groups according to this growth rate, denoted as 'top', 'moderately' and 'weakly' growing countries, and countries showing no growth, respectively.

Table 22.1. Mean annual growth rates for 11 indicators and 20 major countries

1	2	3	4	5	6	7	8	9	10	11	12	13
Coun -try	Total Pr/ 1,000	Mean Annual Growth Rate (MAGR) 1998–2002										
		Pr	% Pr	DA	% DA	Pf	% Pf	Pr/ Pf	Pf/ DA	AS/ DA	FAS /Pr	DAS /Pr
Top growing countries												
PRC	50	12	11	9	7	13	12	3	4	6	0	3
SOK	21	10	10	7	5	11	10	3	3	7	-3	3
BRA	11	10	9	11	9	10	9	-1	-1	1	-2	3
TWN	14	7	6	4	2	5	4	2	1	3	0	1
IND	26	5	4	5	3	4	3	1	-1	1	3	1
Moderately growing countries												
ESP	33	4	3	4	2	3	3	0	-1	0	1	0
ITA	40	3	3	3	1	2	1	1	0	0	1	-1
BEL	12	2	1	3	1	0	-1	0	-2	-1	7	0
AUS	24	2	1	2	0	0	-1	0	-2	0	7	0
ISR	11	2	1	3	1	1	0	-1	-2	-1	-1	0
CAN	41	2	1	1	-1	0	-1	0	-2	0	5	-1
USA	355	2	1	1	-1	0	-1	1	-1	1	5	0
Weakly growing countries												
SWE	18	1	1	1	0	-1	-1	0	-2	-1	5	-1
JPN	82	1	1	2	0	0	0	-1	-2	0	4	1
SWI	16	1	0	1	-1	-1	-2	0	-2	-2	0	-2
NLD	21	1	0	1	-1	-1	-1	0	-1	0	5	0
GER	88	1	0	1	-1	-1	-2	0	-2	-1	5	0
FRA	61	1	0	1	-1	-1	-2	0	-2	-1	5	-1
Countries with no growth												
UK	93	0	-1	1	-1	-2	-3	0	-2	-1	4	0
RUS	25	0	-1	0	-2	-2	-3	0	-2	1	7	1

Data relate to the time period 1998-2002. Countries are ranked by descending mean annual growth rate in the raw number of papers presented in column 3. Mean annual growth rates during 1998-2002 are expressed as a percentage and are rounded to the nearest integer value.
Total Pr/1,000: Raw number of papers during 1998-2002 expressed as a multiple of 1,000.
Pr, %PR: Absolute and relative raw publication counts applying an integer counting scheme.
DA, %DA: Absolute and relative number of domestic authors.
Pf, %Pf: Absolute and relative publication counts applying a fractional counting scheme.
Pr/DA: Raw number of papers per unique publishing domestic author.
Pf/DA: Fractionally counted number of papers per unique publishing domestic author.
AS/DA: Number of authorships per publishing domestic author.
FAS/Pr: The number of foreign authorships per raw domestic paper.
DAS/Pr: The number of domestic authorships per raw domestic paper.
PRC: Peoples Republic of China. SOK: South Korea. BRA: Brazil. TWN: Taiwan. IND: India. ESP: Spain. ITA: Italy. BEL: Belgium. AUS: Australia. ISR: Israel. CAN: Canada. USA: United States of America. SWE: Sweden. JPN: Japan. SWI: Switzerland. NLD: Netherlands. GER: Germany. FRA: France. UK: United Kingdom. RUS: Russia.

It must be underlined that this grouping of countries is *not* designed with the purpose of creating appropriate benchmark groups, but merely to bring some order in the list. The analysis does not primarily aim at comparing countries with one another, but rather at showing how the various indicators behave differently from one another (and from one country to another), what is behind these differences, and why the perception of an 'average' individual scientist on publication productivity may diverge from that of a national evaluating agency. Section 22.5 below presents a detailed discussion of each separate indicator. In order to briefly explain this table, avoiding technicalities, this section focuses on one particular country: the USA.

For the USA, Table 22.1 shows that during the period 1998–2002 the number of papers in which US scientists participated (column 3) increased by 2 per cent per year. But the number of papers the USA can be credited with (applying a fractional counting scheme, column 7) was stable, and its share in the database (column 8) even declined. The US publication productivity ('creditable' or fractionally counted papers per US author, column 10) decreased as well, although an average US scientist added more papers to his or her curriculum vitae in 2002 than he or she did in 1998 (column 11).

What is happening? First, the number of US authors also increased (column 5), though at a lower rate than the number of papers to which US authors contributed (column 3). Hence, there is no evidence that the US active science force shrank during 1998–2002. Secondly, the average size of the US teams participating in the papers (column 13) remained stable. Therefore, it is not true that the papers in which US scientists participated had on average less US authors in 2002 than they had in 1998.

What is happening is that the size of the foreign teams participating in US papers expanded (column 12). In other words, there are *relatively* more foreign authors in US papers (i.e., papers in which US scientists participated) in 2002 than there were in 1998. This is what one would expect to see as globalisation and international collaboration increase. Many other countries show this pattern, but apparently not all of them.

Top growing countries show a different pattern. These countries not only published more raw papers, but the number – and in most cases even the proportion – of domestic scientists in the teams producing them increased as well. This discussion illustrates that one needs the full range of indicators presented in Table 22.1 in order to find an explanation for a country's trend in publication output.

22.4   Conclusions

On the one hand, papers resulting from international scientific collaboration are based on research efforts of scientists from several countries. One can therefore justly argue that it is inappropriate to assign such papers integrally to each contributing country, particularly when one focuses upon what domestic scientists and resources have produced. On the other hand, a crucial issue is whether the efforts involved in internationally collaborative papers are on average similar to that of producing non-collaborative papers.

Stating this issue in more technical terms, if internationally collaborative papers require more input resources than other types of papers, one could argue that it is more appropriate that the contributions of the various participating teams add up to a number *above* one. This point is further discussed in Chapter 27. It is particularly questionable whether a relative increase in the number of *foreign* authors in the papers in which a country participated can be interpreted in terms of a decline in publication output of that country.

It should also be underlined that relative measures or percentage shares, particularly the share of a country's papers or publishing authors relative to the global total, have the property that an increase for some countries (the 'expanding' ones) necessarily lead to a decline in that of at least some others (i.c., established countries).

These considerations lead to the conclusion that, in order to assess the trend in a single country's publication output, an analysis *per publishing author* explored in this chapter is most useful. Informative indicators are the absolute number of publishing domestic authors (column 5 in Table 22.1) and the average number of 'raw' papers per domestic author (column 9). Assuming that the ISI Citation Indexes provide a valid reflection of global scientific activity, these two indicators give an answer to the following questions: did the country's scientific workforce expand or shrink, and did the number of papers in which it participated per (unique publishing) domestic author increase or decline?

Perhaps the most important lesson to be learned from the technical exercise presented in this chapter is that, regardless of the indicators one uses, it is sensible to compare countries from some appropriate comparator group with one another. Focusing on a single country makes it much more difficult to properly interpret trends in indicators. All three studies mentioned in the introduction section actually applied such a comparative viewpoint. A next lesson is that it is crucial to define in the analysis of indicators a clear perspective and to state this explicitly. In order to achieve this, a valuable approach is to present a *series* of indicators and provide them with a consistent interpretation. None of the indicators is perfect and each one indicates a proper, distinct aspect of publication output. Applying any single measure isolated from the others may lead to an incomplete picture and invalid conclusions.

The use of the various types of publication productivity and collaboration indicators does provide a deeper insight into how domestic authors' publication and authoring practices are influenced by trends towards collaboration and globalisation, and thus helps to explain differences between outcomes based on an integer counting scheme and those applying fractional counts. Their application also illuminates how the perception of individual domestic authors regarding trends in their publication productivity may diverge from that of a policy analyst studying the national science system as a whole. An analysis of the type presented in Table 22.1 may therefore be a valuable tool in national science indicators reports for studying trends in national publication output.

This chapter analysed at a macro level a country's publication output, and showed the various ways of incorporating international scientific collaboration in its measurement. The next chapter analyses international scientific collaboration as a separate phenomenon. In addition, it also takes into account the citation impact of a country's papers.

22.5 Afterword: Detailed discussion of Table 22.1

Each indicator is discussed below. This discussion focuses on general patterns rather than on individual cases or exceptions from the general trend.

Pr: Raw publication counts with integer counting scheme (column 3)

If at the end of a year all authors from a country combine their individual publication lists, and ensure that papers published by two or more domestic authors are listed only once, the combined list contains all of the papers with at least one author from that country. In technical terms, an integer counting scheme is applied. This indicator can be denoted as the raw number of papers with at least one domestic author. A scientist tends to consider each paper that he or she authored as 'his' or 'her' paper, regardless of whether it was co-authored by other scientists. Similarly, a national agency or policy maker compiling a list of papers with at least one domestic author can conceive this list as the country's publication list, regardless of whether foreign co-authors were involved. But as is illustrated below, the perception of national trends in publication output obtained at this aggregate level does not necessarily coincide with that of an individual scientist contributing to the list.

The mean annual growth rate (MAGR) for this indicator (Pr) is presented in the third column of Table 22.1. Countries are grouped on the basis of their mean annual increase for this indicator. A first group denoted as 'top growers' with an MAGR of 5 per cent or more includes Peoples Republic of China, South Korea, Brazil, Taiwan and India. These countries could be denoted as the strongly emerging ones, although it is somewhat arbitrary to set the threshold at 5 per cent annual growth.

The next group of countries showing a moderate growth rate of 2 to 4 per cent includes Spain, Italy, USA, Canada, Australia, Belgium and Israel. Spain and Italy show growth rates of 4 and 3 per cent, respectively, whereas all other countries in this group have growth rates around 2 per cent. Next, Germany, Japan France, Netherlands, Sweden and Switzerland all show a weak MAGR of one per cent. Finally, for UK and Russia the MAGR is zero. The UK shows a growth during the first half of the period 1998–2002 and a decline in the second half, so that the mean growth rate for the entire period is approximately zero. Countries showing a moderate or weak growth or no growth at all are denoted below as 'established' countries.

It must be noted at this point that countries with smaller initial annual publication volumes, when they develop, tend to obtain higher growth rates than larger countries. This is a 'natural' phenomenon that one should always take into account when interpreting percentage growth data. Eugene Stanley et al. studied national science systems using models from modern statistical physics, and focused on the standard deviation in annual growth rates rather than on the rates themselves (Amaral et al., 1999; Matia et al., 2005).

In this context the 'displacement' phenomenon highlighted in the NSF Indicators Report and mentioned in Section 22.2 should be briefly discussed. Even when it is true that papers from established countries are displaced by those from emerging ones, it is questionable whether this can be interpreted as a factor that causes a bias. To the extent that this phenomenon takes place in an 'open competition' among established and emerging countries, apparently papers from the former group are not sufficiently significant to be accepted for publication in the international journals covered by the ISI Citation Indexes, and in an analysis of national research performance it would be appropriate that this phenomenon had a negative influence upon national publication counts.

It is also noteworthy that the ISI Citation Indexes do expand their coverage. Not only each year do they include more new journals than they remove previously processed ones, but at the same time established journals tend to publish more papers than they did in the past. It is an open question whether the increase in ISI source papers matches that of the total global literature, but it can be assumed that the ISI Indexes, particularly in the natural and life sciences, cover the most important ones (see Chapter 7).

Relative publication counts with integer counting scheme (%Pr, column 4)

One may argue that a database's coverage may expand or shrink, and that such changes in coverage may affect the absolute number of papers recorded in the database. Or one may claim that it is a global tendency to publish more, so that an increase in absolute numbers is in itself not significant, as most other countries may show the same pattern. Martin et al. (1987) denoted this phenomenon as 'literature inflation'. Following this line of reasoning, one may determine whether the number of papers with at least one domestic author increased faster than the total number of papers in the database under investigation. Due to international collaboration, the sum of percentages over all countries exceeds 100, since a paper with authors from two or more countries contributes integrally to the score of each of these.

The study by King (2004) applied this indicator. The fourth column in Table 22.1 gives for each country its MAGR during 1998–2002. It is approximately equal to the difference between the growth rate in the annual number of raw papers (column 3) and that for the total ISI database. The latter was found to be about one per cent. Hence, growth rates in column 4 tend to be 1 per cent lower than those in column 3. Discrepancies are caused by rounding percentage values to their nearest integer value.

Absolute and relative number of domestic authors (DA, %DA; columns 5, 6)

These indicators count the number of authors linked to a particular country and denoted as domestic authors. Annual growth rates in the absolute number of publishing domestic authors (*DA*, column 5) per country are in most cases equal to that of raw numbers of papers. In the total database the number of authors increased by about 2 per cent per year. As a result, the annual growth rate in a country's percentage of domestic authors, relative to the total number of authors (*%DA*, column 6), tends to be some 2 per cent lower than that calculated for the absolute number of domestic authors.

Interestingly, Peoples Republic of China, South Korea and Taiwan show rather large discrepancies between the MAGR in the absolute number of publishing authors and that for raw papers. This is probably an artefact in the data. As outlined in Chapter 14, in these countries particular family names are so common, e.g., 'Liang' or 'Kim', that even if one takes into account authors' initials, it is practically impossible to determine the number of unique scientists publishing in a year merely on the basis of their author names in a bibliographic database. In principle this problem affects all countries, but not to the same degree. Although this observation touches in a sense merely a detail, it is indicative of the type of measurement errors that may occur and of the knowledge one must take into account in properly interpreting bibliometric indicators.

Absolute and relative publication counts using a fractional counting scheme (Pf, %Pf; columns 7, 8)

A next perspective takes into account international co-authorship. Papers resulting from international scientific collaboration are based on research efforts of scientists from several countries. One can therefore argue that it is inappropriate to assign such papers integrally to each contributing country, particularly when one focuses upon what domestic scientists and resources have produced. Hence, CHI Research decided to apply a so-called fractional counting scheme, assigning a portion of each internationally co-authored paper to a country, based on the fraction of contributing institutions.

In this sense the number of fractionally counted papers can be conceived as the number of papers 'creditable' to a country. Thus, an implicit perspective underlying fractional counting is that of relating 'output' to 'input'. The analysis presented in this chapter calculates the fraction of domestic *authors* rather than that of domestic *institutions*, but a secondary analysis not presented in this chapter showed that for almost all countries the MAGR for the number of papers based on the two fractionation methods are about the same.

Application of a fractional counting scheme has a substantial effect upon the annual growth rate in the absolute (**Pf**, column 7) or relative (*%Pf*, column 8) number of domestic papers. Values in column 3 tend to be two percentage points lower, with some exceptions, particularly for strongly growing countries. For instance, all countries with a weak growth of about 1 per cent in *raw numbers*, except Japan, showed in the number of *fractionally counted* papers an annual decline rate of one per cent. Since the number of papers in the database increased with 1 per cent per year, the annual growth rates in the percentage of a country's fractionally counted papers, relative to the total in the database (*%Pf*), are generally one percentage point lower than that in their absolute numbers.

Author publication productivity using integer or fractional counting scheme (Pr/DA, Pf/DA, AS/DA; columns 9–11)

Productivity in terms of 'numbers of papers per publishing author' is the focus of the next perspective. One may calculate three distinct measures. All three relate to domestic authors publishing at least one paper in a particular year, and it is assumed that this number indicates the number of scientists active in a year. The first two are the number of papers produced per unique publishing domestic author, with papers counted on the basis of an integer (**Pr/DA**, column 9) and a fractional counting scheme (**Pf/DA**, column 10), respectively. The perspective underlying both measures is that of a national system as a whole, and does not coincide with that of individual scientists compiling their annual publication lists. Their MAGR can be estimated by simply subtracting the MAGR for the number of authors (**DA**, column 5) from that for the number of raw (**Pr**, column 3) or fractionally counted (**Pf**, column 7) papers, respectively. It must be remembered that percentages in the table are rounded to the nearest integer.

Focusing on 'established' countries, column 9 shows that for their majority the raw number of papers per domestic author remained constant. The fractionally counted number of papers per domestic author (column 10) declined by 2 per cent for all countries except the USA and the Netherlands, which had -1 per cent, and Italy, for which this indicator remained constant.

A third indicator (**AS/DA**, column 11) can be denoted as the average number of authorships per publishing domestic author. It gives the raw or integer counted number of papers they published on average in a year. These are the papers an 'average' domestic author includes in his or her annual publication list. In order to avoid confusion with the indicator in column 9, the term 'authorship' is used. Its MAGR is one per cent or more for top growing countries. Among established countries, 7 out of 15 showed a decline for this measure, while for another 5 countries it was zero. Only USA and Russia show a positive MAGR of 1 per cent.

The number of foreign and domestic authorships per raw domestic paper (FAS/Pr, DAS/Pr; columns 12, 13)

These indicators serve as a background, and enable one to explain in more detail the differences between several indicators in Table 22.1. The number of authorships of a paper is simply defined as the number of authors included in the paper's byline, and indicates the size of the team producing the paper. The first measure is an indicator of *international*, and the second of *national* collaboration. For established countries, columns 12 and 13 show the following general pattern: the total number of foreign authorships per raw domestic paper (***FAS/Pr***) increased for most countries, whereas the number of domestic authorships per paper (***DAS/Pr***) tended to remain constant or to decline.

In other words, the teams producing papers tended to expand with foreign authors, whereas the number of domestic authors employed in these teams remained constant or declined; hence the share of domestic authors in these teams tended to drop. This phenomenon caused the annual growth rate in the number of fractionally counted papers from these countries to be lower than that for raw numbers of papers. Top growing countries to some extent tended to show the opposite pattern: the number of domestic authorships per paper increased for all 5 countries, in most cases faster than the total number of authorships per paper. Thus, those countries not only published more raw papers, but the number – and in most cases even the proportion – of domestic scientists in the teams producing them increased as well.

AS/DA, the average number of authorships per domestic author (column 11), equals the product of ***DAS/Pr*** (column 13) and ***Pr/DA*** (column 9). Hence, the MAGR in the first is approximately equal to the sum of growth rates of the other two. It should be noted that several countries revealed a slight decline in the latter two indicators with an MAGR between -0.5 and 0.0. In Table 22.1 the growth rates of each of these are rounded up to 0, whereas their sum is lower than –0.5, and therefore lead to rounded growth rates of –1 per cent for the indicator AS/DA.

DAS/Pr thus statistically relates two productivity indicators embodying distinct perspectives. It relates a national view of what all domestic authors have jointly produced (***Pr/DA***) with individual domestic authors' perception of what they have produced in a year, though expressed as an average over all authors (***AS/DA***). The latter two measures may reveal different trends. For instance, the average number of papers in a Japanese author's annual publication list remained constant, whereas the overall raw publication productivity of Japanese authors declined. The explanation for this paradox is that Japanese authors tend to collaborate more with one another. Italy is one of the countries showing a negative trend in national collaboration. Annual publication lists of its domestic researchers did not become longer, but its overall raw publication productivity increased.

Concluding remarks

It should be noted that in this chapter papers from all disciplines are aggregated. In Chapter 21 it is shown that substantial difference exist among disciplines with respect to publication practices expressed in the average number of authors per publication, or the average number of authorships per author. In addition, countries show differences with respect to the distribution of papers among disciplines. Therefore, a more detailed analysis by discipline is expected to provide significant additional information..

Chapter 23

DOES INTERNATIONAL SCIENTIFIC COLLABORATION PAY?

23.1 Introduction

The benefits of international scientific collaboration are heavily debated among scientists and science policy makers, and constitute an important research topic in the field of quantitative science and technology studies. Funding agencies such as the European Commission stimulate collaboration within the European Union by applying it as a funding criterion.

A bibliometric analysis of papers included in the *Science Citation Index* and related Citation Indexes published by the Institute for Scientific Information (ISI, currently Thomson Scientific) revealed that the share of internationally co-authored (IC) papers increased steadily during the past few decades, and reached a level of 16 per cent at the end of the 1990s. It varied among research fields and was highest in *mathematics*, *geosciences* and in *physics & astronomy* (above 20 per cent), and lowest in *clinical medicine* (about 10 per cent). Papers can be categorised according to the number of countries involved in the collaboration. About 85 per cent of IC papers have authors from two countries and reflect bi-lateral international collaboration (BIC). The remaining 15 per cent reflect multi-lateral international collaboration (MIC) involving authors from 3 or more countries.

Various bibliometric studies reported that for specific scientific fields and countries internationally co-authored papers tend to have higher citation rates than those published by authors from a single country. But these studies were rightly cautious in generalising their outcomes and interpreting them in terms of causality (e.g., Narin et al., 1991; Glänzel, 2001; for a review the reader is referred to Glänzel and Schubert, 2004). This chapter further examines how the citation impact of internationally co-authored papers relates to that of other papers. It aims at providing a global, comprehensive analysis, focusing on papers covering the natural and life sciences and resulting from bi-lateral international collaboration.

23.2   Data, methods and results

A citation analysis compared the citation rate of BIC and MIC papers to that of 'purely domestic' papers, i.e., papers published by authors from a single country and hence not resulting from international collaboration (NIC). Publications analysed were published during 1996–2000 and citations were counted according to a fixed citation window of 4 years, i.e., during the first four years after publication date, including the publication year. In order to avoid possible biases due to the fact that multi-authored papers may receive more author self-citations than single-author papers do, citations in which the citing and cited articles have at least one author in common were excluded from the counts.

In all science fields, the citation rate of BIC papers exceeds that of NIC articles, while the average citation impact of MIC papers exceeds that of BIC papers. Table 23.1 shows that the mean citation impact of BIC papers divided by that for NIC papers is 1.24. It is lowest in *chemistry* (1.08) and highest in *clinical medicine* (1.62). For all science fields aggregated, the mean citation impact ratio of MIC compared to NIC articles is 1.64. For articles with authors from at least 10 different countries (MIC 10+) this ratio is 3.23. Thus, in all fields internationally co-authored papers have on average higher citation rates than papers with authors from a single country.

Table 23.1. Citation impact of internationally co-authored papers

Type of paper	Type of collaboration	Citation impact compared to that of NIC papers
BIC papers	Bi-lateral international collaboration, involving authors from 2 countries	1.24
MIC papers	Multi-lateral international collaboration, involving authors from 3 or more countries	1.64
MIC 10+ papers	International collaboration involving authors from 10 or more countries	3.23

But from Table 23.1 it does not follow that international collaboration is a principal factor responsible for this pattern. Countries performing well at the international research front can be expected both to generate more citation impact and to collaborate more intensively than less well performing countries, and may hence be over-represented in the set of internationally co-authored papers. A more detailed analysis focused on bi-lateral international collaboration, and assumed that a country's performance can be validly measured by the citation impact of its purely domestic (NIC) articles.

Table 23.2 presents for the 20 major countries in terms of their number of purely domestic papers, the distribution of NIC and BIC papers in science fields in function of the citation impact of a publishing country. This group of countries contains both scientifically established and emerging countries, and accounts for almost 90 per cent of the global NIC publication output.

It was hypothesised that the order of the countries in a BIC pair is significant. The first country in ISI's corporate address field is normally that of the first or reprint author. Since first or reprint authorship in many fields tends to be attributed to an author (or his or her research group) who made the largest contribution to the work described in the paper, it can be assumed that the first country tends to play a more important role in the collaboration than the second.

Table 23.2. Distribution of NIC and BIC papers by citation impact class of publishing country

Type of papers	Citation impact class of publishing country	% Papers
NIC	High	67
	Low	33
BIC	High–High	48
	High–Low	22
	Low–High	23
	Low–Low	7
	At least one High	93
	At least one Low	52

Data is extracted from the Science Citation Index (SCI) and related Citation Indexes published by the Institute for Scientific Information (ISI, currently Thomson ISI). Publications analysed were published during 1996–2000 and citations were counted according to a fixed citation window of 4 years. Author self-citations were not included. Results relate to bi-lateral international collaboration (BIC) among the 20 countries with the highest number of papers with domestic authors only (NIC). The total number of NIC and BIC papers are about 2,400,000 and 290,000, respectively.

Countries were categorised according to whether they belong to the upper or to the lower half of a ranking of countries by descending average citation impact of their NIC papers. For instance, citation impact class High–Low indicates papers resulting from bi-lateral collaborations in which the first country is in the top 50 per cent and the second country in the bottom 50 per cent of the ranking. This categorisation into high and low impact countries was made by research field, and thus took into account differences in citation practices among research fields. In each research field, the average citation impact of BIC papers published by any pair of countries was evaluated by comparing it to that of NIC papers from those countries in the following two ways.

1. A first approach categorised each pair according to whether the BIC citation rate is lower than the lowest NIC rate among the two contributing countries, lies between the lowest and highest NIC rate, or is higher than the highest NIC rate. In the first case, none of the two countries profits from the collaboration; in the second case the one with the lowest NIC rate profits, whereas the one with the highest does not; finally, in the third case both countries raise their citation impact compared to that of their purely domestic papers.

2. A second approach determined whether the rate for BIC papers is below or above the mean citation rate of NIC papers from the two countries involved in the collaboration. If one conceives the latter mean as an expected value for the citation impact of a pair's BIC papers, one can evaluate the extent to which the collaboration has produced additional value in terms of a citation impact increase compared to this *a priori* expectation.

Table 23.3. Distribution of collaborating country pairs on the basis of the citation impact of BIC papers compared to that for NIC papers

Citation impact publishing countries	*Pairs of collaborating countries*				
	Categorisation 1			*Categorisation 2*	
	$BIC < NIC_{min}$	$NIC_{min} < BIC < NIC_{max}$	$BIC > NIC_{max}$	$BIC < NIC_{mean}$	$BIC > NIC_{mean}$
All	22 %	35 %	44 %	40 %	60 %
High–High	13 %	16 %	71 %	20 %	80 %
High–Low	16 %	41 %	43 %	33 %	67 %
Low–High	25 %	51 %	24 %	57 %	43 %
Low–Low	36 %	28 %	36 %	50 %	50 %

Table 23.3 analyses a total of 3,523 pairs of collaborating countries involving 20 countries in 10 science fields. For instance, the papers in chemistry co-published between USA and UK with first or reprint authors from the USA constitute one pair of collaborating countries, or one 'case'. Such a pair is denoted below as a bi-lateral collaboration pair. Two categorisations were made of pairs according to how the average citation impact of a country pair's BIC papers – denoted as BIC in the table's heading – relates to that of NIC papers published by its constituents. The lower NIC citation rate in a pair is denoted as NIC_{min} and the higher as NIC_{max}. NIC_{mean} is defined as $(NIC_{min} + NIC_{max})/2$. Data are extracted from the Science Citation Index (SCI) and related Citation Indexes published by the Institute for Scientific Information (ISI, currently Thomson ISI). Publications analysed were published during 1996–2000 and citations were counted according to a fixed citation window of 4 years. Author self-citations were not included.

The outcomes are presented in Table 23.3. From Tables 23.2 and 23.3 the following conclusions may be drawn.

– Countries with a high citation impact of their NIC papers are indeed over-represented in the set of papers emerging from bi-lateral international collaboration. They contributed to 93 per cent of all BIC papers, whereas their share of purely domestic papers was 67 per cent. Some 48 per cent of BIC papers resulted from collaboration between two countries that both had a high citation impact, whereas only 7 per cent were from a pair in which both had a low citation impact of their NIC papers.

– In 44 per cent of bi-lateral collaboration pairs, both participating countries increased their citation impact relative to that of their purely domestic papers. In 35 per cent of the cases only the country with the lowest citation impact of domestic papers profited, whereas in 22 per cent of the cases none of the countries raised its impact.

– Considering the mean citation impact of domestic papers of both contributing countries as a norm, it follows that 60 per cent of collaboration pairs generated a citation impact above this norm. When two countries with a low citation impact of their NIC papers collaborated, the latter percentage was 50, whereas for collaboration between two high impact countries it was 80 per cent. An additional analysis by discipline not presented in Tables 23.2 and 23.3 found that this percentage was highest in *biological sciences* and *clinical medicine*, (over 90 per cent) and lowest in *chemistry* and *applied physics & chemistry* (around 70 per cent).

– When a high and a low citation impact country collaborated, their order is indeed significant. When the former came first, and hence delivered the primary author or leading research group, 67 per cent of collaboration pairs produced BIC papers with an average citation impact above the mean citation impact of NIC papers from the two. But when a low impact country came first, this percentage dropped to 43. However, an additional analysis discovered that this decline was found to be much smaller in *engineering* and *mathematics*, which may reflect substantial differences among disciplines, both in author sequence conventions and in the nature of bi-lateral collaboration.

– From the perspective of high impact countries, when they collaborated with low impact nations, the citation impact of their BIC papers was lower than that of their NIC papers in 57 per cent of collaboration pairs when they were first, and in 76 per cent of cases when they were second.

Expanding the set of countries by considering the most productive 40 countries in terms of number of NIC papers, and categorising these into four citation impact classes, the results were qualitatively similar to – but in most cases more pronounced than – those obtained for the 20 country set and two impact classes. For instance, 83 per cent of BIC papers had at least one top impact country, whereas only 20 per cent had at least one country with the lowest citation impact.

Still, for the 40 country set, bi-lateral collaboration among the top 25 per cent countries in terms of NIC citation impact accounted for 30 per cent of all global BIC papers, and in 68 per cent of collaboration pairs these papers generated a citation impact above that of each contributor's NIC impact. When these countries collaborated with the bottom 25 per cent of countries in terms of NIC citation impact, their BIC impact in 76 per cent of cases was lower than that of their NIC papers when they were first, and in 92 per cent when they were second.

23.3   Conclusions

King (2004) and authors of many other studies properly emphasised that "there is a stark disparity between the first and second divisions in the scientific impact of nations". This notion appears to be crucial in any study of scientific impact and international collaboration. The bibliometric analysis of bi-lateral international collaboration presented above shows that when scientifically advanced countries collaborate in a particular research field, they tend – in about 7 out of 10 cases – to profit from the collaboration, in the sense that they raise their citation impact compared to that of their purely domestic publication output. But when countries from the first division contribute in bi-lateral international collaboration to the development of scientifically less advanced countries – and thus to the advancement of science in the somewhat longer term than the time horizon normally adopted in research evaluation – this activity may negatively affect their short-term citation rates, particularly when their role is secondary. Research evaluators should conceive short-term citation impact at the research front and longer term development of scientifically less advanced countries as distinct aspects in their own right, and citation analysts should develop special indicators enabling them to carry out this task.

Chapter 24

DO US SCIENTISTS OVERCITE PAPERS FROM THEIR OWN COUNTRY?

24.1 Introduction

In the debate on the validity of citation analysis in research evaluation, national biases in scientists' reference practices, and particularly national self-preoccupation constitute an important issue. For instance, Seglen claimed that "national bias in reference selection favours North American journals" (Seglen, 1997a). Moed et al. (1983) concluded from interviews that "it is possible that publication and citation practices of US scientists differ from the habits of their European colleagues". In an analysis of citation impact by country, King (2004) stated that "… anecdotal evidence suggests that preferential US citing of US papers may distort the analyses, given the sheer size of the US contribution. It is possible that Japan and Russia, being more scientifically isolated than the other major players, suffer particularly in this respect" (p. 312).

These statements address the possibility that US scientists to some extent may cite other US papers not because of their significance, but for other reasons, such as a limited awareness of foreign research work, or an 'insular' attitude. The implication would be that, if a US paper and a non-US paper have equal cognitive significance to a US author, he or she may tend to cite the former rather than the latter. This tendency could make citation analysis invalid, particularly when US authors or institutions are compared to non-US ones. But qualifications as 'preferential citing', 'overciting', or 'biased referencing' assume that there is a norm or standard in the way authors cite papers from their own country, against which one can assess whether or not a country self-citation rate is 'excessively high', or 'higher than expected'. A crucial task therefore is to search for such a norm, and to define and apply it properly.

A simple measure of the degree of country self-citation can be defined as the proportion of references in a country's papers to other papers published from that country, denoted as its *domestic* papers. Among the many factors that may influence reference behaviour, and particularly country self-citation, this chapter takes into account the size of a country's publication output; the degree of integration of research activities at a national level; and the significance of a country's domestic papers. It is *a priori* assumed that each of these factors positively influences the country self-citation rate as defined above. Thus, a country with a large publication output tends to show a higher self-citation rate than one with a small output, because the former has more domestic papers to cite than the latter. Countries with strongly developed national networks tend to show more intra-national citation links than those in which national scientific networks are poorly developed. Finally, countries publishing papers of high significance tend to cite their own papers more frequently because they are more significant.

The basic question thus becomes: does a country's observed self-citation rate deviate from an expected rate that takes into account the size of the country's output, its strength of national networks, and the significance of its papers? The first factor is analysed fairly extensively in Section 24.3, whereas the other two are illustrated in Section 24.4. The analysis especially compares the USA and Western-European countries. Section 24.2 describes the data used in the study. Section 24.5 summarises the conclusions.

24.2   Data

A detailed analysis was based on the source papers included in the *Science Citation Index* in the year 2003, and all references in these papers to other ISI papers published during the period 1980–2003. Author self-citations, i.e. citations where the cited and citing paper have at least one author in common, were not taken into account, as they influence country to country citation patterns to some extent.

Papers resulting from international collaboration, published by authors from two or more countries, constitute a methodological problem in this analysis. They cannot be uniquely assigned to a country. Moreover, it can be expected that their reference patterns differ from those in articles published by authors from a single country. Therefore, it was decided in this analysis to delete all papers originating from two or more countries. Thus, a file was created with about 500,000 citing papers, containing 8 million references to 13 million citable papers. Both citing and citable papers could be uniquely assigned to the country in which publishing authors' institutions were located, using information from the papers' corporate address field.

24.3 The factor size of domestic publication output

In 1988, Frame and Narin carried out a detailed analysis of referencing practices of US scientists based on publication and citation data from the *Science Citation Index* (SCI), particularly in view of a relative decline during the 1970s in US R&D budgets compared to other major countries. They cited a study conducted by Deutsch (1954), who provided empirical evidence that, in their research papers, Americans were increasingly referencing US work, and perhaps even over-referencing it. Deutsch analysed the country of origin of the papers cited by US scientists in particular journals, including *Physical Review*, and determined the percentage of references to other US work. Frame and Narin (1988) reported that for the latter journal he found that this percentage increased from less than 5 per cent in 1894 to over 70 per cent in 1953.

In an analysis of all SCI papers published during a ten-year period (1975–1984) and citing other papers published in 1975, Frame and Narin found that slightly more than 70 per cent of all references in US papers were to other US papers, almost equal to Deutsch's estimate for *Physical Review*. For other major countries, this percentage of country self-citations was considerably lower.

Frame and Narin argued that one cannot draw conclusions about national self-preoccupation of US scientists from these percentage data, because there is a size effect at stake. Because the US publication output is relatively large – about one-third of the total SCI – US papers constitute a large citation "target". "It is understandable, then, to find scientists in a scientifically large country devoting a substantial portion of their citations to national colleagues, not because of excessive self-preoccupation, but because of the large size of the domestic effort" (Frame and Narin, 1988, p. 207).

If F denotes the proportion of references given by authors from a specific country to papers from the own country – in other words, the fraction of country self-citations – and α the fraction of papers from a country relative to the total number of papers in the entire database, Frame and Narin claimed that the ratio F/α is a more appropriate indicator of national self-preoccupation than the simple proportion F applied by Deutsch. They calculated and analysed this ratio for several countries. They concluded that, although in the past there has been a "*sense* of American insularity, captured in the term 'not-invented-here-syndrome'", (p. 211) in the 1970s and mid-1980s, "bibliometric indicators suggest that American scientists may not be inordinately self-preoccupied. Citation counts indicate that American self references are not dramatically excessive in view of the large size of American research effort ..." (Frame and Narin, 1988, p. 203).

Bookstein and Yitzahki (1999) studied language biases or own-language preferences in scientific publishing. They proposed a simple probabilistic citation model that leads to a new relative citation rate to own-language compared to foreign language papers. Although the authors focused on language in reference behaviour, they emphasised that their model can also be applied to country self-citations, i.e., to measure the extent to which authors from a particular country cite papers from their own country. They noted that the ratio F/α applied by Frame and Narin, which aimed at correcting for size, is itself size-dependent. For instance, for a country publishing one-third of the total collection of papers in the database (thus, α=0.33), the ratio F/α can never exceed a value of 1/0.33=3.0, whereas for a country publishing a fraction of 0.033 or 3.3 per cent of all papers, its maximum value is 30.

If P_o denotes the probability that an author cites any given pertinent paper from his own country, and P_f the probability that an author cites a paper published by scientists from another country, Bookstein and Yitzahki proposed the following probability ratio as a measure of country self-citation:

$$\frac{P_o}{P_f} = \frac{F/(1-F)}{\alpha/(1-\alpha)} = \frac{\dfrac{F}{\alpha}}{\dfrac{(1-F)}{(1-\alpha)}}$$

This probability ratio indicates the odds favouring an author's choosing to cite a publication from his or her own country, relative to what the odds would be if he had chosen at random from the world's literature. For small values of F and α, this probability ratio approaches the earlier ratio F/α, so that this "new measure can be seen as a size-insensitive generalisation of the earlier measure, that agrees with the earlier measure where it served well" (Bookstein and Yitzahki, 1999, p. 344).

Table 24.1 presents the numerical values of all three measures for the degree of country self-citation discussed above for 15 major countries. It also shows ratios for an aggregate of 18 Western-European countries. In this analysis, these 18 countries were conceived as one geographic entity. In this case, degree of 'country self-citation' should be interpreted as that of 'regional self-citation', i.e. the extent to which authors from one of the 18 countries cite papers either from their own country or from another country in the region.

Table 24.1. Three measures for the degree of country self-citation for 15 major countries

Country/Region	Frac-tion of papers (α)	Measures of country self-citation		
		F (Deutsch)	F/α (Frame & Narin)	(F/α)/((1-F)/(1-α)) (Bookstein & Yitzahki)
Results per country				
USA	0.366	0.626	1.71	2.90
UK	0.083	0.180	2.14	2.39
Japan	0.079	0.199	2.52	2.89
Germany	0.063	0.134	2.13	2.31
France	0.045	0.010	2.32	2.48
Canada	0.040	0.099	2.48	2.64
Italy	0.027	0.070	2.63	2.76
Australia	0.027	0.070	5.04	5.55
India	0.021	0.094	4.41	4.77
Peoples Rep China	0.018	0.073	4.14	4.39
Netherlands	0.018	0.073	4.15	4.39
Russia	0.017	0.078	4.45	4.74
Spain	0.016	0.062	3.75	3.93
Sweden	0.014	0.086	6.23	6.72
Switzerland	0.010	0.043	4.07	4.21
Aggregated approach				
USA	0.366	0.626	1.71	2.90
Western Europe	0.330	0.423	1.28	1.49

α: The fraction of citable papers from a country relative to the total number of papers in the entire database.

F: The proportion of references given by authors from a specific country to papers from the own country, in other words, the fraction of country self-citations as calculated by Deutsch (1954).

F/α: Frame and Narin's (1988) measure of country self-citation.

$(F/\alpha)/((1-F)/(1-\alpha))$: Bookstein and Yitzahki's (1999) probability ratio measuring country self-citation.

Outcomes relate to source papers included in the Science Citation Index in the year 2003, and all references in these papers to other ISI papers published during the period 1980–2003. Author self-citations, i.e. citations where the cited and citing paper have at least one author in common, were not included. Papers resulting from international collaboration, published by authors from two or more countries, were deleted.

Western Europe: Aggregate of the following 18 Western-European countries: Austria, Belgium, Denmark, Finland, France, Germany (including East and West Germany prior to 1990), Greece, Iceland, Ireland, Italy, Luxembourg, Netherlands, Norway, Portugal, Spain, Sweden, Switzerland, and the United Kingdom. Data for Russia relates to citable papers published as from 1990.

From Table 24.1 the following observations can be made.

- The value for the Frame & Narin (F&N) measure is greater than one for all countries. This is in agreement with empirical findings presented by Frame and Narin in their study related to the 1970s and 1980s. Apparently, this pattern has not changed in recent years. The Bookstein & Yitzahki (B&Y) measure is also greater than one for all countries
- Among the top 6 countries listed in Table 24.1, the USA scores lowest on the F&N measure but highest on the B&Y measure. This illustrates the size-dependence of the F&N measure, which has the largest consequences for the country with the highest values of F and α, i.e., the USA. The B&Y value for the US is almost equal to that for Japan.
- Major European countries – UK, Germany, France and Italy – have higher F&N values but slightly lower B&Y values than the USA. Smaller countries, in terms of their fraction of citable papers in the database, have both higher B&Y and higher F&N values than the USA. In fact, Table 24.1 reveals a tendency that a country's B&Y measure increases with declining α, the proportion of the country's citable papers in the database.
- The USA on the one hand, and the aggregate of 18 Western-European countries on the other, have similar values of α (0.366 versus 0.330). But F, the proportion of references to the own country (USA) or region (Western Europe), is higher for the USA than it is for the Western-European aggregate (0.626 versus 0.423). The F&A measure for the former is about 34 per cent higher than for the latter, and the B&Y measure even 96 per cent higher.

These outcomes allow for the following conclusions.

- All countries overcite themselves, relative to what one would expect on the basis of their shares of citable papers.
- Focusing on the Bookstein & Yitzahki probability ratio, the US self-citation rate is somewhat higher than that for major Western-European countries, but lower than that for smaller Western-European countries in terms of their proportion of citable papers.
- Thus, at the level of individual countries there is no empirical basis for the general claim that US scientists overcite papers from their own country more than scientists from Western-European countries overcite their domestic papers.
- But US scientists overcite US papers to a much stronger degree than Western-European scientists overcite the total collection of Western-European papers.

24.4 Other factors

A *second* factor of interest is the *degree of integration* of research activities at a national or supra-national level. An attempt was made to assess this aspect by measuring a country's degree of national collaboration. It was expressed as the percentage of a country's papers containing two or more national addresses in the papers' corporate address field, relative to the total number of papers in which it participated. Similarly, the degree of international collaboration was measured by the percentage of papers with at least one foreign address. The latter indicator is added in order to give an integral picture of a country's collaboration patterns. The two measures were also calculated for the aggregate of 18 Western-European countries. In this case, national collaboration is interpreted as collaboration among scientists within the set of 18 countries, i.e., among scientists either from the same country, or from different countries within the set of 18. The results are presented in Table 24.2.

Table 24.2 shows that the USA has a relatively low degree of international collaboration, but a high degree of national collaboration, particularly higher than that for all Western-European countries except Italy. The same observations hold for Japan. Comparing the USA with the aggregate of 18 Western-European countries suggests that there are no large differences between these two systems. The former revealed a slightly higher degree of national collaboration, and a slightly lower degree of international collaboration than the latter. Papers resulting from collaboration among two Western-European countries are categorised in the results per country as internationally co-authored papers, whereas in the analysis of the aggregate set these are defined as 'nationally' co-authored papers. The fact that the degree of national collaboration of the aggregate set is generally higher than that of its constituent countries illustrates the importance of collaboration among Western-European countries.

In view of the imperfection of the national collaboration indicator, one should be careful in drawing definite conclusions from the outcomes. Comparing the USA to major Western-European countries such as the UK, Germany and France, the stronger degree of national collaboration in the USA may at least partially account for this country's higher self-citation probability ratio presented in Table 24.1. Comparing the USA to the aggregate of Western-European countries, the large difference in self-citation ratio could not be attributed to differences in the degree of national collaboration, since the two systems obtained almost identical values for this indicator.

Table 24.2. National and international collaboration for 15 major countries

Country/Region	Int. co-authored papers (%)	Nat. co-authored papers (%)
Results per country		
USA	14.6	39.2
UK	22.6	26.3
Japan	13.6	39.4
Germany	28.8	25.3
France	30.2	35.9
Canada	26.2	31.4
Italy	30.8	46.5
Australia	23.6	28.5
India	12.2	20.5
Peoples Rep China	23.5	32.6
Netherlands	31.9	33.4
Russia	26.4	17.9
Spain	28.4	32.6
Sweden	33.8	36.7
Switzerland	42.1	20.2
Aggregated approach		
USA	14.6	39.2
Western Europe	16.5	37.7

% Internationally co-authored papers: the percentage of papers with at least one foreign address.

% Nationally co-authored papers: the percentage of papers with at least two domestic addresses.

In this table papers that are both internationally and nationally co-authored (i.e., papers with at least one foreign and at least two national addresses) are counted in both indicators.

It should be noted that the indicator of national collaboration applied in this analysis is far from perfect, as it also may reflect structural aspects of a country's science system. For instance, the Centre National de Recherche Scientifique (CNRS) in France and the Centro Nationale della Ricerca (CNR) in Italy play a very important role in the national research system. Papers resulting from research conducted in a CNRS research institute located in a French university may have two addresses in a paper's corporate address field, mentioning CNRS and the university, respectively. Authors of such papers in a sense have two affiliations, and it is questionable whether in all cases this can merely be interpreted in terms of national collaboration. This feature may account for the relatively high values for the percentage of nationally co-authored papers in France and Italy. It must also be emphasised that in this analysis all scientific fields are aggregated, whereas authorship characteristics differ considerably among fields, and the distribution of research papers among fields differs from one country to another.

Nevertheless, in the interpretation of differences in self-citation ratios, it remains crucial which norm one applies. If one adopts the rate at which authors from a Western-European country cite papers from other Western-European countries as a norm, one could argue that US scientists *over*cite papers from their own country, and possibly are not sufficiently aware of – or a least tend to ignore in their referencing – research work abroad. But if one conceives the degree of integration of national research activities within the USA as a norm, it can be argued that Western-European scientists *under*-cite each other and that research activities in this region are not yet sufficiently integrated, notwithstanding the realisation of a level of co-authorship similar to that within the USA.

A *third* factor is the *significance* or *'quality' of the research efforts* in a country from a global perspective. Authors may cite papers from their own country simply because these are more significant. Any attempt to quantify the effect of this factor using citation data is confronted with the problem of how to separate significance from self-preoccupation, insularity or other biases in referencing practices. As the analysis presented in this chapter examines possible biases in referencing behaviour, it cannot *a priori* be assumed in an assessment of the significance of papers based on citation analysis that such biases do not exist.

In order to throw at least some light upon the possible size of the effect of domestic papers' significance upon country self-citation, US papers and Western-European papers are compared to one another with respect to the citation impact they generate upon research activities in the rest of the world, i.e. upon scientists from all countries expect the USA and Western Europe. One may expect that, in view of the large variety of countries from the rest of the world, biases in references practices of their authors to some extent cancel out, although there is no certainty that they cancel out completely.

Papers from the 18 Western-European countries receive from the set of all other countries except Western Europe and the USA on average 0.18 citations, and US papers 0.23 citations, which is about 20 per cent higher than those from Western Europe. This outcome suggests that the observed phenomenon that US scientists cite more US papers than Western-European scientists cite Western-European papers can to a non-negligible degree be attributed to the higher significance of US papers compared to that of Western-European ones, at least in the perception of non-US and non-Western-European scientists.

24.5   Discussion and conclusions

It must be concluded that the analysis presented in this chapter does not provide clear, unambiguous, empirical evidence for biases in US referencing practices compared to those of their Western-European colleagues. A more profound understanding of referencing practices is needed in order to draw more definitive conclusions. The analysis shows in which respects – or according to which norms – US scientists' self-citation behaviour differs from that of their Western-European colleagues. In view of the complexity of the issue, the answer to the question addressed in this chapter's title cannot be answered with a simple yes or no. But partial evidence presented is based on thoroughly conducted empirical research rather than being anecdotal, and may provide a sound basis for further model-building and empirical research on this issue.

It must be emphasised that the analysis presented in this chapter related to reference practices of authors in science, i.e., in the natural, life, applied and technical sciences and mathematics, as represented in ISI's *Science Citation Index*. Reference practices and their biases in social sciences and humanities would certainly deserve a separate, thoroughly conducted study.

In the analyses presented in this chapter, possible language barriers were not discussed as a separate factor. The analysis related to science, and it is assumed that English is the dominant language in this domain of scholarship. In fact, the percentage of SCI source papers processed during 1980-2002 not written in English is only about 4 percent, and the analysis merely related to citations in ISI source papers to other ISI source papers. It cannot be excluded, however, that language barriers to a small degree affect reference practices, particularly the extent to which Western-European scientists from the various language domains (e.g., English, French, German, Spanish) cite each other. Obviously, in a study of reference practices in social sciences and humanities this factor must be taken into account.

It must also be noted that differences among research disciplines may affect the outcomes, as countries may have distinct research profiles. Internationally co-authored papers were deleted from this analysis. The effect of excluding these papers upon the outcomes needs further examination. Further work on generalising and extending the Bookstein–Yitzahki model and applying this new model to citation and co-author relationships among countries is in progress (Bookstein et al., 2005).

PART 2.8

NEW DEVELOPMENTS

Chapter 25

DEVELOPMENT OF NEW INDICATORS

25.1   Introduction

In Chapter 2 it was argued that, in research evaluation, it is not the bibliometric investigator but rather the evaluator who establishes what is valuable in scholarly activity and which dimensions of scholarly quality should have the greatest weight. In the early years of the use of the ISI Citation Indexes in the assessment of research performance, data handling of large files was a complex task. Evaluators had to use more or less predefined indicators. Now that full bibliometric versions of these Indexes are available, bibliometric indicators can become more finely tuned, and therefore more capable to address particular issues raised by policy makers.

At the same time, this development draws the attention more explicitly to theoretical assumptions underlying the various types of indicators, and to the question of which aspects of research performance they actually measure. Discussions about indicators may at first glance seem technical, but there are normally theoretical notions involved that need to be highlighted and further clarified. From this perspective, this chapter presents a number of general notes on the further development of bibliometric indicators, and particularly on citation analysis.

The next section makes suggestions for new indicators. The list is far from exhaustive, and primarily aims at illustrating how theoretical notions are involved in their construction, and how they depend upon what one aims to measure.

25.2   New indicators

The problem of 'size'

An indicator applied in many studies presented in this book is the normalised or relative citation impact indicator. It is defined as a citation per publication ratio for articles published by a group, divided by the same ratio for all articles published worldwide in the subfields in which the group is active. Hence, it takes into account the size of a group's publication oeuvre and aims to enable one to directly compare groups with different publication counts. Researchers commenting on the outcomes of studies applying this indicator have sometimes claimed that it is to some extent distorted by a 'dilution effect', causing large departments that publish many papers to have a normalised citation impact close to a value of one. This tendency is clearly visible in Figure 4.1 in Chapter 4.

There are two issues at stake. The first is, should one aim to analyse citation impact relative to size of publication volume, or should one consider the total citation impact of the entire oeuvre? The second is, assuming that one chooses to assess citation impact relative to size, does the normalised citation impact indicator correct for differences in size in a proper way?

The conceptual issue underlying the first of these is that the volume of a group's publication oeuvre can be conceived as a reflection of its research performance. Groups performing well tend to be able to attract more funding, appoint more researchers and therefore publish more papers than less well performing groups do. By using a normalised citation per publication ratio, *this* manifestation of research performance is ruled out, at least to a considerable extent. Hence, there may be a need to develop indicators expressing the total citation impact of its publication oeuvre, at the same time taking account of differences in citation practices among disciplines.

Aksnes and Taxt (2004) found that an indicator multiplying a department's normalised citation impact with the number of articles it published showed a somewhat higher correlation with peer ratings of departments than the normalised citation impact measure itself, but they underlined that the former indicator may be too strongly determined by the sheer number of articles. More suggestions for such indicators and their technical details will be outlined in future publications.

Regarding the second issue, several authors claimed that a citation per publication ratio does not properly correct for differences in size defined as number of papers published. Katz (1999) found that the total number of citations received by a country's papers (denoted as "recognition"), and the number of papers it published, show a power law relationship with an exponent of around 1.27. He denoted the effect responsible for this relationship as a "Matthew effect": recognition (total citations) appears to *accumulate* with presence (number of papers published) in the science system.

Katz concluded that the comparison of national systems on the basis of their citations per publication ratio can produce misleading results, and suggested that, if the Matthew effect is truly scale-independent, it can also distort citation impact measurements of smaller entities such as national sub-communities. He proposed using the power law relationship to calculate an entity's 'expected' citation impact given the number of papers it published. He apparently assumed that the observed Matthew effect is caused by size, and hence that an appropriate size-independent indicator must rule it out. For large entities this method tends to generate lower citation impact figures than the conventional citation per publication ratio. For a recent, detailed discussion of decreasing power lows in informetrics and bibliometrics, the reader is referred to Egghe (2005).

An entirely different approach in taking into account size can be found in the size-independent measures proposed by Bookstein and Yitzakhi (1999), discussed and applied in Chapter 24. A country's normalised citation impact can be written in the form F/α, where F denotes the fraction of references given by all authors worldwide (in the total collection of citing papers in a database) to a country's papers, and α the fraction of the country's citable papers relative to all citable papers in the database. The critique that Bookstein and Yitzahki formulated against a measure applied by Frame and Narin (1988) for measuring country self-citation (see Chapter 24) also applies to the normalised citation impact indicator. For a country with $\alpha=0.33$, the normalised citation impact cannot exceed 3.0, whereas for a country with $\alpha=0.033$, it ranges between 0 and 30. This point illustrates that the debate on how citation based indicators should properly deal with size continues, and that new measures are expected to be developed in the future (see for instance Bookstein et al., 2005).

Benchmarking

Benchmarking relates to the definition of an appropriate 'reference' set of entities to which a particular unit under evaluation can be compared. The normalised citation impact indicator described in Chapter 4 provides such a reference set by comparing the citation impact of the papers published by some group to the world citation average in the subfield(s) in which it is active. The measure corrects for differences in referencing practices among subfields, and for differences in type of article and in the age of cited papers. Groups can be compared with one another according to the extent to which their citation impact diverges from the world average *in their subfields*.

However, more methodological work could be done to identify more fine-tuned reference sets and benchmarks, which could further enhance both the validity and policy relevance of citation analysis. Kostoff (2002) discussed some of the technical and conceptual difficulties in defining proper benchmarks (he uses the term "normalization set"), and showed how their selection depends upon the aspects addressed in the evaluation. For instance, assessing whether a group performs well within its narrow specialty ("job right?") or whether this specialty itself is relevant from a broader cognitive viewpoint ("right job?") requires different sets of papers in a reference set.

The problem of finding appropriate benchmarks is closely related to the evaluative perspective and the objectives of an evaluation process. Section 1.3 discussed a distinction made by Weinberg (1962) between the internal and external scientific merit of a piece of research. The former is assessed by comparing a particular group active in a specialty to other groups working in the same specialty, whereas the latter involves an assessment of the contribution the specialty made to neighbouring scientific fields. As argued in Chapter 2, in any evaluation process it should be made clear which of these two perspectives is adopted. If both are at stake, they should be clearly distinguished from one another. Each perspective has its own methodologies for selecting proper benchmarks, and one should not inconsiderately use the outcomes based on benchmarking from one perspective in an assessment adopting the other perspective. For a discussion of bibliometric tools for assessing Weinberg's external scientific merit, the reader is referred to the section on cognitive-relational analysis presented below.

Appropriate benchmarking enhances the value of citation analysis, and makes the interpretation of studies of particular departments or institutions easier. In order to properly assess a particular entity's citation impact, normalised citation impact indicators for such entity – comparing its impact with the world citation average in the subfields in which it is active – are beyond any doubt valuable tools. But it is of special interest to analyse the distribution of citation impact among all entities in a field, and to locate a particular entity's impact in that distribution.

For instance, an assessment of all academic institutions in a particular country would be enhanced if one would not merely compare these institutions one with another, but also with institutions from other countries. Technically this can be achieved by showing what their positions are in the citation impact distribution of institutions from a wide set of countries. This would broaden the perspective of both bibliometric researchers and policy officials, and may hold them back from giving too much significance to small numerical differences among institutions from the analysed country itself.

On the one hand, this requires the collection of sufficiently accurate data not only for the entities evaluated, but also for all other entities in the benchmark set, and would therefore substantially expand the efforts involved in a citation analysis. But on the other hand, it is primarily the *shape* of the distribution and *its statistical properties* (especially its percentile values) that are relevant rather than the *names of each individual entity* underlying it. In order to roughly 'locate' a particular institution, such a distribution could be presented and used in such a way that benchmark institutions included are *anonymous*. In that case, the accuracy requirements involved in the data collection for all these institutes can therefore to some extent be relaxed.

Highly cited articles

The normalised citation impact indicator is based on average values of citation distributions that tend to be skewed. An alternative approach is to focus on the 'top' of these distributions, by identifying in a scientific field all highly cited articles – for instance, the 1, 5 or 10 per cent most frequently cited papers – and determining the number of a group's papers in this global set of 'top' articles in terms of citation impact. This method certainly has its merits, and provides a more complete picture of a group's citation impact as it considers parameters of the citation distribution other than its mean value.

In Chapter 16 it is hypothesised that citing authors acknowledging a research group's work do not distribute their citations evenly among all papers emerging from its programme, but rather cite particular papers that have become symbols or 'flags' of such a programme. Following this hypothesis, an analysis of highly cited articles would focus on such flag papers.

It must also be noted that, statistically speaking, large research fields in terms of number for published articles tend to show higher extreme citation rates for individual papers than smaller fields. This tendency was illustrated at the level of scientific journals within journal categories in Chapter 5 (Figure 5-5). The identification of highly cited articles *in a field* thus depends upon how a field is defined, particularly in terms of broadness of substantive contents. A group's paper may be among the top 1 per cent in its narrow specialty, but not even among the top 5 or 10 per cent in the wider sub-discipline.

How to deal with co-publications

A crucial methodological issue is in an evaluation of a particular entity (e.g., an individual scholar, research department, or national science system) how to deal with publications co-authored by members of that entity and those from other entities. Chapters 21, 22 and 23 illustrated three counting schemes, briefly denoted as 'integer', 'fractional' and 'first author' counting. All three methods assumed that the size of the contribution that a collaborative article makes to scientific production is in principle equal to that of a non-collaborative one. On the one hand, one can argue that this is appropriate, since it is not the effort itself but rather the outcome of it that is relevant in this context, and one of the ways to assess the outcome is through citation analysis.

But one can also argue that a paper published by large international consortia of research groups requires efforts and tends to represent contributions that are larger than any group could ever achieve alone. Following this line of reasoning, one may therefore question whether in a bibliometric analysis such paper should be counted as 'one' publication. From the point of view of a fractional counting scheme, the contributions made by the various units involved in a collaborative paper should in that case add up to a number higher than one.

Assuming that papers by larger teams generally represent larger contributions than those by smaller author groups, the analyses presented in Chapter 21 would indicate that scientists' publication productivity in a sense did increase over the years. However, further reflection and empirical analysis is needed. It must be underlined that such an assumption would also have implications for counting of citations. In order to develop a consistent approach, one should also consider whether or not citations from certain types of collaborative papers should receive a higher weight than those from other types of articles.

Indicators of breadth, persistence, coherence and depth of a knowledge base

Citation analysis is not used to measure merely scientific excellence of the various sub-units in a national science system. Brusoni and Geuna (2004) gave an overview of the study of knowledge specialisation and integration processes in science and technology, both at the level of institutions and in national S&T systems. Knowledge specialisation is characterised in terms of a unit's breadth and persistence, and integration in terms of coherence and depth. Breadth is measured through the number of fields (i.e., journal categories) in which a unit has achieved a certain minimum level of activity or specialisation. Persistence is defined on the basis of the length of the time period during which a unit was active in a field. Coherence relates to the 'cognitive distance' between fields, and depth to the unit's involvement in different types of research in terms of basic versus applied.

All aspects were measured with the help of bibliometric indicators derived from the publication and patent literature. The general issue is how these aspects are interrelated and how they influence the performance of the various sub-units individually and that of the system as a whole. For instance, in order to make a significant contribution in a field, a unit needs to specialise. On the other hand, if it is too strongly specialised, particularly in technical or scientific fields with a low opportunity, it will be difficult to refocus its specialisation pattern in the short term in order to pick up recent promising developments.

Productivity analyses relating output to input

Publication and citation based indicators reflect the output of scholarly research and are becoming more and more available to evaluators and policy makers. The availability of reliable and useful 'input' data on scholarly activity, however, is to some extent lagging behind. Although several international organisations put enormous efforts into generating standardised statistics on R&D input, relating these aggregate measures to bibliometric indicators is a difficult task, and is hampered for instance by the fact that they are based on different subject classification systems (Luwel, 2004). Much more work has to be carried out to collect reliable input data. To the extent that useful input and output data are available, various econometric approaches to the measurement of productivity or efficiency of S&T systems are fruitful (Bonaccorsi and Daraio, 2004).

Training of scientists

If the extent to which research groups from Western countries contribute to the education of researchers and to building up a research infrastructure in developing countries is a relevant dimension of research performance, citation analysts should enable evaluators to assess this aspect properly, and distinctly from other dimensions such as the short-term citation impact at the international research front. As argued in Chapter 23, new indicators could be developed which assess these aspects separately, rather than merely using methodologies that express both aspects in a single measure.

If the extent to which research groups contribute to the education of trained scholars is a valuable aspect, methodologies could be developed which analyse the further research career of scholars who started as PhD students in those groups. Thus, apart from analysing the citation impact of the articles published by a group, one could, using appropriate time fames, determine the number of PhD students in a group who, in later phases of their careers, made important contributions to scholarly progress.

Further developing 'qualitative' citation analysis through contextual and cognitive-relational analysis

Quantitative analysts of science could develop more 'qualitative' citation based indicators, along a contextual or a cognitive-relational viewpoint, thus abandoning the principle underlying most citation analyses that "all citations are equal". Such indicators potentially have an enormous value, both in the sociology of science and in a research evaluation context, but are currently generally unavailable.

Contextual indicators are derived from the passages in the full text of scholarly documents in which a particular document or set of documents is cited. It would be necessary to develop initially simple, and in a later phase more sophisticated, classifications of 'how' documents are cited from the perspective of research evaluation rather than from that of information retrieval.

Although during the past few decades several attempts to 'objectively' and quantitatively characterise such citing passages were described (for a review see Small, 1982; Cronin, 1984; Liu, 1993), substantial progress in a direction that make it a useful tool in the assessment of research performance has thus far not been achieved. One reason for this has perhaps been a technological one: no methods for analysing relatively large amounts of full texts by computer were available. Nowadays, however, more and more scholarly publications become available in electronic form, and software for processing full texts enters the market.

A second reason why citation context analysis may not yet have provided usable tools lies in the conceptual difficulties in developing some kind of classification system of citation contexts. It would be a challenge to develop such systems, not primarily from the point of view of information use and rhetorical analysis, but from a much broader evaluative perspective. A first step could be a further, large-scale categorisation of references on the basis of their location in the citing text, as was proposed by Cano (1989). In the end, citation analysis of a set of documents would not only give information on how frequently they were cited, but also provide some descriptive, statistical summary of 'how' they were cited.

Development of cognitive-relational citation indicators could particularly follow the lines described by Henry Small, along which the diffusion of scientific concepts is studied and their citation impact on more 'distant' areas is being assessed. Referring to the case of the controversial paper on 'cold fusion '(see Chapter 4 of this book), he argued:

> There appears to be no difference between the way supposed "invalid" and "valid" science is cited. However, looking within a field and looking across fields provides a new perspective on this question: what appears valid within a narrow specialty might fail to find support or validation in neighboring areas, and this might be the decisive factor (Small, 1998).

Such an approach explicitly aims at providing tools to assess the *scientific merit* of research as defined by Weinberg (1962) and discussed in Section 1.3.

Weighted citation counts

As outlined in Chapter 5, Pinski and Narin (1976) developed a methodology for calculating measures of influence or impact of particular units (e.g., scientific journals), based on citation relationships among such units, and assigning to citations from a prestigious unit a higher weight than to a citation from a less prestigious or peripheral unit. Based on their notions, a recurrent citation measure would not *a priori* count a citation as 'one', but rather assign a weight to the citation, based on the number of times the citing document was itself cited. Such a notion also underlies for instance the Search Engine Google's measure of PageRank. The "value" of a web page is measured by the number of other web pages linking to it, but in this value assessment, links from pages that are themselves frequently linked to have a higher weight than links from those to which only few other pages have linked.

It is expected that Pinski and Narin's notions will play an important role in the development of new citation impact indicators, particularly in wide universes of scholarly documents that are strongly heterogeneous in terms of their scholarly quality or significance. This actually seems to be the case in a universe embracing all documents freely available through the Internet. The potentialities and limitations of recurrent citation impact indicators need to be thoroughly assessed. For recent applications of such indicators in research performance assessments the reader is referred to van Raan (2004a) and van Leeuwen (2004a).

Historical research: conducting bibliometric studies covering several decades

Most bibliometric studies conducted during the past few decades apply time horizons of between five and ten years in performance assessments.

Now that bibliometric data from the ISI Citation Indexes are available for a time span of an entire century, it would be fruitful to conduct more studies of a primarily historical nature, in which developments in scholarly disciplines are studied over much longer periods than the 5 to 10 years normally taken into account in research assessment studies. The historiographic methods developed by Eugene Garfield (HistCite software) could play an important role in this type of research (e.g., Garfield et al., 2003).

A particular challenge would be to give an historical account of the cognitive developments in a subfield, identify its main contributors, and create bibliometric profiles of them during a number of years. Bibliometric assessments should be made at various points in time, particularly those focusing on citation impact generated in a short term, and discuss the outcomes of those assessments in relation to the size of the participants' contributions identified in the historical overview.

Such studies could examine the extent to which bibliometric indicators were successful in forecasting important contributions made to a field, and particularly whether other types of indicators than those currently applied may be more appropriate forecasting tools.

Scholarly communication research: analysing relationships between formal and informal use

Nowadays more and more scholarly publishers make their publications available through the internet, by offering subscribers access to their large electronic warehouses that not only include basic bibliographical information on all published items such as titles or authors, but also their full texts. Though subject to strict privacy rules, the use of such warehouses can in principle be monitored. The practices of users, such as their search paths and documents retrieved in a full text format, are stored in log files that can be subjected to computerised statistical analysis.

If citations in journal articles reflect *formal* use of scholarly documents, the analysis of the use of a publisher's electronic warehouse can provide insight into their *informal* use. A comparison of formal and informal use is not only expected to provide an insight into informal usage practices, but may also yield a deeper understanding of formal referencing behaviour and the validity of citation based indicators.

The working hypothesis adopted in such studies could be that informal use can to a certain extent be structured and analysed in the same way as formal use, applying an analogy model relating users of electronic journals to (collections of) publishing authors, user sessions to scientific papers and retrieved documents to formal cited references. This type of study is further discussed in the next chapter.

Chapter 26

ELECTRONIC PUBLISHING, NEW DATABASES AND SEARCH ENGINES

26.1 Electronic publishing

During the past few decades more and more scholarly documents have become available in electronic form. In past years publishers of scientific and scholarly information have made their journals and articles available through the Internet to universities, corporations and government institutes. At the same time, scholars are more and more encouraged to self-archive their documents and deposit them in publicly accessible websites, by inserting metadata such as date, author-name, title, journal-name, and then attaching the full-text document. A special protocol was developed by the *Open Archive Initiative* for collecting metadata about data files in separate archives, so that users can process the data in separate archives as if they were contained in a single archive.

Electronic archives may contain either peer reviewed or non-peer reviewed documents. They may even include a non-refereed preprint version and a final, accepted, and possibly revised version of the 'same' document. Moreover, they may offer *open* or *toll access*. Open access allows anyone, anywhere, with a connection to the Internet to read, download, print, copy, and redistribute any deposited article. Toll access means that only subscribers paying subscription fees are permitted to use an archive.

Within the context of this book it is of special interest that recent studies start to examine the extent to which open access documents generate higher citation impacts than non-open access ones, using data from the ISI Citation Indexes. Harnad and Brody (2004) found that 10 per cent of journal articles in physics published during 1992–2001 and indexed by the Institute of Scientific Information were made open access by self archiving in *ArXiv*, an e-print service in the fields of physics, mathematics, non-linear science, computer science, and quantitative biology. They found that the ratio of the average citation impact for the open access articles to that for non-open access articles was around 3.0. Antelman (2004) found for articles in philosophy, political science, electrical engineering and mathematics that the difference in mean citation impact between open access and non-open access articles was between 50 and 90 per cent.

Apart from type of access, the effects of other relevant factors, including the type of information carrier (print versus Eprint), type of publication (e.g., peer reviewed or non-peer reviewed, journal versus proceedings paper), the status of the scholars depositing their papers in an open access archive (do prolific authors tend to self-archive their papers more frequently than less prolific ones?), and size and composition of the universe of citation sources need to be studied more closely.

In an electronic archive one can in principle monitor and analyse how it is used by someone accessing it. Particularly downloads of articles can be monitored by collecting and analysing data on document downloads captured by a web-server. Data on downloads from an archive can be correlated with citation data extracted from that archive itself, or from ISI Citation Indexes. A key issue is how the number of times a document is downloaded in full text format from an electronic archive statistically relates to the number of times it is cited in the reference lists of other documents, particularly those published in journals processed for the ISI Citation Indexes.

Interesting analyses on the relationship between citations and downloads were based on *Citebase*, a citation and impact-ranked search service from the Open Citation Project, indexing papers deposited in *ArXiv*. Results of this work can be found in Hickman (2000) and in many related publications including Hitchcock et al. (2002), Brody et al. (2002), and Harnad et al. (2003). These studies reported evidence that downloads influence citations and that citations influence downloads. More and more case studies are published that examine these relationships for particular journals, fields and electronic archives. Perneger (2004) found for the *British Medical Journal* a Pearson correlation coefficient of 0.5 between downloads of papers during the first week after their publication in the journal and the number of times they were cited during certain later time periods in journals processed for the ISI Citation indexes. Other interesting work regards analyses of the use of the *NASA Astrophysics Data System* (e.g., Kurtz et al., 2005).

It should be noted that huge electronic archives with a broad coverage – such as Elsevier's *ScienceDirect* and many databases offering open access – may have an influence that is not properly reflected in citations from the journal literature. One might argue that specialists in a field tend to succeed in purchasing relevant documents in their specialty regardless of whether they are included in such archives or not, and that multi-disciplinary archives particularly enhance the visibility and availability of their documents to a wider, non-specialist scholarly audience. It can be expected that a large proportion of citations is given by specialists, and that the influence of such documents upon the wider community, particularly in the short term, may go unnoticed.

The author of this book conducted a case study examining how the number of times an article published in the journal *Tetrahedron Letters* is downloaded from *ScienceDirect* statistically relates to the number of times it is cited in journals processed for the ISI Citation Indexes (Moed, 2005). *ScienceDirect* is a data warehouse owned by Elsevier, which provides access to over 1,600 peer reviewed academic journals published by Elsevier. He found a weak Spearman rank correlation of 0.11 between downloads made during the first three months and citations during the first two years after publication.

He hypothesised that the number of paper downloads and received citations measure different concepts. If the number of downloads of a paper is a valid indicator of the number of scientists it is read by, authors are apparently highly selective in what they formally cite in reference lists. Downloads and citations relate to different phases in the process of collecting and processing relevant scientific information that eventually leads to the publication of a journal article, the former being located more in the beginning, and the latter more towards the end of it.

The outcomes suggest that the primary factors responsible for variation in downloads among individual papers are different from those influencing the papers' citation rates. Future bibliometric research could quantify such factors and correlate these to the number of downloads, as well as citation patterns. Therefore, it is still an open question as to whether indicators of perceived significance of research articles can be based on the number of times they are downloaded from electronic archives.

During the past few years a new field has emerged, studying the nature of the World Wide Web, termed as webometrics or cybermetrics (e.g., Ingwersen and Björneborn, 2004). It applies informetric and bibliometric methodologies to the study of the Web's contents, link structures and search engines. In the analysis of link structures among web pages, the latter are conceived analogously to scientific papers, and their incoming and outgoing links analogously to citations and references, respectively. Impact factors of web sites are calculated and link motivation studies are carried out. The number of links to web sites of an academic scholar or institution is conceived as a (potential) measure of prominence, and correlated with bibliometric impact measures (e.g., Thelwall and Harries, 2003).

26.2   New databases and search engines

Beyond any doubt electronic publishing, and the electronic availability and indexing of scholarly documents, have an enormous positive influence upon scholarly communication, and hence on scholarly progress in general. During the past decade several important scientific literature databases were created that include cited references of indexed documents and citation search tools. The *ArXiv* database, founded by Paul Ginsparg in 1991, was mentioned above. Another physics database including cited references and citation search tools is the *Spires HEP* literature database, covering high energy physics and related fields. *ResearchIndex* (or *CiteSee*r), founded by Steve Lawrence of NEC Research, is a full-text archive covering computer science. Recently *Chemical Abstracts (CAS)* substantially enhanced its online citation search capabilities.

Very recently Google has introduced a test version of *Google Scholar*. According to its tutorial, it enables users to find scholarly documents, published from a wide variety of academic publishers, professional societies, preprint repositories and universities, as well as scholarly articles available across the web. *Google Scholar* also automatically extracts citations and presents them as separate results, even if the documents they refer to are not online. Ranking of search results is partly based upon the frequency at which a document is cited in other indexed documents.

As more and more scholarly documents become available in electronic form through the Internet, their use as sources in bibliometric or citation analysis is expected to increase in the near future. From the perspective of research evaluation, it is essential to make clear that including more sources does not necessarily lead to more valid assessments of the contributions scholars make to the advancement of scholarly knowledge. In assessing the contribution to scholarly progress, the importance of (citing) sources in a field, and the extent to which the contents of their documents contain new knowledge and meet professional quality standards, are crucial criteria. A combination of peer review and citation analysis can be fruitfully used to assess these issues, following the lines developed by Eugene Garfield when he created the *Science Citation Index*.

Recently, the scientific publisher *Elsevier* launched *Scopus*, a new and promising online search engine covering abstracts and cited references from about 14,000 scientific journals covering all sciences. Similar to the ISI Citation Indexes, *Scopus* covers the primary, serial, peer reviewed literature. Its potentialities and limitations for bibliometric analysis in general, and for citation analysis in a research evaluation context in particular, need to be assessed in the same careful and critical way as the ISI Citation Indexes were examined during the past few decades by many bibliometric investigators.

Chapter 27

FURTHER RESEARCH

27.1   Introduction

This chapter highlights two important issues of a more general nature as regards the use of citation analysis in research evaluation, that need to be further studied in future research. Section 27.2 stresses the need to carry out systematic studies of the conditions under which citation analysis is actually used in research evaluation, and of the effects of its use upon the scholarly community, its evaluators and the policy arena. It underlines that insights obtained from such studies could play an important role in the development of new indicators.

Section 27.3 discusses the phenomenon that outcomes of citation analysis are often presented to the 'outside world' in the form of *rankings* of entities such as individual scholars, research departments or institutions. It is argued that the concept of scholarly quality cannot be fully captured by a quantitative measure. Moreover, it is emphasised that such rankings tend to draw attention away from how the performances of the various ranked entities may depend upon one another.

27.2   Assessment of the actual use of citation analysis and its effects

Many evaluators believe that all evaluation mechanisms to some extent distort the processes they purport to evaluate (e.g., Warner, 2003). The effects of the use of bibliometric indicators in research evaluation – ranging from crude publication counts to sophisticated citation impact measures – upon the scholarly community and upon scholarly progress in general undoubtedly deserves careful attention, not only from bibliometric investigators, but also from other members of the scholarly community and the research policy arena. Although some evidence for such effects on scholars' publication and referencing practices is rather informal, or even anecdotal, recent studies examine these in a systematic way.

Chapter 21 identified at a global level patterns that, when further analysed, may reveal traces of changes in publication practices and authorship conventions. An important topic is the effect of formulaic use of bibliometric indicators in the allocation of research funds upon scientists' publication practices (Butler, 2003; 2004).

It is essential to make clear that the crucial issue at stake is not whether or not scholars' practices change under the influence of the use of bibliometric indicators, but rather whether or not the application of such measures as a research evaluation tool enhances research performance and scholarly progress in general. On the other hand, studies of motives, impressions and expectations of scholars and policy makers must play a role in such an assessment. Anecdotal, informal, and unsubstantiated evidence evidently has a limited value. Instead, systematic research needs to be undertaken, covering longer time periods and taking into account longer term effects.

It is often argued that a particular evaluation procedure should not be carried out over a very long period of time. A time period of ten years is sometimes suggested as an appropriate duration. After that, new procedures and criteria need to be developed. If this is a valid argument, it could have consequences for the use of bibliometric indicators as well. From this perspective one may consider modifying the indicators applied in research performance assessments every ten years or so, or replacing the types of indicators normally applied by new types. Insights into how current indicators were actually used and their effects upon the evaluated community have to play an important role in the construction of such new indicators.

Steve Woolgar defined citation analysis as a "measurement technology". He proposed carrying out sociological research on the dynamics and effects of the application of this technology in research evaluation.

> We urgently need to understand the dynamics which affect the adoption of one or other measurement technology, and the role the different social agencies in the appropriation of such technologies for their own ends (Woolgar, 1991, p. 325).

The author of this book feels that the type of research proposed by Woolgar could indeed make a valuable contribution to a deeper understanding of the actual and future role of citation analysis in research evaluation. This understanding would contribute to the further development of the 'critical' potential of citation analysis as a research evaluation tool.

27.3   Rankings versus relational indicators

Outcomes of citation analysis often appear in the policy domain in the form of rankings of evaluated entities on the basis of their citation impact. Such rankings tend to focus the attention upon individual entities, particularly upon those appearing at the top and bottom. To the extent that research evaluation processes carried out within the scholarly system aim at providing instruments to the 'outside' world to discern what is excellent and what is less so, it is understandable that their outcomes are easily interpreted and presented in the form of rankings. After all, in many domains of society, rankings of entities according to their performance play an important role.

Rankings based on citation analysis are readily conceived as tools showing research policy makers and administrators which entities need additional support, and for which entities support should be reduced or even abandoned. Moreover, they may be tools for those who are themselves not active members of the scholarly community, but who are about to enter the scholarly system, to identify their best entry point, This is the case, for instance, for students choosing an academic institution for their further training, or for managers of firms in search of particular scholarly knowledge. It must be noted that outcomes of peer reviews such as those conducted within the framework of national research assessment exercises, may also be presented and easily interpreted as rankings.

On the one hand, the need of policy makers and the wider public to obtain insight into the scholarly quality of the various groups is legitimate, and there is definitively a positive role for citation analysis as a tool in addressing this type of issue. On the other hand, it must be emphasised that scholarly quality is not as straightforwardly measured as performance in many other societal domains. As argued in Chapters 2 and 17, it cannot be measured in the same way as practitioners in physics or other areas of science measure their concepts. Moreover, rankings disregard the relationships among entities and how these relationships influence an entity's citation impact or research performance. Bibliometric investigators should look for means to express these notions in the outcomes they produce. This is a matter both of developing new indicators, and of presentation of their outcomes.

This book further develops such a relational perspective at various levels of aggregation. It proposed in Chapter 16 to conceive individual articles as elements of publication oeuvres of research groups, and highly cited articles as symbols of their research programmes. It showed in Chapter 5 that journals with high and low citation impact journals may show a considerable overlap in publishing author populations, so that one cannot simply claim that top authors publish in top journals and less prolific authors in journals with a lower citation impact. It underlined in Chapter 4 that the performance of an individual scientist working in a research group is related to that of other colleagues in the group. At the level of national science systems it illustrated in Chapter 22 how a nation's citation impact is influenced by international scientific collaboration, and thus how one nation's performance may depend upon that of another.

The relationship between genuine scientific excellence and 'ordinary' or 'good (yet not excellent)' research is complex. On the one hand, excellence builds upon achievements made both by excellent and by good research. In addition, excellence seeks for an acknowledgement of its status from both excellent and good researchers. This is in fact a base assumption of citation analysis as a research evaluation tool. In this sense, excellence depends upon good research. On the other hand, excellence attracts and directs both excellent and good research. Good research seeks for involvement in excellent research, and for an acknowledgement of its quality both from good and excellent researchers. In this sense, good research depends upon excellence. However, much more research is needed into such relational aspects, and proper ways must be developed to present the insights obtained from this research in a way that is understandable to a wider public.

References

Abt, H.A. (2004). Some incorrect journal impact factors. *Bulletin of the AAS*, 36, 576.

Aksnes, D.W., and Taxt, R.E. (2004). Peer reviews and bibliometric indicators: a comparative study at a Norwegian university. *Research Evaluation*, 13, 33–41.

Albert, M.B., Avery, D., Narin, F., and MacAllister, P. (1991). Direct validation of citation counts as indicators of industrially important patents. *Research Policy*, 20, 251–259.

Amaral, L.A.N., Gopikrishnan, P., Matia, K., Plerou, V., and Stanley, H.E. (2001). Application of statistical physics methods and concepts to the study of science and technology systems. *Scientometrics*, 51, 9–36.

Anonymous, Nature (2002). Errors in citation statistics. *Nature,* 415, 101.

Antelman, K. (2004). Do Open-Access articles have a greater research impact? *College and Research Libraries*, 65(5), 372–382.

Arunachalam, S. (2004). Science on the periphery: Bridging the information divide. In: Moed, H.F., Glänzel, W., and Schmoch, U. (2004) (eds.). *Handbook of quantitative science and technology research. The use of publication and patent statistics in studies of S&T systems.* Dordrecht (the Netherlands): Kluwer Academic Publishers, 163–184.

Bakker, C.J.G. (1977). *Electronenmicroscopie in Nederland.* Utrecht (the Netherlands): Stichting Fundamenteel Onderzoek der Materie, FOM-Report 43105.

Bassecoulard, E., and Zitt, M. (2004). Patents and publications. In: Moed, H.F., Glänzel, W., and Schmoch, U. (2004) (eds.). *Handbook of quantitative science and technology research. The use of publication and patent statistics in studies of S&T systems.* Dordrecht (the Netherlands): Kluwer Academic Publishers, 665–694.

Bhattacharya, S., and Basu, P.K. (1998). Mapping a research area at the micro level using co-word analysis. *Scientometrics*, 43, 359–372.

Bonaccorsi, A., and Daraio, C. (2004). Econometric approaches to the analysis of productivity of R&D systems. In: Moed, H.F., Glänzel, W., and Schmoch, U. (2004) (eds.). *Handbook of quantitative science and technology research. The use of publication and patent statistics in studies of S&T systems.* Dordrecht (the Netherlands): Kluwer Academic Publishers, 51–74.

Bookstein, A., and Yitzahki, M. (1999). Own language preference: A new measure of "relative language self-citation". *Scientometrics*, 46, 337–348.

Bookstein, A., Moed, H.F., and Yitzahki, M. (2005). *Measures of international collaboration in scientific literature. Part 1 and Part 2*. Forthcoming.

Bordons, M., Morillo, F., and Gómez, I. (2004). Analysis of cross-disciplinary research through bibliometric tools. In: Moed, H.F., Glänzel, W., and Schmoch, U. (2004) (eds.). *Handbook of quantitative science and technology research. The use of publication and patent statistics in studies of S&T systems*. Dordrecht (the Netherlands): Kluwer Academic Publishers, 437–456.

Borgman, C.L. (1990). Editors' Introduction. In: Borgman, C.L. (ed). *Scholarly communication and bibliometrics*. Newbury Part: Sage, 10–27.

Borgman, C.L., and Siegfried, S.L. (1992). Getty's Synoname and its cousins: A survey of applications of personal name-matching algorithms. *Journal of the American Society for Information Science*, 43, 459–476.

Bourke, P., and Butler, L. (1998). Institutions and the map of science: matching university departments and fields of research. *Research Policy*, 26, 711–718.

Braam, R.R., Moed, H.F., and van Raan, A.F.J. (1991). Mapping of science by combined co-citation and word analysis, I: Structural Aspects. *Journal of the American Society for Information Science*, 42, 233–251.

Bradford, S.C. (1953). *Documentation*, 2nd ed. London: Lockwood.

Braun, T., Glänzel, W., and Schubert, A. (1988). World flash on basic research – The newest version of the facts and figures on publication output and relative citation impact of 100 countries 1981–1985. *Scientometrics*, 13, 181–188.

Braun, T., Glänzel, W., and Schubert, A. (1989). Assessing assessments of British science: some facts and figures to accept or decline. *Scientometrics*, 155, 165–170.

Braun, T. (2004). Keeping the gates of science journals. In: Moed, H.F., Glänzel, W., and Schmoch, U. (2004) (eds.). *Handbook of quantitative science and technology research. The use of publication and patent statistics in studies of S&T systems*. Dordrecht (the Netherlands): Kluwer Academic Publishers, 95–114.

Breschi, S., and Lissoni, F. (2004). Knowledge networks from patent data. In: Moed, H.F., Glänzel, W., and Schmoch, U. (2004) (eds.). *Handbook of quantitative science and technology research. The use of publication and patent statistics in studies of S&T systems*. Dordrecht (the Netherlands): Kluwer Academic Publishers, 613–644.

Brody, T., Carr, L., and Harnad, S. (2002). Evidence of hypertext in the scholarly archive. *Proceedings of HT'02, the 13th ACM Conference on Hypertext, University of Maryland*, June. http://opcit.eprints.org/ht02-short/archiveht-ht02.pdf.

Brooks, T.A. (1986). Evidence of complex citer motivations. *Journal of the American Society for Information Science*, 37, 34–36.

Brusoni, S., and Geuna, A. (2004). Specialisation and integration. In: Moed, H.F., Glänzel, W., and Schmoch, U. (2004) (eds.). *Handbook of quantitative science and technology research. The use of publication and patent statistics in studies of S&T systems*. Dordrecht (the Netherlands): Kluwer Academic Publishers, 733–758.

Butler, L. (2003). Modifying publication practices in response to funding formulas. *Research Evaluation*, 17, 39–46.

Butler, L. (2004). What happens when funding is linked to publication counts? In: Moed, H.F., Glänzel, W., and Schmoch, U. (2004) (eds.). *Handbook of quantitative science and technology research. The use of publication and patent statistics in studies of S&T systems*. Dordrecht (the Netherlands): Kluwer Academic Publishers, 389–406.

Callon, M., Courtial, J.P., Turner, W.A., and Bauin, S. (1983). From translations to problematic networks: an introduction to co-word analysis. *Social Science Information*, 22, 191–235.

Callon, M., Law, J., and Rip, A. (1986). How to study the force of science. In: Callon, M., Law, J., and Rip A. (eds.), *Mapping the dynamics of science and technology*. London: MacMillan Press, 3–18.

Cano, V. (1989). Citation behavior: classification, utility and location. *Journal of the American Society for Information Science*, 40, 248–290.

Carpenter, M.P., and Narin, F. (1981). The adequacy of the Science Citation Index (SCI) as an indicator of international scientific activity. *Journal of the American society for Information Science*, November 430–439.

Carpenter, M., and Narin, F. (1983). Validation study: patent citations as indicators of science and foreign dependence. *World Patent Information*, 5, 180–185.

Chang, K.H. (1975). *Evaluation and survey of a subfield of physics: Magnetic resonance and relaxation studies in the Netherlands*. Utrecht (the Netherlands): Stichting Fundamenteel Onderzoek der Materie, FOM-Report 37175.

Chubin, D.E., and Moitra, S.D. (1975). Content analysis of references: Adjuct or alternative to citation counting? *Social Studies of Science*, 5, 423–441.

Cicchetti, D.V. (1991). The reliability of peer review for manuscript and grant submissions: a cross-disciplinary investigation. *Behavioral and Brain Sciences*, 14, 119–186.

Clark, K.E. (1957). The APA study of psychologists. *American Psychologist*, 9, 117–120.

Cole, S., and Cole, J.R. (1967). Scientific output and recognition: A study in the operation of the reward system in science. *American Sociological Review*, 32, 377–390.

Cole, J.R., and Cole, S. (1971). Measuring the quality of sociological research: Problems in the use of the Science Citation Index. *The American Sociologist*, 6, 23–29.

Cole, S., Rubin, L., and Cole, J.R. (1977). Peer review and the support of science. *Scientific American*, 237, 34–42.

Cole, S., Cole, J.R., and Simon, G.A. (1981). Chance and consensus in peer review. *Science*, 214, 881–886.

Cole, S. (1983). The hierarchy of the sciences? *American Journal of Sociology*, 89, 111–139.

Cole, S. (1989). Citations and the evaluation of individual scientists. *Trends in Biochemical Sciences*, p. 9 a.f..

Cozzens, S.E. (1982). Split citation identity: A case-study in economics. *Journal of the American Society for Information Science*, 33, 233–236.

Cozzens, S.E. (1989). What do citations count? The Rhetoric First model. *Scientometrics*, 15, 437–447.

Cronin, B. (1984). *The Citation Process. The role and significance of citations in scientific communication*. London: Taylor Graham.

Cronin, B., and La Barre, K. (2004). Mickey Mouse and Milton: Book publishing in the humanities. *Learned Publishing*, 17, 85–98.

Da Motta e Albuquerque, E. (2004). Science and technology systems in less developed countries. In: Moed, H.F., Glänzel, W., and Schmoch, U. (2004) (eds.). *Handbook of quantitative science and technology research. The use of publication and patent statistics in studies of S&T systems*. Dordrecht (the Netherlands): Kluwer Academic Publishers, 759–778.

De Bruin, R.E., and Moed, H.F. (1990). *The unification of addresses in scientific publications*. In: Egghe, L. and Rousseau, R. (eds.), Informetrics 89/90. Selection of papers submitted for the 2nd International Conference on Bibliometrics, Scientometrics and Informetrics, London, Ontario, Canada, 5–7 July 1989, Elsevier Science Publishers, Amsterdam, 65–78.

Deutsch, K.W. (1954). Is American attention to foreign research results declining? Submitted for the Committee on International Relations of the American Academy of Arts & Sciences, June 9, 1954. Reference copied from Frame and Narin (1988).

Diamond, N., and Graham, H.D. (2000). How should we rate research universities? http://www.physics.northwestern.edu/graduate/Graham_Diamond.html.

EC (2003). European Commission (EC). *Third European Science and Technology Indicators Report*. EUR 20025. Luxembourg: Office for Official Publications of the European Communities, 451 pp.

Egghe, L., and Rousseau, R. (1996). Averaging and globalizing quotients of informetric and scientometric data. *Journal of Information Science*, 22, 165–170.

Egghe, L. (2005*). Power laws in the information production process: Lotkaian informetrics*. Oxford (UK); Elsevier.

Frame, J.D., and Narin, F. (1988). The national self-preoccupation of American scientists. An empirical view. *Research Policy*, 17, 203–212.

Garfield, E. (1964). The Citation Index,– A new dimension in indexing. *Science,* 144, 649–654.

Garfield, E. (1972). Citation Analysis as a tool in journal evaluation. *Science,* 178, 471–479.

Garfield, E. (1974). Some comments on pure and applied research – stimulated by a list of works cited by applied chemists. *Current Contents*, December 4, 1974. In: *Essays of an information Scientist*, 2, 184–197. Philadelphia: ISI Press.

Garfield, E. (1976). *Characteristics of highly cited publications in the engineering sciences. Current* Contents, March 22, 1976. In: *Essays of an Information Scientist*, 2, 441–446. Philadelphia: ISI Press.

Garfield, E. (1979). *Citation Indexing. Its theory and application in science, technology and humanities*. New York: Wiley.

Garfield, E. (1980). Premature discovery or delayed recognition – Why? *Current Contents*, 21, May 26, 5–10.

Garfield, E. (1983a). How to use citation analysis for faculty evaluation, and when is it relevant. Part 1. *Current Contents*, 44, 5–13, October 31, 1983. In: *Essays of an Information Scientist,* 6, 354–362. Philadelphia: ISI Press.

Garfield, E. (1983b). How to use citation analysis for faculty evaluation, and when is it relevant. Part 2. *Current Contents*, 45, 5–13, November 7, 1983. In: *Essays of an Information Scientist*, 6, 363–372. Philadelphia: ISI Press.

Garfield, E. (1985). Uses and misuses of citation frequency. Current Comments, October 28, 1985. In: *Ghostwriting and other essays. Essays of an Information Scientist*, 8, 403–409. Philadelphia: ISI Press.

Garfield, E. (1986). The 250 most-cited authors in the Arts and Humanities Citation Index, 1976–1983. *Current Contents*, 48, 3–10. In: *Essays of an Information Scientist*, Vol. 9, 381–388. Philadelphia: ISI Press.

Garfield, E. (1990). Forcasting the Nobel Prize winners: Some caveats are in order. *The Scientist*, 4. Also published in: Garfield, E. (1991). *Essays of an Information Scientist: Science Reviews, Journalism Inventiveness and Other Essays*, 14, p.382–383. Philadelphia: ISI Press.

Garfield, E., and Welljams-Dorof, A. (1992a). Of Nobel class: A citation perspective on high impact research authors. *Theoretical Medicine*, 13, 118–126.

Garfield, E., and Welljams-Dorof, A. (1992b). Of Nobel class: A citation perspective on high impact research authors (Part 2). *Theoretical Medicine*, 13, 128–136.

Garfield, E. (1996). How can impact factors be improved? *British Medical Journal*, 313, 411–413.

Garfield, E. (1998). Random thoughts on citationology. Its theory and practice. *Scientometrics,* 43, 69–76.

Garfield, E., Pudovkin, A.I., and Istomin, V.S. (2003). Why do we need Algorithmic Historiography? *Journal of the American Society for Information Science and Technology,* 54(5), 400–412.

Gilbert, G. N. (1977). Referencing as persuasion. *Social Studies of Science,* 7, 113–122.

Glänzel, W. (1996). A bibliometric approach to social sciences, national research performances in 6 selected social science areas, 1990–1992. *Scientometrics,* 35, 291–307.

Glänzel, W. (2001). National characteristics in international scientific co-authorship. *Scientometrics,* 51, 69–115.

Glänzel, W., and Moed, H.F. (2002). Journal impact measures in bibliometric research. *Scientometrics,* 53, 2, 171–194.

Glänzel, W., and Meyer, M. (2003). Patents cited in the scientific literature: An exploratory study of 'reverse' citation relations. *Scientometrics,* 58, 415–428.

Glänzel, W., Schlemmer, B., and Thijs, B. (2003). Better late than never? On the chance to become highly cited only beyond the standard bibliometric time horizon. *Scientometrics,* 58, 571–586.

Glänzel, W., and Schubert, A. (2004). Analysing scientific networks through co-authorship. In: Moed, H.F., Glänzel, W., and Schmoch, U. (2004) (eds.). *Handbook of quantitative science and technology research. The use of publication and patent statistics in studies of S&T systems.* Dordrecht (the Netherlands): Kluwer Academic Publishers, 257–276.

Godin, B. (2005). Measurement and Statistics on Science and Technology: 1920 to the Present. London: Routledge.

Goldberger, M.L, Maher, B.A, and Flatteau, P.E. (1995). *Research-doctorate programs in the United States: Continuity and change.* National Academy Press.

Grupp, H., and Mogee, M.E. (2004). Indicators for national science and technology policy. In: Moed, H.F., Glänzel, W., and Schmoch, U. (2004) (eds.). *Handbook of quantitative science and technology research. The use of publication and patent statistics in studies of S&T systems.* Dordrecht (the Netherlands): Kluwer Academic Publishers, 75–94.

Harnad, S., Carr, L., Brody, T., and Oppenheim, C. (2003). Mandated online RAE CVs linked to university Eprint archives: Improving the UK Research Assessment Exercise whilst making it cheaper and easier. *Ariadne,* 35 (April 2003).

Harnad, S, and Brody, T. (2004). Comparing the impact of Open Access (OΛ) vs. non-OA articles in the same journals. *D-Lib Magazine,* 10 (6).

Hickman, I. (2000). *Mining the social life of an eprint archive.* http://opcit.eprints.org/ijh198/index.html.

Hicks, D., Tomizawa, H., Saitoh, Y., and Kobayashi, S. (2004). Bibliometric techniques in the evaluation of federally funded research in the United States. *Research Evaluation,* 13, 78–86.

Hicks, D. (2004). The Four literatures of social science. In: Moed, H.F., Glänzel, W., and Schmoch, U. (2004) (eds.). *Handbook of quantitative science and technology research. The use of publication and patent statistics in studies of S&T systems.* Dordrecht (the Netherlands): Kluwer Academic Publishers, 473–496.

Hitchcock, S., Bergmark, D., Brody, T., Gutteridge, C., Carr, L., Hall, W., Lagoze, C., and Harnad, S. (2002). Open citation linking: The way forward. *D-Lib Magazine,* 8 (10).

Holcombe, R.G. (2004). Investigating the apparatus: The National Research Council ranking of research universities. Its impacts on research in economics. *Econ Journal Watch,* 1, 498–514.

Holton, G. (1978). Can science be measured? In: Elkana, Y., Lederberg, J., Merton, R.K., Thackray, A., and Zuckerman, H. (Eds.).*Toward a metric of science: the advent of science indicators*. New York: John Wiley, 39–68.

Hooten, P.A. (1991). Frequency and functional use of cited documents in information science. *Journal of the American Society for Information Science*, 42, 397–404.

Hull, D.L. (1998). Studying the study of science scientifically. *Perspectives on Science*, 6, 209–231.

Ingwersen, P., and Björneborn, L. (2004). Methodological issues of webometric studies. In: Moed, H.F., Glänzel, W., and Schmoch, U. (2004) (eds.). *Handbook of quantitative science and technology research. The use of publication and patent statistics in studies of S&T systems*. Dordrecht (the Netherlands): Kluwer Academic Publishers, 339–370.

Jin, B., and Rousseau, R. (2004). Evaluation of research performance and scientometric indicators in China. In: Moed, H.F., Glänzel, W., and Schmoch, U. (2004) (eds.). *Handbook of quantitative science and technology research. The use of publication and patent statistics in studies of S&T systems*. Dordrecht (the Netherlands): Kluwer Academic Publishers, 497–514.

Katz, J.S. (1999). The self-similar science system. *Research Policy*, 28, 501–517.

King, D.A. (2004). The scientific impact of nations. *Nature*, 430, 311–316.

Kostoff, R.N. (2002). Citation analysis of research performer quality. *Scientometrics*, 53, 49–71.

Kurtz, M.J., Eichhorn, G., Accomazzi, A., Grant, C., Demleitner, M., Murray, S.S., Martimbeau, N., and Elwell, B. (2005). The bibliometric properties of article readership information. *Journal of the American Society for Information Science and Technology*, 56, 111–128.

Langfeldt, L. (2001). The decision-making constraints and processes of grant peer review, and their effects on the review outcome. *Social Studies of Science*, 31, 820–841.

Law, J., and French, D. (1974). Normative and interpretative sociologies of science. *Sociological Review*, 22, 581–595.

Lawrence, P.A. (2003). The Politics of publication. *Nature*, 422, 259–261.

Le Pair, C. (1988). The citation gap of applicable science. In: van Raan, A.F.J. (ed.). *Handbook of quantitative studies of science and technology*. Amsterdam: Elsevier/North-Holland, 537–553.

Lewison, G. (1999). The definition and calibration of biomedical subfields. *Scientometrics*, 46, 529–537.

Lewison, G. (2001). Evaluation of books as research outputs in history of medicine. *Research Evaluation*, 10, 89–95.

Lewison, G. (2004). Citations to papers from other documents. In: Moed, H.F., Glänzel, W., and Schmoch, U. (2004) (eds.). *Handbook of quantitative science and technology research. The use of publication and patent statistics in studies of S&T systems*. Dordrecht (the Netherlands): Kluwer Academic Publishers, 457–472.

Leydesdorff, L., and Amsterdamska, O. (1990). Dimensions of citation analysis. *Science, Technology and Human Values*, 15, 305–335.

Leydesdorff, L. (1998). Theories of citation? *Scientometrics*, 43, 5–25.

Liu, M. (1993). Progress in documentation the complexities of citation practice: a review of citation studies. *Journal of Documentation*, 49, 370–408.

Lok, C.K.W., Chan, M.T.V., and Martinson, I.M. (2001). Risk factors for citation errors in peer-reviewed nursing journals. *Journal of Advanced Nursing*, 34, 223–229.

Luwel, M. (1999). Is the Science Citation Index US biased? *Scientometrics*, 46, 549–562.

Luwel, M., Moed, H.F., Nederhof, A.J., De Samblanx, V., Verbrugghen, K., and van der Wurff, L.J. (1999). Towards indicators of research performance in the social sciences and humanities: An exploratory study in the fields of law and linguistics at Flemish universities. Brussel: Vlaamse Universitaire Raad, Depot nr. d/1999/2939/9.

Luwel, M. (2004). The use of input data in the performance analysis of R&D systems. In: Moed, H.F., Glänzel, W., and Schmoch, U. (2004) (eds.). *Handbook of quantitative science and technology research. The use of publication and patent statistics in studies of S&T systems*. Dordrecht (the Netherlands): Kluwer Academic Publishers, 315–338.

Mabe, M., and Amin, M. (2001). Growth dynamics of scholarly and scientific journals. *Scientometrics,* 51, 147–162.

Mabe, M., and Amin, M. (2002). Dr Jekyll and Dr Hyde: Author-reader asymmetries in scholarly publishing. *Aslib Proceedings*, 54, 149–157.

Mabe, M. (2003). The growth and number of journals. *The Journal for the Serials Community*, 16, 191–197.

MacRoberts, M.H., and MacRoberts, B.R. (1987). Testing the Ortega hypothesis: Facts and artifacts. *Scientometrics,* 12, 293–296.

MacRoberts, M.H., and MacRoberts, B.R. (1996). Problems of citation analysis. *Scientometrics*, 36, 435–444.

Marshakova-Shaikevich, I. (1996). The standard impact factor as an evaluation tool of science and scientific journals. *Scientometrics*, 35, 283–291.

Martin, B.R., and Irvine, J. (1983). Assessing basic research: some partial indicators of scientific progress in radio astronomy. *Research Policy*, 12, 61–90.

Martin, B.R., Irvine, J., Narin, F., and Sterritt, C. (1987). The continuing decline of British science. *Nature*, 330, 123–126.

Matia, K., Amaral, L.A.N., Luwel, M., Moed, H.F., and Stanley, H.E. (2005). Scaling phenomena in the growth dynamics of scientific output. *Journal of the American Society for Information Science and Technology*, 55, to be published.

McCain, K.W. (1990). Mapping authors in intellectual space. A technical overview. *Journal of the American Society for Information Science*, 41, 433–443.

Merton, R.K. (1957). Priorities in scientific discovery: a chapter in the sociology of science. *American Sociological Review*, 22, 635–659.

Merton, R.K. (1968). The Matthew Effect in science: The reward and communication systems of science are considered. *Science,* 159, 56–63.

Merton, R.K. (1972). The institutional imperatives of science. In: Barnes, B.S. (ed.), *The Sociology of Science*, 35–39.

Merton, R.K. (1977). The sociology of science: an episodic memoir. In: Merton, R.K. and Gaston, J. *The sociology of science in Europe,* 3–141. Carbondale: Southern Illinois University Press.

Merton, R.K. (1996). The Matthew Effect in Science, II: Cumulative Advantage and the Symbolism of intellectual property. In: Merton, R.K., *On Social Structure and Science*. Chigaco: The University of Chicago Press, 318–336. Also in *ISIS,* 79, 607–623, 1988.

Meyer, M. (2000). Does science push technology? Patents citing scientific literature. *Research Policy*, 29, 409–434.

Moed, H.F., Burger, W.J.M., Frankfort, J.G., and van Raan, A.F.J. (1983). *On the measurement of research performance: The use of bibliometric indicators*. Leiden: University of Leiden, 199 pp.

Moed, H.F., and Vriens, M. (1989). Possible inaccuracies occurring in citation analysis. *Journal of Information Science*, 15, 95–107.

Moed, H.F., de Bruin, R.E., and van Leeuwen, Th.N. (1995). New bibliometric tools for the assessment of national research performance: database description, overview of indicators and first applications. *Scientometrics*, 33, 381–442.

Moed, H.F., and van Leeuwen, T.N. (1996). Impact factors can mislead. *Nature*, 381, 186.

Moed, H.F., van Leeuwen, T.N., and Reedijk, J. (1998). A new classification system to describe the ageing of scientific journals and their impact factors, *Journal of Documentation*, 54, 387–419.

Moed, H.F. (2000). Bibliometric indicators reflect publication and management strategies. *Scientometrics*, 47, 323–346.

Moed, H.F. (2002a). The impact-factors debate: the ISI's uses and limits. *Nature*, 415, 731–732.

Moed, H.F. (2002b). Measuring China's research performance using the Science Citation Index. *Scientometrics*, 53, 281–296.

Moed, H.F., Luwel, M., and Nederhof, A.J. (2002). Towards research performance in the humanities. *Library Trends*, 50, 498–520.

Moed, H.F., Glänzel, W., and Schmoch, U. (2004) (eds.). *Handbook of quantitative science and technology research. The use of publication and patent statistics in studies of S&T systems*. Dordrecht (the Netherlands): Kluwer Academic Publishers, 800 pp.

Moed, H.F., and Garfield, E. (2004). In basic science the percentage of 'authoritative' references decreases as bibliographies become shorter. *Scientometrics*, 60, 295–303.

Moed, H.F. (2005). Statistical relationships between downloads and citations at the level of individual documents within a single journal. *Journal of the American Society for Information Science and Technology, to be published*.

Moravcsik, M.J., and Murugesan, P. (1975). Some results on the function and quality of citations. *Social Studies of Science*, 5, 86–92.

Mulkay, M.J. (1974). Methodology in the sociology of science: some reflections on the study of radio astronom. *Social Science Information*, 13, 107–119.

Naldi, F., Luzi, D., Valente, A., and Vannini Parenti, I. (2004). Scientific and technological performance by gender. In: Moed, H.F., Glänzel, W., and Schmoch, U. (2004) (eds.). *Handbook of quantitative science and technology research. The use of publication and patent statistics in studies of S&T systems*. Dordrecht (the Netherlands): Kluwer Academic Publishers, 299–314.

Narin, F. (1976). *Evaluative bibliometrics: The use of publication and citation analysis in the evaluation of scientific activity*. Washington D.C.: National Science Foundation.

Narin, F., Stevens, K., and Whitlow, E.S. (1991). Scientific co-operation in Europe and the citation of multinationally authored papers. *Scientometrics*, 21, 313–323.

Narin, F. (1994). Patent bibliometrics. *Scientometrics*, 30, 147–155.

Narin, F., Hamilton, K.S., and Olivastro, D. (1997). The increasing linkage between US technology and public science. *Research Policy*, 26, 317–330.

Narin, F., Breitzman, A., and Thomas, P. (2004). Using patent citation indicators to manage a stock portfolio. In: Moed, H.F., Glänzel, W., and Schmoch, U. (2004) (eds.). *Handbook of quantitative science and technology research. The use of publication and patent statistics in studies of S&T systems*. Dordrecht (the Netherlands): Kluwer Academic Publishers, 553–568.

Nederhof, A.J., and van Raan, A.F.J. (1987). Peer review and bibliometric indicators of scientific performance: A comparison of cum laude and ordinary doctorates in physics. *Scientometrics*, 11, 329–236.

Nederhof, A.J. (1988). The validity and reliability of evaluation of scholarly performance. In: van Raan, A.F.J. (ed). (1988), *Handbook of quantitative studies of science and technology*. Amsterdam: Elsevier/North-Holland, 193–228.

Nederhof, A.J., and Zwaan, R.A. (1991). Quality judgements of journals as indicators of research performance in the humanities and the social and behavioral sciences. *Journal of the American Society for Information Science*, 42, 332–340.

Nederhof, A.J., and van Raan, A.F.J. (1993). A bibliometric analysis of six economics research groups: A comparison with peer review. *Research Policy*, 22, 353–368.

Nederhof, A.J., Luwel, M., and Moed, H.F. (2001). Assessing the quality of scholarly journals in Linguistics: An alternative to citation-based journal impact factors. *Scientometrics*, 51, 241–265.

Norris, M., and Oppenheim, C. (2003). Citation counts and the Research Assessment Exercise:V: Archeology and the 2001 RAE. *Journal of Documentation*, 59, 709–730.

NOWT (2004). Netherlands Observatory of Science and Technology (NOWT). *Science and Technology Indicators 2003 (in Dutch)*. CWTS/MERIT report to the Netherlands Ministry of Education, Culture and Science.

Noyons, E.C.M., Moed, H.F., and van Raan, A.F.J. (1999). Integrating research performance analysis and science mapping. *Scientometrics*, 46, 591–604.

Noyons, E.C.M., Buter, R.K., van Raan, A.F.J., Schmoch, U., Heinze, T., Hinze, S., and Rangnow, R. (2003). *Mapping excellence in science and technology across Europe. Nanoscience and nanotechnology*. Leiden: CWTS.

Noyons, E.C.M. (2004). Science maps within a science policy context. In: Moed, H.F., Glänzel, W., and Schmoch, U. (2004) (eds.). *Handbook of quantitative science and technology research. The use of publication and patent statistics in studies of S&T systems*. Dordrecht (the Netherlands): Kluwer Academic Publishers, 237–256.

NSF (2002). National Science Foundation (NSF). *Science and Engineering Indicators 2002*. www.nsf.gov/sbe/srs/seind02/start.htm.

OECD Group on the Science System (1998). *University research in transition*. Paris: Organization for Economic Cooperation and Development (OECD), 103 pp.

Oppenheim, C., and Renn, S.P. (1978). Highly cited old papers and the reasons why they continue to be cited. *Journal of the American Society for Information Science*, 29, 227–231.

OST (2004). Observatoire des Sciences et des Techniques (OST). *Indicateurs de sciences et de technologies*. Edition 2004. Paris: Economica, 576 pp.

Peritz, B.C. (1983). A classification of citation roles for the social sciences and related fields. *Scientometrics*, 5, 303–312.

Perneger, T.V. (2004). Relation between online "hit counts" and subsequent citations: prospective study of research papers in the BMJ. *British Medical Journal*, 329, 546–547.

Persson, O., Glänzel, W., and Danell, R. (2004). Inflationary bibliometric values: the role of scientific collaboration and the need for relative indicators in evaluative studies. *Scientometrics*, 60, 421–432.

Persson, O., and Danell, R. (2004). Decomposing national trends in activity and impact. In: Moed, H.F., Glänzel, W., and Schmoch, U. (2004) (eds.). *Handbook of quantitative science and technology research. The use of publication and patent statistics in studies of S&T systems*. Dordrecht (the Netherlands): Kluwer Academic Publishers, 515–528.

Pinski, G., and Narin, F. (1976). Citation influence for journal aggregates of scientific publications: theory, with application to the literature of physics. *Information Processing and Management*, 12, 297–312.

Price, D.J.D. (1961). *Science since Babylon*. New Haven: Yale University Press.

Price, D.J.D. (1963). *Little Science, Big Science*. Columbia Univ. Press, New York.

Price, D.J.D. (1970). Citation measures of hard science, soft science, technology, and nonscience. In: Nelson, C.E. and Pollock, D.K. (Eds.), *Communication among scientists and engineers*, 3–22.

Price, D.J.D. (1978). Towards a model for science indicators. In: Elkana, Y., Lederberg, J., Merton, R.K., Thackray, A., and Zuckerman, H. (Eds.).*Toward a metric of science: The advent of science indicators*. New York: John Wiley, 69–95.

Price, D.J.D. (1980a). The citation cycle. In: Griffith B.C., *Key papers in information science*, 195–210. White Plains, NY: Knowledge Industry Publications.

Price, D.J.D. (1980b). *Towards a Comprehensive System of Science Indicators*. Paper presented to the Conference on Evaluation in Science and Technology – Theory and Practice, Dubrovnik, July, 1980.

Pudovkin, A.I., and Garfield, E. (2004). Rank-normalized impact factor. A way to compare journal performance across subject categories. Paper presented at the ASIST meeting, November 17, 2004. Available at: http://www.garfield.library.upenn.edu/papers/asistranknormalization2004.pdf.

Rinia, E.J., van Leeuwen, Th.N., van Vuren, H.G., and van Raan, A.F.J. (1998). Comparative analysis of a set of bibliometric indicators and central peer review criteria. Evaluation of condensed matter physics in the Netherlands. *Research Policy*, 27, 95–107.

Rinia, E.J., van Leeuwen, Th.N., van Vuren, H.G., and van Raan, A.F.J. (2001). Influence of interdisciplinarity on peer–review and bibliometric evaluations. *Research Policy*, 30, 357–361.

Salter, A.J., and Martin, B.R. (2001). The economic benefits of publicly funded basic research: a critical review. *Research Policy* 30, 509–532.

Salton, G. (1963). Associative document retrieval techniques using bibliographic information. *J Assoc. Comp. Mach.*, 10, 440–457.

Sampat, B.N., and Ziedonis, A.A. (2004). Patent citations and the economic value of patents. In: Moed, H.F., Glänzel, W., and Schmoch, U. (2004) (eds.). *Handbook of quantitative science and technology research. The use of publication and patent statistics in studies of S&T systems*. Dordrecht (the Netherlands): Kluwer Academic Publishers, 277–298.

Sandqvist, A.A. (2004). The A&A experience with impact factors. arXiv:astro-ph/0403184 v1 8 Mar 2004. Also to be published in: Heck, A. (ed). *Organizations and Strategies in Astronomy* – Vol. 5. Dordrecht (the Netherlands): Kluwer Academic Publishers.

Schmoch, U. (1993). Tracing the knowledge transfer from science to technology as reflected in patent indicators. *Scientometrics*, 26, 193–211.

Schmoch, U. (2004). The technological output of scientific institutions. In: Moed, H.F., Glänzel, W., and Schmoch, U. (2004) (eds.). *Handbook of quantitative science and technology research. The use of publication and patent statistics in studies of S&T systems*. Dordrecht (the Netherlands): Kluwer Academic Publishers, 717–732.

Schwechheimer, H., and Winterhager, M. (2001). Mapping interdisciplinary research fronts in neuroscience: A bibliometric view to retrograde amnesia. *Scientometrics*, 51, 311–318.

Seglen, P.O. (1992). The skewness of science. *Journal of the American Society for Information Science*, 43, 628–638.

Seglen, P.O. (1994). Causal relationship between article citedness and journal impact. *Journal of the American Society for Information Science*, 45, 1–11.

Seglen, P.O. (1997a). Citations and journal impact factors: Questionable indicators of research quality. *Allergy*, 52, 1050–1056.

Seglen, P.O. (1997b). Why the impact factor of journals should not be used for evaluating research. *British Medical Journal*, 314, 498–502.

Sen, B.K. (1992). Documentation Note: Normalised impact factor. *Journal of Documentation*, 48, 318–325.

Simkin, M.V., and Roychowdhury, V.P. (2002). *Read before you cite*. http://www.arxiv.org/ftp/cond-mat/papers/0212/0212043.pdf

Simonton, D.K. (2004). Psychology's status as a scientific discipline: Its empirical placement within an implicit hierarchy of the sciences. *Review of General Psychology*, 8 (1), 59–67.

Small, H. (1973). Co-citation in the scientific literature: A new measure of the relationship between publications. *Journal of the American Society for Information Science*, 24, 265–269.

Small, H.G. (1977). Co-citation model of a scientific specialty: – a longitudinal study of collagen research. *Social Studies of Science*, 7 (2), 139–166.

Small, H.G. (1978). Cited Documents as concept symbols. *Social Studies of Science*, 8, 327–340.

Small, H. (1982). Citation context analysis. *Progress in Communication Sciences* 3, 287–310.

Small, H., and Sweeney, E. (1985). Clustering the Science Citation Index using co-citations, I: A comparison of methods. *Scientometrics*, 7, 393–404.

Small, H., Sweeney, E., and Greenlee, E. (1985). Clustering the Science Citation Index using co-citations, II: Mapping science. *Scientometrics*, 8, 321–340.

Small, H. (1987). The Significance of bibliographic references. *Scientometrics*, 12, 339–342.

Small, H. (1998). Citation analysis: Do we need a theory?. *Scientometrics*, 43, 141–142.

Smith, A.T., and Eysenck, M. (2002). *The correlation between RAE rankings and citation counts in psychology*. Technical Report, Psychology, University of London, Royal Holloway. http://cogprints.ecs.soton.ac.uk/archive/00002749/01/citations.pdf

SOOS (2003). Steunpunt O&O Statistieken (SOOS). *Flemish Indicator Book 2003*. In Dutch. Leuven: Steunpunt O&O Statistieken.

Spiegel-Rösing, I.S., Fausen, P.M., and Baitsch, H. (1975). Beiträge zur Messung von Foschungsleistungen, *Schriftenreihe Hochschule*, 16, Bonn.

Stang, P.J. (2005). JACS policy on manuscript processing. *Journal of the American Chemical Society*, 127, 1.

Stock, W.G. (2004). International and German language library and information science journals. Testing the Garfield hypothesis. In German. In: Pipp, E. (Ed.), *Ein Jahrzehnt World Wide Web*. Tagungsberichte ODOK'03. Wien, Phoibos, 53–62.

Swygart-Hobaugh, A.J. (2004). A citation analysis of the quantitative/qualitative methods debate's reflection in sociology research: Implications for library collection development. *Library Collections, Acquisitions, and Technical Services*, 28 (2), 180–195.

Thelwall, M., and Harries, G. (2003). The connection between the research of a university and counts of links to its web pages: An investigation based upon a classification of the relationships of pages to the research of the host university. *Journal of the American Society for Information Science*, 54, 594–602.

Tijssen, R.J.W., Buter, R.K., and van Leeuwen, Th.N. (2000). Technological relevance of science: validation and analysis of citation linkages between patents and research papers. *Scientometrics*, 47, 389–412.

Tijssen, R.J.W. (2004). Measuring and evaluating science–technology connections and interactions. In: Moed, H.F., Glänzel, W., and Schmoch, U. (2004) (eds.). *Handbook of quantitative science and technology research. The use of publication and patent statistics in studies of S&T systems*. Dordrecht (the Netherlands): Kluwer Academic Publishers, 695–716.

334   *Citation Analysis in Research Evaluation*

Van Den Berghe, H., de Bruin, R.E., Houben, J.A., Kint, A., Luwel, M., Spruyt, E., and Moed, H.F. (1998). Bibliometric indicators of research performance in Flanders. *Journal of the American Society for Information Science*, 49, 59–67.

Van Leeuwen, Th.N., Moed, H.F., Tijssen, R.J.W., Visser, M.S., and van Raan, A.F.J. (2000). First evidence of serious language-bias in the use of citation analysis for the evaluation of national science systems. *Research Evaluation*, 9, 155–156.

Van Leeuwen, Th.N., Moed, H.F., Tijssen, R.J.W., Visser, M.S., and van Raan, A.F.J. (2001). Language biases in the coverage of the Science Citation Index and its consequences for international comparisons of national research performance. *Scientometrics*, 51, 335–346.

Van Leeuwen, Th.N., Visser, M.S., Moed, H.F., and Nederhof, A.J. (2002). Bibliometric profiles of academic chemistry research in the Netherlands, 1991–2000. In: VSNU, *Chemistry and Chemical Engineering*. Utrecht (the Netherlands): Association of Universities in the Netherlands (VSNU), 151–177.

Van Leeuwen, Th.N. (2004a). *The second generation of bibliometric indicators*. Thesis, Leiden University.

Van Leeuwen, Th.N. (2004b). Descriptive versus evaluative bibliometrics. In: Moed, H.F., Glänzel, W., and Schmoch, U. (2004) (eds.). *Handbook of quantitative science and technology research. The use of publication and patent statistics in studies of S&T systems*. Dordrecht (the Netherlands): Kluwer Academic Publishers, 373–388.

Van Raan, A.F.J. (1990). Fractal dimension of co-citations. *Nature*, 347, 626.

Van Raan, A.F.J. (1996). Advanced bibliometric methods as quantitative core of peer review based evaluation and foresight exercises. *Scientometrics*, 36, 397–420.

Van Raan, A.F.J (1998). In matters of quantitative studies of science the fault of theorists is offering too little and asking too much. *Scientometrics*, 43, 129–139.

Van Raan, A.F.J. (2000). On growth, ageing, and fractal differentiation of science. *Scientometrics* 47, 347–362.

Van Raan, A.F.J., and van Leeuwen, T.N. (2002). Assessment of the scientific basis of interdisciplinary, applied research – Application of bibliometric methods in Nutrition and Food Research. *Research Policy*, 31, 611–632.

Van Raan, A.F.J. (2004a). Measuring Science. In: Moed, H.F., Glänzel, W., and Schmoch, U. (2004) (eds.). *Handbook of quantitative science and technology research. The use of publication and patent statistics in studies of S&T systems*. Dordrecht (the Netherlands): Kluwer Academic Publishers, 19–50.

Van Raan, A.F.J. (2004b). Sleeping beauties in science. *Scientometrics*, 59, 461–466.

Van Vianen, B.G., Moed, H.F., and van Raan, A.F.J. (1990). An exploration of the science base of recent technology. *Research Policy*, 19, 61–81.

Vinkler, P. (1986). Evaluations of some methods for the relative assessment of scientific publications. *Scientometrics*, 10, 157–178.

Visser, M.S., and Moed, H.F. (2004). Measuring the impact of non-ISI source items. Paper presented at the S&T Indicators Conference, Leiden (the Netherlands), 25–28 September 2004.

Visser, M.S., and Moed, H.F. (2005). Developing bibliometric indicators of research performance.in computer science. Paper submitted to the ISSI 2005 Conference, Stockholm (Sweden), 24–28 August, 2005.

Warner, J (2003). Citation analysis and research assessment in the United Kingdom. *Bulletin of the American Society for Information Science and Technology*, 30 (1), October/November.

Weinberg, A. (1962). Criteria for scientific choice. *Minerva*, 1, 158–171.

White, H.D., and Griffith, B.C. (1981). Author co-citation – a literature measure of intellectual structure. *Journal of the American Society for Information Science*, 32, 163–171.

White, H.D. (1990). Author co-citation analysis: Overview and defense. In: Borgman, C.L. (ed). *Scholarly Communication and Bibliometrics*, 84–106. Newbury Park: Sage.

White, H.D., and McCain, K.W. (1998). Visualizing a discipline: An author co-citation analysis of information science, 1972–1995. *Journal of the American Society for Information Science*, 49, 327–355.

Widhalm, C., Topolnik, M., Kopcsa, A., Schiebel, E., and Weber, M. (2001). Evaluating patterns of co-operation: application of a bibliometric visualisation tool to the Fourth Framework Programme and the Transport Research Programme. *Research Evaluation*, 10, 129–140.

Woolgar, S. (1991). Beyond the citation debate: Towards a sociology of measurement technologies and their use in science policy. *Science and Public Policy* ,18, 319–326.

Wouters, P. (1999). *The Citation Culture*. Thesis, University of Amsterdam.

Zitt, M., and Bassecoulard, E. (1998). Internationalization of scientific journals: a measurement based on publication and citation scope. *Scientometrics*, 41 (1–2), 255–271.

Zitt, M., Perrot, F., and Barré, R. (1998). Transition from national to transnational model and related measures of countries performance. *Journal of the American Society for Information Science*, 49 (1), 30–42.

Zitt, M., Ramanana, S., and Bassecoulard, E. (2003). Correcting glasses help fair comparisons in international science landscape: country indicators as a function of ISI database delineation. *Scientometrics*, 56, 259–282.

Zitt, M., and Bassecoulard, E. (2004). Internationalisation in science in the prism of bibliometric indicators. In: Moed, H.F., Glänzel, W., and Schmoch, U. (2004) (eds.). *Handbook of quantitative science and technology research. The use of publication and patent statistics in studies of S&T systems*. Dordrecht (the Netherlands): Kluwer Academic Publishers, 407–436.

Zuckerman, H. (1987). Citation analysis and the complex problem of intellectual influence. *Scientometrics*, 12, 329–338.

Index of Keywords, Cited Works and Cited Authors

Information Knowledge and Science Management